Richard Deacon is one of
writers on espionage matte
the British, Russian, Chi
Services.

25ᵀᴴ

To Phillip

lots of love

Grant, Sue,
Benjamin, Hannah + Miriam

XXX
XX

RICHARD DEACON

The French Secret Service

GRAFTON BOOKS

A Division of the Collins Publishing Group

LONDON GLASGOW
TORONTO SYDNEY AUCKLAND

Grafton Books
A Division of the Collins Publishing Group
8 Grafton Street, London W1X 3LA

A Grafton Paperback Original 1990

ISBN 0-586-20673-6

Printed and bound in Great Britain by
Collins, Glasgow

Set in Times

Contents

Glossary

Abwehr   German External Secret Service

Algérie Française   'Algeria for the French' movement

Barbouzes   Unofficial agents of the French Secret Service

BCRA (M)   *Bureau Centrale de Renseignements et d'Action Militaire*, a section of the wartime Gaullist Secret Service

BDPA   *Bureau pour le Développement de la Production Agricole*, an organization for aiding underdeveloped countries, but said to have had links with French Intelligence

BMA   *Bureau des Menées Anti-Nationales*, an organization created by the Vichy Government to combat anti-nationalism, but also used for undercover espionage

CFLN   *Comité Français de Libération Nationale*, World War II Gaullist organization

CNES   *Centre Nationale d'Étude Spatiale*, centre for outer space studies

Deuxième Bureau   The organization which analyses intelligence reports

DGER   *Direction Général des Études et Recherches*, the re-creation of French Intelligence in 1944

DGSE   *Direction Générale de la Sécurité Extérieure*, the new title given to the French Secret Service in 1982

DGSS   *Direction Générale des Services Spéciaux*, the title given to the Gaullist Secret Service in 1943

DST   *Direction de la Surveillance du Territoire*, the French equivalent of Britain's MI5 counter-espionage organization

FARL   *Factions Armées Révolutionnaire Libanaises*, a terrorist organization

FLN   *Force de Libération Nationale*, formed by the Algerian rebels to combat French rule

Gendarmerie   Police

GEPAN Groupe d'Études des Phénomènes Aerospatiaux Non-Identifiés, a body set up to study UFO reports

GIGN Special anti-terrorist group of the *Gendarmerie*

GRU Soviet Military Intelligence

Haute Police The highest branch of the French police, with which the earlier French Intelligence Services maintained close links

KGB The branch of the Soviet Secret Service specializing in external intelligence-gathering as well as disinformation and some counter-espionage

MI5 British counter-espionage organization, mainly for detecting foreign agents in British territory

MI6 British service specializing in intelligence-gathering outside the country

OAS Organisation de l'Armée Secrète The organization set up by Algerian settlers and some of the military in order to preserve Algeria as part of Metropolitan France

OSS Office of Strategic Services (American), set up during World War II and later replaced by the CIA

Préfet (Prefect) Chief of Police

SAC Service d'Action Commune, founded on the return to power of General de Gaulle, which later became notorious for its recruitment of gangsters

SDECE Service de Documentation Extérieure et de Contre Espionage, the title of the French Secret Service until 1982

Service Action This is a title which from time to time recurs in French Intelligence, sometimes just as *Action*, sometimes as *Action Civique*, or *Service Action Commune*. In effect it implies some kind of undercover operation which can sometimes, but not always, be compared to the type of work in which the British SAS engages

SOE Special Operations Executive; the British World War II organization set up to form links with Resistance movements on the Continent and to engage in sabotage against the enemy

SR Services de Renseignements, the bureau concerned with intelligence-gathering, linked to the *Deuxième Bureau*. For a while the *SR* also had an *SCR*, which was concerned with counter-espionage

SSM   Service of Military Security which replaced the BMA in 1942

Sûreté The French Security and Criminal Investigation Department

TR   Travaux Ruraux (Office of Rural Works), set up under the wartime Vichy government as an undercover espionage service

Introduction

'You think when you have slain me you will conquer France, but that you will never do. Though there were a hundred thousand Goddammees [English soldiers] more in France than there are, they will never conquer that kingdom.'

attributed to Joan of Arc, *circa* 1430

Throughout history and up until the present day the French Secret Service in all its various branches has consistently remained one of the most highly rated of all intelligence services in the world. This standard has been maintained, in good times and bad, in the same almost romantic spirit of determination as expressed by Joan of Arc in the fifteenth century. France is still a nation of great importance to the whole of the Western world, and its intelligence-gathering makes a fascinating story.

France has enjoyed a system of intelligence-gathering on a national scale since the thirteenth century; it was in operation some two hundred years before the creation of a British intelligence network under Henry VII. What is perhaps less well appreciated is that in addition to establishing this early lead, the French maintained a high degree of efficiency *during defeat and occupation*. I have put these words in italics because they need to be stressed. One of the reasons I wrote this book is because the often quixotic gallantry and enterprise of some of France's intelligence officers and agents in their country's darkest days has most unfairly been overlooked by historians. For example, the French Secret Service not only continued to operate after France was partially occupied following Bismarck's campaign of 1870, but completely reorganized itself the following year to a high degree of efficiency, not least by creating from scratch the now world famous *Deuxième Bureau*.

Similarly, after the partial occupation of the country by the Germans in 1940, the French Secret Service under the Vichy Government carried on with tremendous courage and against great odds. This was done sometimes with the cognizance of the heads of governments and the Services, sometimes without. French Intelligence waged its own undercover war against the Nazis and was at times better informed about the enemy than the British Secret Service was.

In one section of French Intelligence between 1940 and 1944 no fewer than 134 lost their lives, while in the counter-espionage section 104 agents were reported as either dead or missing. This is, of course, in no way intended to belittle the gallantry of those Frenchmen who were working from outside the country on the side of General de Gaulle's Free French forces. In due course they formed their own intelligence service which ultimately was married to those elements of French Intelligence proper which continued to serve the government of Vichy. But it cannot be denied that some of the successes of the Americans and British from 1942 onwards would not have been achieved without some help from French Intelligence officers still serving Vichy.

It may be that early experience of the cynical brutality of the intelligence game has enabled the French to ride out the storms of occasional espionage scandals in modern times rather better than most other Western powers. Another important factor is that the strong sense of realism in the French character never allows inhibitions or humbug to hamper their intelligence undertakings. When things begin to go wrong in this sphere, when some scandal is unearthed, especially if national security or prestige is involved, the French usually manage skilfully to play it down.

Invariably the tactics of those in control of such situations is to make the *affaire* complicated and mysterious so that nobody else can get to the bottom of it. These are, of course, the tactics which enabled French Intelligence to disguise from the nation the truth about the notorious Dreyfus affair for more than ten years at the turn of the century. Never do the French allow themselves to get into time-wasting, futile and unnecessarily prolonged scandals like the Americans with Watergate and

Irangate and the British with *Spycatcher*, clumsily tackling
Peter Wright and turning his tentative revelations into a
bestseller.

The handling of the disastrous sinking of the Greenpeace
vessel, *Rainbow Warrior*, by two French Secret Service agents
was a classic example of French skill in such matters, something
both Americans and British could usefully learn from and
digest. Had either of these nations suffered a similar scandal,
one can be sure that because of protests by the green lobby,
futile commissions or committees of inquiry would have been
set up, ministers would have resigned and perhaps even governments been defeated. And all to no useful purpose.

To study the people of any nation through examining the
secret service of that state is an illuminating operation. When
applying this thesis to the French one begins to understand
their ability to think that much faster than most other peoples.
Undoubtedly they thought fast and realized the inevitable in
1940 when their allies unfairly blamed them for capitulating.
Meanwhile the British only managed to survive by a remarkable
combination of good luck and the resilience and instinctive
courage of the whole nation. But they were much closer to
total defeat than most people still imagine.

Fast thinking may sometimes enable the French to cover up
mishaps and espionage errors better than most other Western
powers. In 1987, commenting on the case of one Maryse
Villard, who had been charged with passing secret documents
to her Iranian lover, the *Daily Telegraph*'s correspondent in
Paris posed the question, 'How was it possible to keep secret
for more than a year the arrest and imprisonment of a woman
employed by M. Chirac, the Prime Minister?'[1] On the other
hand the French have never had the obsessive, almost paranoid
and frequently ridiculous passion for secrecy which has so often
made the British Secret Service look foolish. There is still a
pretence, against all the evidence, that the latter does not exist.
But the French make no such pretences. The *Deuxième Bureau*
makes no secret of its address, and its telephone number is in
the directory. True, the *Deuxième Bureau* is not the Secret
Service proper, but it is the top, vital organization which
collects and interprets intelligence for the use of the High

Command or other organizations, civilian and military, who may need its advice. Nor have the French made any attempt to disguise the fact that there are a *Troisième* and a *Cinquième Bureau* as well and that periodically the names of their various intelligence organizations and sections are changed. The addresses of all are clearly indicated.

Another remarkable feature of the French Secret Service has been the intelligent use of female agents, mainly in war, but sometimes in peace. Some of their escapades make outstanding stories of ingenuity and courage. If a recurring criticism of the service is to be found in these pages, it is that on occasions some highly unsuitable and rigid military officers have been given high commands with disastrous effects, such as the Dreyfus case at the turn of the century. There was also a tendency to ignore intelligence findings by civilians in the years between the wars.

What is fascinating is how Britain and France have from the earliest times been involved in an espionage war against one another. This was the case almost constantly until the end of the nineteenth century, when the Germans became a threat to both nations and the situation changed. The relationship was so complicated in the earlier period that frequently there have been occasions when Britons have been spying for the French and the French have been spying for the British.

For most of this century, the notable exception being during World War II, both nations have after centuries of hostilities co-operated with each other. Nevertheless, a continuation of the traditional rivalry occasionally causes one nation to try to exploit the other for its own ends.

What seems singularly significant, however, is that, despite temperamental and cultural differences, the two nations are, according to most of France's spymasters, past and present, natural allies. When a spymaster makes such a deduction one cannot be other than impressed. Yet Cardinal Richelieu, Dubois, Fouché and some more recent chiefs of French Intelligence have risked not merely their careers, but their lives in asserting this. Fouché nearly lost his head in doing so when challenged by Napoleon I.

Perhaps the greatest talent of the French Secret Service –

and this has been even more marked since World War II – is their ability swiftly to correct mistakes and make major changes when needed. The title of the French Secret Service proper has been changed four times since World War II: a small point but a significant one. No other nation has quite this same talent for quick thinking and carefully planned changes in organization. With the French these qualities add up to the name of the game which is Intelligence. Change, yes; secrecy, only where necessary, and a talent for covering up errors which amounts almost to genius, yes.

1

The Cabinet Noir

To promote the security of the state for the happiness of the people.
                                                        Charles V of France

There were few formal intelligence systems in the modern sense
in Europe prior to the fourteenth century. What few there were
seemed largely haphazard. Charles V, known as The Wise,
when he came to the throne in 1364 gave France her first
intelligence organization actually under the state. It is important to understand that he did this with the laudable aim quoted
at the head of this chapter. In fact the new service ended up by
achieving something quite different, as Charles's network of
spies and police operating across the nation merely deprived
the people of much of the liberty they had previously enjoyed.
Charles perhaps was never aware of this, but the system he
introduced soon became one of oppression. The movement of
people from place to place, or even job to job, was restricted.

It was in fact a Cardinal, Armand Jean du Plessis, Duc de
Richelieu, who created France's first truly effective secret
service 250 years later. Richelieu would never have been so
naïve as to believe one could promote the security of the state
– at least in those days – for the happiness of the people. In this
respect Richelieu had an enormous advantage: it was the
Catholic Church which, in the seventeenth century, had the
most widespread and efficient espionage system in the world.
No single nation could compete with it. Generally speaking,
throughout Europe until the late sixteenth century, guidance in
the collection of intelligence was sought from the Catholic
Church. It was for this reason that European nations chose
princes of that Church, usually Cardinals, to organize their
secret services.

It should be explained that in this period 'intelligence' covered very many activities and often there was no dividing line between those who organized the collection of intelligence and those who formulated policy. Quite often a minister could act as an intelligence agent, while an agent could be allowed to negotiate treaties and form policies. Nor was there as yet any clear distinction between military, naval and other forms of intelligence-gathering. The words 'Secret Service' covered a multitude of activities and departments. The first military intelligence organization which existed in France was the Statistic Section of the Depot of War, created by Michel le Tellier, Marquis de Louvois, during the reign of Louis XIV. Louvois was Under-Secretary of State for War and one of the great reorganizers of the French Army.

Born in Paris in 1585, Richelieu was consecrated as Bishop of Luçon at the remarkably early age of twenty-two. From then onwards he was never far from the heights of power, learning the hard way how to get the better of his enemies. First of all the Queen Mother of France, Marie de Médicis, appointed him a Minister of State, but shortly after this Richelieu was driven from office following the assassination of Concini, the Italian adventurer, in 1617. Concini and his wife had exercised a great influence over Marie de Médicis, who made Concini a Marshal. It was their advice to the Queen Mother which paved the way for the dismissal of Richelieu. Then, after having been made a Cardinal two years later, Richelieu was recalled to the service of the state by Louis XIII. From then until the end of his life he virtually ruled France, largely, it must be admitted, through his astute manipulation of the intelligence service he created and which was controlled by his *Cabinet Noir*. Ruthless he may have been, but his great virtue was that all his scheming was done entirely for what he saw as the good of France, never for his personal advantage.

The *Cabinet Noir* consisted of a carefully chosen number of what Richelieu considered to be 'advisers' on the analysis of intelligence. The purpose of the Cabinet was to analyse intercepted correspondence, the work of the police, and information provided by a network of spies in all quarters of Paris so that plots could be destroyed before they were fully developed.

Many of these plots were solely related to family feuds in the aristocracy, but occasionally they threatened the King himself, even if indirectly. Thus much of the *Cabinet Noir*'s work was to keep the government in touch with thinking and scheming in all sectors of French aristocratic society. Richelieu feared the machinations of those in high places far more than the revolutionary instincts of the Paris mobs. The actual numbers of members of the *Cabinet* varied from a very few in 1620 to perhaps not more than twelve or fifteen from 1624 onwards. His chief adviser and mentor was the Capuchin priest, François le Clerc du Tremblay, more generally known as Father Joseph, who was in effect director of Richelieu's secret service.

There was, and still is, a close link in France between the intelligence services and the police, even though the relationship has been and occasionally still is uneasy and difficult. Sometimes the two work together quite well, sometimes there is positive hostility. In Richelieu's time the French made a distinction between the 'high police' and the 'low police'. The latter concerned themselves with mundane matters such as controlling the markets, public sanitation and prostitution, but otherwise interfered very little with the life of the masses. The *Haute Police* had full authority to spy at will, penetrating private households by underground passages and devising means of being present everywhere important people were gathered together without being seen. Sometimes people were secretly detained without trial in the interests of their families, either to avoid scandals or because there were no grounds for a successful prosecution in the normal courts.

All such intelligence-gathering might seem extraordinarily parochial for a man of Richelieu's character. But he wanted to ensure that he had adequate internal intelligence before extending such operations overseas. Behind this planning was his belief that through this espionage system he could force the various aristocratic families to accept the authority of the crown. Richelieu was a French statesman first and foremost and a man of the Church second, for he made his judgements almost entirely upon expediency and governmental interest. If he had a philosophy regarding his work it was, firstly, a belief that intelligence, both internally and externally, enabled France to remain a first-class power. Richelieu had a cosmopolitan mind. He had a high opinion of the English as intelligence-gatherers and employed a number of them as agents, commenting that they were 'fearless, reliable and without bias'.[1]

The Cardinal ordered the kidnapping of an English agent, Montague, and, as a result of information he extracted, was able to thwart the schemes of George Villiers, First Duke of Buckingham, who had become entranced by the French Queen as well as involving himself in the affairs of France. Richelieu's lack of any religious prejudice in ruthlessly pursuing his policies was admirably demonstrated when he stirred up Gustave Adolphus, King of Sweden, to support the Protestant cause in Germany in the Thirty Years War, enabling the French to seize Alsace. He invariably based all his policies overseas on what he had gleaned from intelligence; later he aimed at weakening the power of Spain by encouraging a rebellion in Portugal and a rising in Catalonia. His overall aim was to keep France as the major power in Europe.

Richelieu held almost as much power, if not more, as the King. He not only had total access to all intelligence reports, but also the skill to make accurate assessments. The composition of the *Cabinet Noir* and especially its censorship of the informal postal system which then existed were for a long time kept secret from all but a very few. Richelieu had one major cause of concern within the secret service: the conspiratorial Marie de Rohan, Duchess of Luynes and Chevreuse, who, though his chief assistant after Father Joseph, ultimately proved to be a mischievous intriguer who caused more trouble than she was worth. Maybe Richelieu's one weakness was in retaining her services, as it is reported that on his deathbed he said her passion for intrigue had shortened his life.

Another of Cardinal Richelieu's great achievements was to discover the best of the early cryptographers in Antoine Rossignol, a young student of mathematics who took up ciphers as a hobby. Rossignol was recommended to Richelieu by the Prince of Condé, and when the great Huguenot stronghold of La Rochelle was being attacked by the King's forces messages were received which nobody could decipher, until Rossignol broke the code. Richelieu later sent for Rossignol and gave him full powers to set up a new academy (Richelieu's own description of it) to deal with secret correspondence. Prior to this there had been few outside the ranks of scholarly monks and priests who could handle deciphering. From then on France led the world in cryptography, working on Rossignol's teachings, but adding to them all the time. Rossignol invented the safest cipher of all in those days, known as the *Vigenère*. In an age in which messages could so easily be intercepted (and especially once people began to suspect that this occurred) cryptography was all important, not least in the underworld. So highly did Richelieu regard Rossignol that one of his last commands shortly before his death in 1642 was that his cryptographer should be kept in the forefront of French Intelligence circles, and it is said that Louis XIII before his own demise made much the same comment. Even today in France a device used to open a lock when the key is missing is called a 'Rossignol'.

Unquestionably, through his powerful secret service, Richelieu not only strengthened and united the nation internally, but actually enabled the French to wrest power in Europe from the gradually declining Holy Roman Empire. It was his success in quelling internal disorders which gave the French monarchy its despotic power. His greatest success in foreign policy was the ending of Spain's maritime superiority, achieved partly through the stirring up of the insurrection in Portugal. Not least, Richelieu should be remembered as the founder of the French Academy, but perhaps the most surprising aspect of the Cardinal's character was the way in which he continued to lead and to dominate, despite almost permanent ill health.

2

Mazarin the Enigmatic

Mazarin made himself the absolute master of all the outward effects
which passion usually produces, so much so that neither by his speech,
nor the least change in his countenance, could one discover his real
thoughts.

François de Callières[1]

Richelieu's successor as chief of intelligence was the able if
enigmatic Cardinal Jules Mazarin. A handsome man of Sicilian
parentage, Mazarin was educated in a Jesuit college in Rome
where he took the degree of Doctor of Laws, later joining the
Papal Army in which he specialized more in learning the
diplomatic than the military arts. In 1636 he became Richelieu's
secretary. The shrewd comment on Mazarin made at the head
of this chapter came from a contemporary French diplomat,
François de Callières, who had dealings with him over a long
period. Another facet of Mazarin's mastery of the game of
intelligence is mentioned by de Callières in his memoirs. He
describes how Mazarin was sent on a mission to Milan to see
the Governor, the Duca de Feria, to try to find out his true
feelings on a certain matter: 'He thus had the cunning to
inflame the Duke's anger and so discover what he would never
have known if the Duke had maintained a wise hold over his
feelings.'[2]

Mazarin's real name was Giulio Mazarini and one reason
why he never commanded the same authority as Richelieu was
that the French had reservations about his Italian background.
Nevertheless he had impressed Richelieu with his ability in
handling on behalf of Italy the negotiations which led to the
Treaty of Cherasco in 1631. The Pope made him legate of
Avignon some time after this and in 1634 he was sent to Paris

as nuncio-extraordinary. In 1639 he became a naturalized French subject and it was his skill as ambassador to Savoy which led Richelieu to demand for him a Cardinal's hat. He never quite achieved the same power as Richelieu did, despite the fact that when Louis XIII died only a year after Richelieu's death Mazarin immediately devoted his attention to winning the ear of Louis' widow, Anne of Austria. It was she who appointed him first minister of the crown. This success he achieved by sweet words and much flattery and soon the Queen was under his spell. During the minority of her son, Louis XIV, she had, of course, considerable influence. It was even whispered that Mazarin had arranged a secret marriage ceremony with her, but of this there is no proof.

Mazarin probably failed to be as effective as Richelieu not only because of the disadvantage of his Italian ancestry, but also because he failed to assert his authority strongly enough over the new king. Mazarin also suffered from the fact that when Louis XIV came of age, he at first seemed to take little interest in using intelligence as a means of gaining a tighter political control of events. The result – perhaps an inevitable one – was that some of the leading families started to set up their own private intelligence agencies, sometimes to spy upon one another, often to find out what went on at court.

It was in this period that the British achieved a great improvement in their own secret service under Cromwell's brilliant spymaster, John Thurloe. This unostentatious Essex lawyer, under the cover of Postmaster-General, built up one of the most efficient intelligence services in the whole of Europe. So much so that Mazarin frequently confessed himself to be baffled, because even when the French Cabinet met behind locked doors their secrets leaked to Thurloe within a few days. Mazarin's own agents in London told him as much. An important factor here was that London managed to establish relations with one of the French private intelligence services. A major blow to Mazarin was that suddenly the English had developed an intelligence service which competed with Richelieu's creation.

Money was a factor: previously England had shown a parsimonious attitude towards its intelligence services, often, as in the case of Walsingham, expecting the chief of the service to provide his own finances. Thurloe succeeded because Cromwell allowed far more money to be spent on intelligence-gathering than had the Stuart kings. Also he had extended his network of spies to cover far distant places, making particular use of Jewish agents. Mazarin, however, soon found the answer to some of his failures: the secrets were being leaked by courtiers to some in ecclesiastical circles and Thurloe had taken full advantage of this. A Puritan himself, he was convinced of the greed and corruption of senior members of the Catholic Church. To his agent in Leghorn he once wrote: 'These people cannot be gained but by money, but for money they will do anything . . . Such intelligence must be procured from a Monsignor, a secretary or a Cardinal . . . I should say 1,000 pounds a year were well spent . . .'[3]

Mazarin's cunning did not always enable him to get his own way, even when he wished to reward his own agents. For much of his intelligence he relied upon an agent named Ondedei, whom he even visualized as a future Cardinal. The anonymity of the priesthood still provided the best cover for French spies in this era. Yet when he arranged for Ondedei to be made Bishop of Fréjus there were loud howls of protest. Those in influential circles close to the throne knew that Ondedei was a spy, and suddenly even priestly spies had become unpopular.

Some of Mazarin's intelligence-gathering was devoted to plots to extend France's territorial possessions, one of his schemes being to try to make the young Louis XIV Emperor of Germany as well as King of France. He sent out agents with bags of gold and masses of pro-French propaganda to try to achieve this aim. But these efforts were eventually wasted: the German princes were in no mood to back the French on this project. However, Mazarin did win one victory out of all this, managing to extract a promise that the Germans and their allies would not provide any aid to Spain against France.

After Mazarin died in 1661 Louis XIV at last forced himself to take a more positive interest in intelligence work. This was not so much due to any shrewd insight into intelligence affairs as to his insistence that '*L'état, c'est moi*'. Not unnaturally this frequently made life difficult for those handling intelligence on behalf of the state, but where England was concerned he achieved a notable success. Being a cousin of Charles II of England, Louis was well aware of that monarch's fondness for attractive women, so in 1669 he dispatched Louise de Keroualle to London to make friends at court. She soon became a mistress of Charles and, with the secretly conducted Treaty of Dover in 1670 which made him an ally of France, Louise proved herself to be an intelligent agent and useful informant. Meanwhile Charles II made her Duchess of Portsmouth, and she seems to have drawn almost as much from the funds of the English Treasury as from that of France. Certainly she was instrumental, in 1672, in persuading Charles to declare war on the Dutch at Louis XIV's bidding.

Louis XIV was also helped by the fact that after the abdication of James II and the end of the Stuart dynasty in England there was a period of some thirty years of Jacobite plotting by supporters of the exiled Stuarts in England, Scotland and France. That there was a kind of Jacobite secret service is evident from the extensive archives of the Scots College at St Germain. France took full advantage of the Jacobite movement by enlisting many of its members as spies for her own service. Often Scottish Jacobites were used by the French for espionage in foreign courts, especially those who had been banished from their own home territory.

It was in this period that a new figure emerged in the French Intelligence Service, that of the able military leader, Maurice de Saxe (1696–1750), who wrote: 'Spies and guides . . . are as useful as the eyes in your head, and, to a general, are quite indispensable . . . You cannot spend too much money in order to obtain good ones. They must be obtained from the country in which war is being waged.'[4]

Marshal de Saxe was the illegitimate son of Augustus the Strong, King of Poland and Elector of Saxony. After being made Duke of Courland he was expelled from the duchy by the Russians in 1727 and thereafter he fought for the French, ultimately being created a Marshal and given command of the French Army in Flanders.

When Louis XIV died in 1714, his successor and great grandson, Louis XV, was only five years old, and the Duke of

Orleans was appointed Regent. The Duke chose as his secretary and chief of civilian intelligence Cardinal Guillaume
Dubois, who was to prove almost as effective an adviser on
intelligence as Richelieu or Mazarin. Born at Brives-la-Gail-
larde in the Limousin in 1656, Dubois became known as the
'Little Abbé' when he took the tonsure at the age of thirteen.
His good fortune was to have been tutor to the future Duke of
Orleans. In due course Dubois became one of the most
prominent statesmen in Europe.

The early years of Louis XV's reign were difficult ones for
France as this nation was mistrusted by Austria and Spain and
regarded with deep hostility by England. The Regent decided
to make the improvement of relations with England his first
priority and, with this in mind, he ordered Dubois, then sixty
years old, to go to London in the disguise of a Dutch gentle-
man. Dubois' role was sometimes to pose as an invalid travelling for his health, at others to be a book collector in quest of
rare editions. It may seem unusual to employ a spymaster as a
travelling spy, but Dubois was made for the part. He managed
to acquire a great deal of information from sources close to the
government and King George I himself. Dubois used various
aliases during his lengthy visit to Britain, but became best
known under the pseudonym of St Alban.

Eventually, such was his talent for infiltrating the highest
circles in London, he joined a party accompanying George I to
Hanover. It was then he made his shrewdest move, cultivating
the acquaintance of Stanhope, England's Secretary of State,
and giving him a secret letter from the Regent proposing an
alliance between England and France. The two men met at The
Hague and immediately established a warm accord. Nevertheless Dubois erred when he offered Stanhope a bribe of 600,000
livres which was politely refused. Dubois was, however, persistent: he merely changed his tactics. He requested the dispatch
from France of sixty cases of the finest wines, giving thirty of
these to Stanhope and thirty to George I. This time the bribe
seemed to work, for Stanhope agreed to persuade the King to
agree to an alliance, though only on the grounds that this would
protect his beloved Hanover from the intrigues of Prussia and
Austria.

During all these negotiations Dubois was still operating under one or other of his pseudonyms to all except Stanhope. Once, when Stanhope gave a state dinner to diplomats accredited to the Hanoverian court, Dubois, who could not be invited, sat in an adjacent room with the door ajar, taking notes of the indiscreet table talk which he heard. 'The wine of the Secretary of State was gay and talkative,' Dubois wrote to the Regent of France.[5]

In his memoirs Dubois admitted that he had worn various disguises and that his original mission had been simply that of a spy. He lived at an address in Westminster, but secret dispatches and other correspondence were sent to him at another address, to '*Dubusson, maître à danser, chez M. Hamton, maître charpentier à St Martin, derrière l'église proche Cherincross*.'[6] Thus did the versatile Cardinal take on the identity of a French dancing teacher living close to St Martin's Church near Charing Cross. He also cultivated the company of various English ladies with relations or friends in diplomatic circles, plying them with all manner of presents which he had shipped over from Paris. Through one such lady with a husband in the Spanish Embassy in London he learned of a Spanish plot to compromise and exploit an attaché named Buvet in King Louis' library. Dubois' lady friend also handed him copies of letters which the Spanish Ambassador to France had sent to the Spanish Embassy in London.

Before leaving London Dubois wrote to the Duke of Orleans outlining what should be the future programme for obtaining intelligence from England which, he said, 'often meant intelligence upon Spain, Austria, Hanover, Sweden and other nations as well . . .' To win the trust of the English, he urged, one must not make direct proposals 'which might make them think we regard them as capable of being bribed, but proceed by the practice of noble manners'.[7] Despite this, Dubois indulged in quite a lot of bribery among the English, giving 100,000 francs worth of jewels to Lord Stair, the English Ambassador to France.

There was perhaps more Francophobia in England than Anglophobia in France in the seventeenth and eighteenth centuries. Certainly French Intelligence had since the days of

Richelieu kept an open mind on relations with England. In the higher spheres of society the two countries maintained a civilized, if wary relationship. It was among the masses that open hostility was to be found.

Unhappily for Dubois the Treaty of Hanover, intended to strengthen her influence throughout Europe and Scandinavia, did not greatly help France in the end; it cost her much to subsidize Sweden as an ally in Scandinavia, provoked Russian hostility and ended in a war with Spain. Thereupon Dubois changed his tack and aimed for an alliance with Spain and England.

Dubois died in 1723. In many respects he had perhaps been even better as an agent in the field, playing his role in various disguises and getting information, than he had been as an analyst of intelligence. On occasions, of course, he filled both roles at the same time. No doubt his ecclesiastical upbringing had enabled him to fit in at all levels of society, whether in a humble role or as a diplomat, and this may have helped him to be a supremely good psychologist-cum-secret agent. In Dubois one had a Cardinal in his sixties suddenly engaging in espionage, who declared that to obtain the best information from English ladies of good breeding 'one needs to find out very quickly any faults in their husbands (their version of these being more accurate than other people's) and then one must find out what they most miss in life, even if this means ascertaining how their husbands fail to please them in the bedchamber'.[8]

There is no direct evidence that the Cardinal himself conducted espionage in bedchambers, but it was certainly fashionable in that century. As the eighteenth century progressed so did the power of women in public affairs. There was the Marquise de Pompadour, mistress of Louis XV, who made one of her favourites chief of the secret police on the understanding that he discovered all the gossip about her that was going the rounds. Probably more time was spent on finding out this kind of tittle-tattle than in obtaining worthwhile information, but the Marquise was a power in the land and she even decided who should be sent as spies to foreign courts.

3

The Rise and Fall of the Secret Correspondence

I had discovered the very secret correspondence of Louis XV's private politics, a correspondence perfectly concealed from his Council and above all from his Minister of Foreign Affairs.

> The Abbé Georgel, *Mémoires*
> *pour servir à l'histoire des événements de*
> *la fin du 18ième siècle 1760–1810*

Dubois was succeeded by another Cardinal, Fleury, as chief of France's formal intelligence service. Fleury had previously been tutor to Louis XV, who eventually made him a minister. He, too, sought to preserve an alliance between France and Britain. He saw this as being in France's long-term interests, believing that as neighbours separated by a narrow channel they should live at peace with one another. But he, and the Secret Service, had to contend with the influence of a powerful war party who eventually forced him to enter the Polish Succession War of 1733–5, as a result of which Louis gained Lorraine.

The Secret Correspondence was a system of intelligence-gathering and also of manipulating policy conducted solely for the King. It was not only absolutely separate from the official Secret Service, but often operated against the findings of that service. In short, these two services never worked together and for many years the official Secret Service had no idea that the Secret Correspondence existed. The creation of this ultra-secret royalist intelligence service developed out of an idea by the Prince de Conti, a friend of Louis XV. It was decreed that nobody but the King and his own secret agents must know about this organization. Conti's idea was that the King should form a secret cabinet which would function independently of all ministries, including the Foreign Ministry. It was formed in

1748 when Conti became the King's personal adviser on foreign affairs. The members of the Secret Correspondence had their own Black Chamber in Paris which set out to ascertain details of all official dispatches without those in government knowing anything about it. Not only did the Secret Correspondence have its own cipher, but it had agents all over Europe spying on Louis' own ambassadors.

Everyone who was admitted to the Secret Correspondence had to be approved personally by the King. There were about forty men involved in the control of the service. Initially the key people were the Prince de Conti; Tercier, the chief clerk at the Foreign Office who, unknown to his master, was secretary of the Correspondence; and Lebel, Louis XV's valet. Naturally, with men such as Tercier working for this service, it soon had access to official ciphers. Nevertheless the organization was a recipe for chaos and disaster. It couldn't be otherwise in the long run when it was often working against the official policies of the Foreign Ministry and advice from the real Intelligence Service.

The Prince de Conti was succeeded as head of the Correspon- dence by François-Marie, the Duc de Broglie. Other members included the Chevalier de Saint-Priest and Des Rivaux, sec- retary to the French envoy in Warsaw. The problems the King's secret service created came largely out of French policy towards Poland. France's official policy in the middle of the eighteenth century was not to interfere in matters concerning Poland and to regard the Poles as allies against the Hapsburg monarchy. But the Correspondence had different views. Its plan was to infiltrate Poland with agents who would use bribes to persuade Polish leaders to join with France in opposing the Russians. Meanwhile France's official Intelligence Service was still using its agents to impress upon the Poles that the French had no intention of interfering in Polish politics. Not surprisingly the Poles began to wonder what French policy really was and this puzzlement increased when Catherine the Great of Russia sent an army into Poland to try to bring about the election of Stanislas Poniatowski as King of Poland. This situation was further complicated when Poniatowski passed a message through to Choiseul, the French Foreign Minister, offering an alliance if France would support his cause. Choiseul asked General Monnet to go to Poland to negotiate on his behalf, completely ignorant of the fact that the General was a member of the Correspondence, and that he had firm instructions to oppose any deals with Poniatowski.

In the end the Russian troops managed to put down all opposition to Poniatowski and he was duly elected King in 1764. Louis XV withdrew his ambassador from Poland and declined to recognize the new King.

There are few parallels in history to this situation in eighteenth-century France when two intelligence services were operating independently of each other and pursuing different policies. The nearest one can get to such a situation in modern times was in World War II when Britain's MI6 and SOE (Special Operations Executive) were on occasions at loggerheads with one another. But at least each knew of the other's existence and they shared the same aim – winning the war.

It was after the Polish catastrophe that French ministers began to suspect the existence of a secret intelligence organization which might be working against them with the King's tacit approval, but for some years they were unable to find any proof of this. Eventually, through a leakage of information from someone inside the Austrian Black Cabinet, an organization comparable to the French *Cabinet Noir*, the full implications of Louis XV's Secret Correspondence were revealed. The discovery was made by the Austrian Chancellor, Prince Kaunitz, a friend of Choiseul, but though he kept the secret to himself somebody else inside the Black Cabinet passed the news to Paris. Shortly after the King learned that his intrigues had been unmasked he became ill and died. Thus in 1774, twenty-six years after it was created, the Secret Correspondence was wound up. The man chiefly responsible for unmasking its activities was the Abbé Georgel, a Jesuit priest, who was secretary to the French Ambassador to Vienna.

Probably the main reason why this service had lasted so long was that it had been extremely efficient in recruiting reliable agents and had maintained a surprising degree of security in its activities. That it remained so effective in its purpose of giving the King an intelligence service of his own reflected the official

Secret Service's failure in not detecting its existence sooner.
But its winding up was not the end of the affair. The cost of
hushing things up and avoiding public scandal was high, and
doubtless some gentle blackmailing contributed to this. The
new King, Louis XVI, reluctantly agreed that pensions should
be paid to members of the Correspondence. This meant a drain
of some 100,000 livres a year on the Foreign Ministry for some
years to come. But many of the brilliant people recruited by
the Secret Correspondence continued to work for French
Intelligence afterwards. The French, being realists in all things,
took note of the fact that Tercier, as the chief clerk of the
Foreign Office, had passed on all Foreign Office messages to
the King's private service. Their immediate reaction was to
consolidate, to bring the best of the rival service into their own
official service.

French Intelligence was, however, beginning to lose its
effectiveness at this time, not least through being permanently
bogged down solely in snuffing out royal scandals. Apart from
this, latterly the Secret Correspondence had been misused
foolishly by the King. One example of how amateurish and
blatantly foolish it had become was when Louis XV, acting
entirely on his own, offered the Marquis François de Bonnac,
his Ambassador at The Hague, 180,000 livres a year to find a
first-class agent in England. Bonnac's response was to produce
one Maubert, an unfrocked priest and a former convict who
was offered the job of chief French spy in London. Maubert
was urged to bribe British members of Parliament in order to
find out governmental plans. Yet, as far as can be seen, little
was achieved by this ploy. Maubert, who operated in England
under the name of Botteman, had ideas of his own, chief of
which was his personal plan to ruin the Bank of England. This,
as outlined to Bonnac, was as follows:

In England there exists a hundred million pounds sterling in the form
of paper notes and some eighteen million in coins. If one produced
more paper, then more claimants would make demands than the Bank
could satisfy . . . I know of a man here who can make superb copies,
imitating the engraving in every small detail . . . The plan would be to
buy a thousand bills and make copies which one would pass to the
counterfeiters on condition they presented them to the Bank for

payment. The originals would remain with me. Some two weeks later I should arrange for them to be presented at the Bank. The bills would be seized and so, too, would be the carrier, but we should have proof of legitimate possession of same. Then I should make the matter one of public concern and all will be alarmed . . . But you must arrange for this to be initiated in France . . .[1]

Louis XV instantly rejected this plan on the grounds that this was an appalling swindle: 'This proposition,' he wrote, 'to counterfeit the bills of the Bank of England is regarded with all the indignation and horror it deserves.'[2]

Most of the failures in French espionage during the latter part of Louis XV's reign and almost the whole of Louis XVI's could be attributed to the use of unscrupulous types for the work and an over-reliance on bribery. The spies tended to strike ridiculously hard bargains with their paymasters, and the latter sometimes tended to recover some of the heavy fees paid for information by sharing intelligence gains with other friendly powers, for example the Austrians.

An Englishman named Robinson, who operated in London and was also chosen by ambassador-cum-spymaster Bonnac, was ineptly clumsy and soon found himself imprisoned in the Tower as a result of his blatant attempts to gain confidential information. He was succeeded by a French physician, Dr Hensey, the brother of the Abbé Hensey, who was in the French Diplomatic Service. Dr Hensey sent his reports on intelligence gained in London to Bonnac via the diplomatic bag of the Austrian Ambassador in London. He thought this procedure was safe, but in due course Hensey was watched and all his messages were intercepted. The British suspected him not merely of working for France, but of selling his secrets to the Spaniards as well. He was arrested, brought to trial, and sentenced to be hanged, mainly as a warning to other would-be spies, but it is not absolutely certain whether this sentence was carried out.

The secret papers of Louis XV and the documents of the French Ministry of Foreign Affairs of the 1750s reveal numerous instances of blunders in the recruitment of spies by the French. An Italian named Philipi made some outrageous suggestions of how he could create chaos in Britain. He had been employed as a French spy in London for some years without providing any worthwhile intelligence, but in 1760, apologizing for his silence, he said he had a plan to kidnap the English King and his family, seize the Tower of London and capture the artillery magazine at Woolwich, claiming that he would use several hundred Corsicans to carry this off. Cardinal Bernis, then French Foreign Minister, effectively clamped down on this proposal, declaring Philipi to be a scoundrel who would be summarily dealt with when he arrived in France for further talks. He was as good as his word: when Philipi went to Paris, he was given twenty-four hours to get out of the country and ordered to go to The Hague where he was to continue as an agent for the French, but on no account to return to England. As a result France was without a major agent in London for quite a long time.

Yet another example of incompetence in the field of intelligence occurred in the 1780s when French troops dressed in civilian clothes were secretly sent into Holland, yet had their military rank indicated on their passports.

Much of France's intelligence-gathering was organized from their Embassy at The Hague in this period. One target for the French in the Dutch capital was Count Ivan Golovskin. Golovskin's father was Russian Ambassador to The Hague and a friend of the Duke of Cumberland and so had access to some British state secrets. Golovskin was in dire trouble as a result of gambling debts and, as he was secretary to his father and privy to many of the latter's secrets, he offered to sell them to the French. But this offer was referred back to the King who, suddenly revealing a moral double standard (bearing in mind the Secret Correspondence), promptly rejected the offer on the grounds that it would be highly dangerous to trust either a gambler or a man prepared to betray his own father.

4

The Transvestite Spy

They have ordered me to be a woman and I wear petticoats by command of the King.

The Chevalier d'Eon de Beaumont

The story of the Chevalier d'Eon de Beaumont is one of the most remarkable in the history of espionage. It shows how the French intelligence services have the courage to pursue some wildly improbable ploys to gain information.

The Chevalier Charles d'Eon de Beaumont was one of the earliest recruits to Louis XV's Secret Correspondence. Born at Tonnère in 1728, into a family of well-known lawyers, the young Chevalier was, on the instructions of his mother, made to dress in female attire until his early teens. Being of slim build, with delicate features and a pretty face, he was able to masquerade as a woman quite easily, which he often did. Yet in many respects he was thoroughly masculine, proving himself not only to be an accomplished swordsman, but actually being elected to the senior position of *grand prévôt* of the *Salle d'Armes* as a result.

Louis XV chóse him not only as a member of his private intelligence service, but in 1754 sent him on a remarkable mission. This was probably one of the few imaginative ideas which Louis ever had. What he proposed was that the Chevalier should once again don women's clothes and pose as a female. He was to go to the court of the Tsarina Elizabeth at St Petersburg using the name of Mlle Lia de Beaumont. D'Eon told his old friends, 'I am proud to be able to serve him in any capacity.'[1]

D'Eon's brief was to try to prevent the Russians from adopting a pro-British policy and to win them over as allies of

France. He was also urged to seek support for the Prince de Conti's pretensions to the Polish crown. These were formidable tasks for any secret agent on his first mission, but Charles Geneviève Louis Auguste André Timothée d'Eon de Beaumont was a young man almost totally without fear and with a love of practising deception.

Even in those days intelligence services used what in modern espionage parlance is known as a 'control'. D'Eon was given as his control a Jacobite Scotsman named MacKenzie Douglas, who sometimes called himself the Chevalier Douglas. The French believed that a Scotsman as chaperon for 'Mlle Lia' would be less likely to arouse suspicion than a Frenchwoman. So Douglas was given precise orders that he was to pose as the uncle of 'Lia' on the journey to St Petersburg, where on arrival he was to contact the English Ambassador in an effort to disabuse anyone who might think he was other than a loyal British subject. He had been supplied with an ordinary British passport. 'To avoid being interrogated at any of the great courts of Germany en route to St Petersburg, his presence perhaps exciting curiosity, it is desirable that he should enter Germany through Swabia, whence he will pass into Bohemia under the pretext for this journey.' His official instructions then gave details as to how he should go from Bohemia to Saxony and then by Silesia to Russia: 'He must never risk anything through the ordinary post except notice of his arrival.'[2]

It must be said that at this time the Secret Correspondence planned such missions in great detail even if later on there were a number of blunders. D'Eon took with him to Russia a copy of Montesquieu's *L'Esprit des Lois*, in the binding of which was hidden a letter from Louis XV to the Tsarina. When d'Eon (dressed as Lia) and Douglas arrived in 1755, the Tsarina promptly took Lia into her entourage where she became so popular on account of her looks that soon a number of painters begged permission to paint this ravishing young lady from Paris famed for her pink and white complexion. Douglas was not so fortunate. He reported to the English Ambassador who made inquiries about him and learned he had Jacobite connections which immediately made him suspect. The Russian police were tipped off and Douglas was arrested and put in prison where he remained until 1757. Only then was the French Ambassador able to intervene on his behalf.

Gradually d'Eon managed to change the Tsarina's attitude towards the French and even persuade her not to sign a treaty with Britain. Eventually, carefully choosing a propitious moment, d'Eon told the Tsarina who he really was and she not only forgave him for his deception, but offered him an important post at her court. D'Eon, faithfully keeping to his brief, declined her offer graciously and returned to France. He carried with him private letters from the Tsarina to Louis XV, as well as taking to the courts of Versailles and Vienna the Tsarina's official but friendly assurances that the Treaty of Subsidies with England (largely a commercial arrangement) was no longer effective and that some 80,000 men she had assembled in Livonia and Courland would henceforth act in concert with the forces of Austria and France. D'Eon was also charged with delivering the ratification of the Treaty of Versailles which in effect made Russia an ally of the French. For his role in all this the Chevalier was awarded the Grand Cross.

After this success d'Eon was sent on various spying missions, sometimes in the disguise of a woman, but more often as a man. He went to Russia again on three occasions, not attempting the role of Lia again! For his services he was promoted to the rank of a captain of dragoons, given a permanent post and a substantial salary to be paid out of secret funds. What is not altogether clear is to what extent he served both the Secret Correspondence and the official Secret Service. His salary was reputed to be in the region of 3,000 livres. For a time he was aide-de-camp to the Duc de Broglie, who was then head of the official secret service. Sometimes he served with the French Army, and was wounded in the head and thigh in a reconnaissance action at Ultrop.

In between his military and espionage duties he not only established himself as an authority on economics, but wrote two books touching on this and other subjects. But he must have been greatly disappointed when his early success with Tsarina Elizabeth was largely nullified when Catherine came to the throne. Records suggest that his last significant report from Russia was the detailed account of the new Tsarina's close friendship with the British Ambassador, and her fondness for England and hostility to France. He was able to pinpoint how the French could make themselves more popular in St Petersburg by reporting that the British were making an alliance with Prussia whose King the new Tsarina thoroughly detested. As a result d'Eon regained French influence in St Petersburg.

In 1762 d'Eon was sent to England, ostensibly as secretary to the French Ambassador, but chiefly as the Secret Correspondence agent. His instructions were to assist in a scheme for the invasion of England. Louis told him, 'Take up my orders on the surveys to be made in England, whether on the coasts or the interior of the country . . . and on the designs of England as regards Russia and Poland, the north and whole of Germany.'[3]

While in England d'Eon patiently and meticulously made a study of the home counties to work out the best routes for a French army to take if and when it invaded. The Duc de Nivernois wrote that, 'D'Eon is at work from morning to night. I cannot sufficiently extol his zeal, vigilance, amiability and activity.'[4]

But prejudice against d'Eon was building up, despite his splendid record. Already the official secret service was becoming suspicious that their work was being undermined by a rival whom they had not yet tracked down. This might have made the official secret service doubtful about d'Eon. But his one fatal error had been to fall foul of the Marquise de Pompadour, the King's mistress and still a powerful figure behind the scenes in France. She was intensely jealous of d'Eon's influence with the King and plotted against him while d'Eon was in London. Meanwhile the French Foreign Office had appointed to London an enemy of d'Eon's who was obviously intended to supersede him. Here, one suspects, the hand of La Pompadour was all important. A wave of that hand often changed policy.

Suddenly d'Eon was peremptorily ordered to return to France and to put on 'women's garments' once again, a carefully calculated insult as there was no question of his being involved in a mission calling for this kind of disguise. By this time it was made clear to him that he had lost his post in London, and d'Eon promptly accused the man chosen to succeed him, the Comte de Guerchy, of attempting to murder him.

Having returned to France, d'Eon was confronted with a libel action from the Comte de Guerchy. He was then outlawed from France for failing to appear for judgment. He escaped to England, taking with him as a sensible precaution against future poverty or further mischief a collection of compromising papers and documents which revealed the duplicity of the King and his minister, Choiseul, in making certain peace moves; they had tried to make an alliance with Britain at the same time that they were planning to invade her.

For years after this attempts were made not merely to discredit d'Eon, but even to murder him. He was given sanctuary in England and made many friends there, including that rabble-rousing Radical, John Wilkes. It was even rumoured that he became a member of the secret society known as the Knights of St Francis of Wycombe, more popularly called the Hell-Fire Club, whose headquarters were caves underneath the church on the hill at West Wycombe. There is, however, no firm proof of this.

The French even went so far as to engage an English chimney-sweep to hide in the chimney of d'Eon's London home and to make loud groaning noises to suggest the house was haunted. Their aim was to make d'Eon imagine the place was inhabited by a ghost and then to report him to the authorities in the belief that he would be put away as insane. Such a plot seems extraordinarily far-fetched and bizarre. But d'Eon was not so easily trapped; he suspected the presence of an intruder, thrust his sword up the chimney and threatened whoever was hiding there with death unless he came down. The sweep lost no time in climbing out of the chimney and immediately confessed that he had been hired by the French. D'Eon let him go, but took his revenge by publishing revelations about the private life of the French King. He told how one of the members of a subsidized harem in the Parc aux Cerfs had discovered the identity of her royal lover and how the King had silenced her by having her declared insane and shut up in an asylum.[5]

In 1774 d'Eon was allowed to return to France only on

condition that he delivered up the state papers in his possession and wore women's dress. Despite the odds against him obtaining a fair deal, the Chevalier still managed to outwit his enemies, even dictating his own terms for the return of the documents. But by this time recent events had helped him: the Secret Correspondence had been discovered and wound up and Louis XVI had succeeded to the throne. The new King fully appreciated d'Eon's past services to the state and eventually he was allowed to return to England where he lived until his death at the age of eighty-two.

In the meantime the French sent a mysterious 'Monsieur Norac' to London to try to persuade d'Eon to spy for France once again. He rejected the offer, even though it included quite a useful salary. Later he revealed to the British the identity of 'Monsieur Norac': he was none other than the famous playwright, Caron de Beaumarchais, who wrote *The Barber of Seville* and *The Marriage of Figaro*. This versatile character had been apprenticed to his watchmaker father at the age of thirteen and had swiftly shown his talent by creating a design for very small watches, which greatly appealed to the ladies of Versailles. As a result the young de Beaumarchais was appointed watchmaker to King Louis XV. Then, having married a wealthy widow some years older than himself, he decided to become a music teacher and gave instruction to the daughters of the King. His versatility seemed endless: next he was to become agent of the banking firm of Duverny in Paris. He owed the post to the fact that he was a tutor to the King's daughters, as Duverny hoped he could interest them in various philanthropic schemes.

Curiously enough it was the public disgrace of de Beaumarchais which led him to become an ace secret agent. Suddenly he was accused of using his wife to try to bribe a judge to obtain a verdict of acquittal in a particularly complicated case. As a result he was condemned by the French *Parlement* and deprived of all civil rights as well as his French citizenship. Yet the very night on which he was condemned he was entertained by some of his friends in royal circles and the next day he was inundated with letters of sympathy and promises of support. Even more impressive was the response of the Minister of Police, de Sartines, who was the confidant of another of the

King's mistresses, Madame du Barry. It was de Sartines who enlisted de Beaumarchais as a secret agent, first of all on purely domestic matters concerning the King and his mistresses, but mainly in buying the silence of one Morande, who had once had du Barry as a mistress. De Beaumarchais later had his civil rights restored and was used as an agent to deal with d'Eon.

But if de Beaumarchais did not succeed in his mission to bring d'Eon back into the fold, he proved himself in other ways. Charm was his greatest asset and provided him with informants in the most unexpected circles. It was he who won over the confidence of Arthur Lee, who was then representing the American colonies in London. This friendship resulted in a pledge of French support for the Americans against the British.

When the Chevalier d'Eon died in 1810 there was still considerable doubt about whether he really was a man or a woman. His body was examined by several medical and surgical men. Two of them signed a certificate which stated that they 'found the male organs in every respect perfectly formed'. About the same time the *Gazette de Santé* of Paris stated:

It is singular that while all Europe was making a woman of this dubious character, there existed in Paris many unimpeachable witnesses who would have vouched for his manhood long before it was put in question . . . What reason could have induced the Government to condemn a soldier who had obtained military orders and a respectable diplomatic character to assume the dress of a woman? Some politicians think that they have found the reason for this strange conduct on the part of the Government . . . in his secret diplomacy, and that the discovery of his real sex might have lowered the dignity of the French Government and disturbed the peace as well as sullied the honour of many families, in which d'Eon had been received with that unbounded confidence which women grant to women only. They strengthen their opinion by the report current in Paris that, when the Chevalier was ordered to resume female attire, he had the alternative of obeying, or ending his days in the Bastille.

There can be no denying that after studying all sources – British, French and Russian – on d'Eon's brilliant coup in St Petersburg in the era of the Tsarina Elizabeth, that this was one of the most remarkably effective uses of disguise in all history.

5

The French Revolution

The plan of the Jacobins was to stir up the rich against the poor and the poor against the rich.

Fantin Désodoards[1]

At the very time that the forces were slowly being created which would launch the French Revolution, France was still dithering over whether to make an alliance with Britain, or to go to war with her. The belligerent Duc de Choiseul, the French Foreign Minister, actually began to plan for such a war by increasing French naval strength and formulating a plan of attack. His aim was to make the capture of London the first priority. For this purpose he needed a survey of the southeastern coasts of Britain. The agent chosen to carry out this ambitious survey was a somewhat mysterious Colonel Grant of Blairfindy, a Scotsman whose actual identity as a member of the family of Grant of Blairfindy remains something of a mystery, because he was disowned by his relatives. However, it would seem that he was also known as Baron Grant and that he was a nephew of one Alexander Grant (1723–91), who went to France and married the Comtesse d'Ancelet.

We know that Colonel Grant carried out this survey because of the diligence of the British Secret Service who had been alerted to the fact that the French were planning an invasion of Britain. In 1767 Lord Chatham organized the theft from the French Ministry of War in Paris of the surveys which had been made. Today those reports are in the British Public Record Office. They show that Grant had done detailed surveys, revealing the exact number of landing places which would be available to French troops. Colonel Grant opened his report with details of each of these sites, even suggesting that after arrival at Deal (his favourite location for an initial landing) the French Army should march in two columns to London. Grant's report was wildly optimistic: he had the Scotsman's traditional contempt for the English – the people, he said, would offer no resistance. Choiseul was rather more cautious, and he ordered Grant to make a further reconnaissance the following year. But even after receiving a similarly optimistic report, Choiseul was still doubtful. To make sure, he sent another agent to investigate. This time a Frenchman was employed to make his assessments and they were much more cautious. The new spy was Lieutenant-Colonel de Beville, whose reports were extremely reliable and detailed, covering not merely southeast England, but the southwest and many places inland. His final assessment was that the French should not concentrate on occupying London, but first and foremost on destroying the British navy. In the end it was not Choiseul who decided French tactics, but the King, who made it clear that he was not in favour of war. So the invasion of England was once again called off.

Meanwhile the underground forces plotting revolution in France were steadily building up their own intelligence networks. Few historians have managed to pinpoint how all this began. True, much of it came from the people's feeling they were being exploited, especially by some of the aristocratic families. But without doubt the plans of how such a revolution should be started and exploited came from outside the country, especially from Germany, and from divers secret societies professing a new kind of brotherhood. As early as 1793 the *Journal de Vienne* stated that, 'It is not the French who conceived the great project of changing the face of the world; this honour belongs to the Germans. The French can claim the honour of having begun its execution, and of having followed it out to its ultimate consequences . . . whence comes the eternal Jacobin refrain of universal liberty and equality.'

The actual formation of the revolutionary intelligence networks is still largely wrapped in obscurity, but to some extent they were based on a study of the tactics employed by the Illuminati, a republican secret society founded by Adam Weishaupt in Bavaria in 1776. These tactics included the deliberate use of disinformation in order to foment rebellion and revolution. The great mass of French subjects still had a high regard for the sovereign, despite the inherent weakness of Louis XVI, and this included the peasantry who were more exploited than were the industrial workers. Those who exploited them were the landowning aristocracy. The first main thrust of positive plotting came from the Jacobins, the revolutionary Club founded at Versailles in 1789 on the very eve of the revolution. It was their campaign in July of that year which was designed to whip up the peasants against the aristocracy, while assuring them that such a move would be supported by Louis XVI. Agents were sent out all over the country to tell the people that, 'The King desires you to burn down the châteaux. He only wishes to keep his own.' Sometimes such disinformation took the form of placards bearing this slogan and headed 'Edict of the King'. There was, of course, no such edict, though it was true that Louis had been critical of the behaviour of some of the aristocratic landowning families. Disinformation became a major tactic in exploiting and developing the revolution and, inevitably, became a major feature of the new state secret service as it somewhat slowly and haphazardly emerged. It was the teaching of Weishaupt and the Jacobins which most influenced the new intelligence service.

The French Revolution followed the pattern of most revolutions in leading to criminal excesses and an atmosphere of hatred and malevolence. This was, of course, heightened by the tactics of disinformation. The official intelligence service simply collapsed: it was not taken over, but totally replaced by a repressive secret police system. One of the most unpleasant characters it produced was Héron, of the *Haute Police*. After Louis XVI was executed in 1793 the new government of the revolutionaries began to organize its own intelligence service, spending vast sums of money on this while doing very little for the welfare of the masses. Héron was involved in setting up this organization which, though nominally under the control of the Ministry of Foreign Affairs, sent its reports to the Committee of Public Safety and the Paris Commune. Héron became a double agent who, while serving on the Committee of General Security as a paid official, was also paid by the Committee of

Public Safety to spy upon his employers. For a while he seems to have had the best of both worlds by ensuring the elimination of his own enemies, real or imagined, by denouncing them to one or other of the committees for which he worked. It was Héron who was the real spymaster of the reign of terror of 1793–4. Essentially a police spy with no particular talents, Héron had a persecution mania and suspected many of his own colleagues of plotting against him. He had the backing of Maximilien de Robespierre, the leader of the Jacobins and a member of the Committee of Public Safety, and for that reason his career lasted longer than would otherwise have been the case. It is impossible to say how many people he condemned to the guillotine.

The new Intelligence Service was far more interested in internal espionage than reports from overseas. However, it must be said that while it employed a smaller number of agents than France had previously, they were of a markedly higher calibre than those of the decade before the revolution. Most of them were used inside France: twelve of them concentrated on Paris alone. As far as the employment of foreign agents was concerned, much greater caution was shown and in the main intelligence reports were left to the discretion of the diplomats on the spot. They were required to make regular reports to the Foreign Ministry in Paris under various headings, including 'Report on the condition of the people, their virtues, vices and progress in civilization'.

The revolution and the Terror which followed brought to the fore two remarkable if contradictory characters in the field of intelligence, both of whom played a leading role in the power game. They were the Baron Jean de Batz and François Noel Babeuf. De Batz was a royalist of the privileged class who deliberately joined in the campaign of terror with the aim of ending the revolution by condemning leading revolutionaries and sending them to the guillotine. De Batz, after being commissioned in the Queen's Dragoons, had been appointed a Deputy in the States General in 1789. It was he who was most insistent that the new Intelligence Service should proceed slowly on its overseas information-gathering, relying on diplomats' advice and eschewing the services of double agents and

foreigners as much as possible. His plan of using the revolution
to get his own way was a subtle scheme which called for
courage, resourcefulness and tremendous cunning, and he
managed to protect himself with a network of personal spies,
sustained by his own system of bribery, mostly drawn from
police agents.

He had many narrow escapes from death during the Terror,
not least when he tried to save both the King and Queen from
the guillotine, but he miraculously preserved his authority. In
the end he was arrested by a detective who declined to be
bribed, but he did not remain in detention for long. By that
time the excesses of the Terror had resulted in what de Batz
hoped for, the end of the revolution, thus paving the way for
the Bonapartist takeover. To a large extent he prevented the
new Intelligence Service from becoming anything as all-powerful or effective as, for example, the Cheka after the Russian
Revolution.

Babeuf was a totally different character. Born in 1762, he
held the post of commissary in the supply department of the
Commune in the early days of the revolution. He seems to have
been another adept at disinformation, as he incurred the wrath
of the Committee of Public Safety by publishing a pamphlet
accusing it of driving people to revolt by means of a fictitious
famine, thus creating an excuse for killing them off.[2] For a
short time after this he was imprisoned. After the fall of
Robespierre in 1794 and the end of the Jacobin republic,
however, he came into his own and decided to form a 'Secret
Directorate' which seems to have been based on the workings
of that mysterious German secret society already mentioned,
the Illuminati. Just as Weishaupt had employed twelve agents
to direct operations in Germany, so Babeuf appointed twelve
agents to cover the various districts in Paris. It was laid down
that these men were not even to know the names of those who
formed the central committee of four on the Directorate.
Babeuf's intention was to bring about something very like a
communist dictatorship, but he was eventually betrayed and
brought to trial. He denied that he was the leader of the
conspiracy, insisting that, 'I had only a secondary and limited

part in it . . . The heads and leaders needed a director of public opinion, and I was in a position to enlist this opinion.'[3]

Babeuf himself was executed in May 1797, but it was never proved to what extent the Illuminati might have been behind his plans for a second revolution. Naturally, the scheming and double-dealing of people like Babeuf and Baron de Batz helped to create a paranoia which pervaded the ranks of those concerned with intelligence and counter-espionage: everyone began to suspect everyone else, or at least to mistrust one another.

James Tilley Matthews, tea-merchant, hypnotist and amateur diplomat, went over to Paris to try to negotiate a private peace between England and France in 1793. Why anyone on either side would think there was any chance of his succeeding is hard to believe. He failed and was then jailed for three years by the Jacobins. When Matthews left prison and returned to England, it was as an embittered man who felt he had been betrayed and exploited by the French. He reported that a team of French 'magnetic spies', armed with machines for transmitting waves of 'animal magnetism', were planning to overthrow the British Parliament and paralyse the Navy. These machines, he asserted, could inflict various forms of long-distance torture: 'foot-curving, lethargy-making, spark-exploding, knee-nailing, eye-screwing, fibre-ripping'.[4]

Undoubtedly, Matthews had become the victim of disinformation cunningly fed to him by the French, though it hardly seemed in their interests to frighten a nation in which they had at least a few allies at a time when they had not yet put their own house in order. In an interview with Lord Liverpool, then at the Foreign Office, Matthews warned of these alleged perils, but no notice was taken of him. Thereupon Matthews wrote to Liverpool, saying: 'I pronounce your Lordship to be in every sense of the word a most diabolical traitor.' A month later he was committed to an asylum. Anglophobia and Francophobia reached lunatic heights in this era.

6

Fouché the Incomparable

Fouché was a remarkable genius who inspired in Napoleon something akin to terror.

Honoré de Balzac

Joseph Fouché, Duke of Otranto, was in many ways incomparable as head of intelligence and as Minister of Police, and he undoubtedly revolutionized French intelligence-gathering and laid the foundations of a modern espionage system. Under Louis XV and Louis XVI the intelligence system had been marred by rivalries and competing services, while during the revolution it had deteriorated to little more than a ruthless counter-espionage service such as one associates with an absolute police state.

Born at Nantes in 1754, Fouché was originally destined for the Church and he took the robe of the Oratorian Order in 1779, but eventually refused to take the vows of the Order or to be ordained. In 1792 he abandoned his clerical dress and was elected to the National Convention. From that moment he also switched his political sympathies from those of a cautious conservative to those of a radical. He first won favour with the radicals when he urged the execution of the King. Two years later he made a name for himself by forcibly putting down a revolt in Lyon and this paved the way to his appointment as Minister of Police in 1799. He was quick to seize power not only in this role, but as a spymaster-extraordinary who created a nationwide network of agents as well as beginning to build up a service overseas.

Fouché was one of the first to realize how the French secret service had failed in the previous half century, most especially in its total inability to protect the French crown. It was for this reason that a Ministry of Police was created after the establishment of the Republic and Fouché insisted it should have the dual mission of uncovering and dissolving opposition to the established authority from within France as well as the various plots of exiled royalists and foreign agents. This policy of Fouché's was absolutely right, especially after Napoleon came to power and confirmed his appointment. The First Consul, Napoleon Bonaparte, was in perpetual danger of assassination in those early days of post-revolutionary France. It is true that to some extent such tasks had always been the principal concern of French intelligence and police services since Richelieu, but in Bonaparte's early days they were more necessary than ever. Royalists, soldiers and unscrupulous adventurers alike plotted to kill him under the guidance of one Hyde de Neufville. It was Fouché alone who stamped out these plots by building up a state-controlled combination of police and spies. Such was Fouché's authority and power that he was able to acquire a large budget for running his service. Not only did he increase the number of agents almost twofold, but by his policy of defending the new regime at all costs he developed an espionage system which included police, magistrates, inspectors and spies in all walks of life, and he insisted on control over espionage and counter-espionage equally.

Bonaparte had made his name through his military prowess, his success in 1795 in suppressing a rising in Paris, and his organization of Lombardy into a republic. Fouché had developed an espionage system which covered not only the police, the military, and the Foreign Ministry but also Napoleon's personal household staff. But, to make matters more difficult for Fouché, Napoleon himself employed his personal spies, usually women in his entourage or in Parisian society circles such as Madame de Genlis. Napoleon would also interfere personally, sending off missives to the secret police such as 'They tell me that very seditious talk goes on at a wine-shop in the Rue St Honoré . . . Pay a little attention to these small taverns.'[1]

Fouché was, of course, fortunate in that he had the full backing of the *Conseil des Cinq Cents* (the key administrative council of the Republic from 1795 to 1799) when he was given his post. This council had decided it was essential for a ministry of defence to have as its top priority the protection of the republic, and to some extent Fouché based his secret service on that of Richelieu's *Haute Police*. He had a nose for sniffing out bribery and it was this gift which enabled him to stamp out one of the worst features of the intelligence services in France. Bribery of one kind or another is always used by secret services, but once its use becomes a widespread policy it leads to betrayal and disaster. Fouché insisted that bribery must be used sparingly and only when worthwhile results seemed assured. Once even he was duped when Louis XVIII in exile managed to infiltrate one of his own agents into the republic's service and for a considerable time used part of this agent's pay as a supplement to his own modest income. Fouché was a man who believed that results should come first and bribes only secondarily, whereas for many years police and espionage policies had been the other way round.

He used the revolution to guarantee his own future and then promptly closed down all the Jacobin clubs. But if some have condemned him for his opportunism and corruption, it is doubtful whether he was any more corrupt than Prince Maurice de Talleyrand, Napoleon's Foreign Minister, described by Lord Acton as 'the money-getting sybarite, the patient auxiliary of the conqueror and tyrant'.[2]

Balzac said of Fouché that he was 'a remarkable genius who inspired in Napoleon something akin to terror'. It was this so-called terror which prompted Napoleon to force Fouché's resignation from office in 1802 on the grounds that he had become too powerful and had exceeded his powers. There were never any adequate reasons given for what amounted to Fouché's dismissal, but the general impression was that Napoleon thought his intelligence and police chief was becoming too autocratic. Balzac claimed that Napoleon had misconstrued one of the most brilliant and exceptional men around him. Naturally, Fouché had many enemies who sought the ear of Napoleon and they probably made allegations against him. There was jealousy, too, as Fouché had become Duke of Otranto, a millionaire, and the second richest man in France.

But within two years Fouché was reinstated in power. In 1804 Napoleon had been made Emperor of France following the discovery of a plot headed by one Georges Cadoudal which was checked immediately, and greatly strengthened Napoleon's position. But this incident made him aware of the fact that Fouché's talents were much needed and he recalled him to his former offices.

From then on, Fouché set out to make the French Secret Service so efficient and indispensable that he himself would be indispensable. At the same time he set out to please Napoleon in every possible way. Each evening for the next ten years as Minister of Police he wrote reports for the Emperor, covering all that had happened in the Empire over the previous twenty-four hours. These reports included hard news, gossip, reports from agents and terse comments on ambassadors, merchants, politicians and clergy ('intolerant priests' as he often described them). They surveyed events from the Pyrenees to the Baltic, from the Atlantic to the Gulf of Naples and as far afield as St Petersburg, Vienna, London, Lisbon and Hamburg. The documents, which are deposited in the French National Archives, make fascinating reading even today.

One of the first things Fouché did after he was reinstated was to discover what errors had been committed in his absence. He ascertained that the British intelligence agents were using continental banking houses for sending their messages to London and that intelligence-gathering on British affairs needed to be improved. Consequently he proposed the establishment of a select corps of 117 men, the *Guides-Interprètes de l'Armée d'Angleterre*, to be stationed at various points along the coasts. Their mission was to find out everything possible about British naval and military movements. At the same time, knowing that Napoleon had become something of a hero to the Irish revolutionaries of the day, Fouché was not slow in coming to terms with the Irish intriguers and recruiting them to his own ranks.

Many of Fouché's reports to the Emperor related to surveillance of the coastlines and especially the Channel ports and, of course, intelligence concerning Britain. War between France and England had started in 1803 (another very good reason for Fouché's recall). On 17 July 1804, there was a report on pensions paid by the British to various emigrants to France who

were acting as agents, as well as news of the purchase of a ship
to survey the enemy coast from Jersey.[3]

'Mingaud declares that England often employs Russian,
Swedish and Spanish spies,' reported Fouché the following
month. This was confirmed in another bulletin which asserted
that 'such spies were directed against France'.[4]

On another occasion the spymaster informed his Emperor
that he was told that, 'The English government employs as
spies women, merchants, colporteurs [hawkers] and Jews.
Those in the interior address their reports to the agents who
live on the coast for the latter to pass on to English ships as
they go alongside them in their own boats.'[5]

Fouché worked closely with Colonel Jean Savary, who later
became a general and Duke of Rovigo. Savary was an aide of
Napoleon who headed the military intelligence section of the
General Staff at the Emperor's headquarters. This branch of
intelligence was separate from that of Fouché's, but he had
access to it. For a long period the two services worked well
together. Savary owed a great deal to an agent named Karl
Schulmeister, whom he discovered in 1799. Schulmeister, who
was born in a small town on the Rhine, had been a scribe to
the Prince of Darmstadt near Strasbourg, and had served for a
short period in the French cavalry. He had also indulged in
smuggling from time to time. Little is known of him between
the years 1800 and 1804, but it is believed that he had done
some work for the Austrians and became very knowledgeable
about their armies. Then it would seem that he became a
double-agent, working for the French while keeping this secret
from the Austrians. There seems to be confirmation for this in
that when he left Vienna he received travel documents from
Austria's Marshal Mack. Thus he had entry papers to both the
Austrian and French camps. Officially, however, he only
became an agent of General Savary in 1804.

His first assignment for the French was in connection with a
French plan to abduct Louis de Bourbon, Duc d'Enghien, who
lived in exile in Baden. This unfortunate young man took no
interest in politics whatsoever and certainly did not interfere in
French affairs: his sole crime in Napoleonic eyes was that he
lived on funds provided by the British. Therefore an example

must be made of him to warn other royalist exiles of the old regime. Louis de Bourbon often visited a young woman in Strasbourg and Schulmeister learned of these meetings and reported the matter to Savary. With the latter's agreement Schulmeister arranged for the woman to be detained and removed to Belfort near the frontier on the grounds that she was a suspicious person. The crafty double-agent's next move was to forge a letter from the young woman to Louis, begging him to come to her aid and try to obtain her release.

The gallant Duc responded exactly as Schulmeister had anticipated. He honestly thought he could bribe her captors to let him take her away from Belfort to the territory of his great friend, the Margrave of Baden. As soon as Louis approached the frontier he was seized by Schulmeister's assistants and abducted to Vincennes. A week later he was condemned to death by a court martial and executed by a firing squad. Schulmeister is said to have been paid a sum of money equivalent then to at least £4,000 for making these arrangements.

But it was in the following year, 1805, that Schulmeister proved his worth as a master-spy in the military field. For a lengthy period he supplied to the Austrians false information on the deployment and order of battle of the French armies, the intention being to deceive the Austrian Marshal Mack, a somewhat dull and unperceptive soldier.

Mack was in fact an easy prey for the astute and cunning Schulmeister, who spoke several languages fluently and ingratiated himself with the Marshal by claiming to belong to the Hungarian aristocracy. Lapping up all that the agent had to say, Mack introduced Schulmeister to exclusive clubs in the Austrian capital and even made him a member of his personal staff. Meanwhile Schulmeister was giving the French almost daily details of Austrian military plans and movements. They in return, with Napoleon's permission, printed copies of a French newspaper containing masses of false information which was passed on for Schulmeister to show to Mack.[6]

Ultimately Mack was lured into dispatching an army of 30,000 men in the expectation of pursuing and defeating the retiring army of Marshal Ney of France. What he found himself facing was a strong advancing army headed by Ney and on 2 December 1805 the united Austrian and Russian forces were defeated at Austerlitz. The Austrians were forced to capitulate and Marshal Mack, at first suspected of having betrayed Austria, was deprived of his rank and sent to prison.

It was long afterwards that the machinations of Schulmeister were discovered, thus paving the way for Mack's release. For even after the collapse of the Austrian armies Schulmeister was still conducting his intrigues in Vienna. As doubts about the double-agent were being whispered in the clubs of the Austrian capital such behaviour on his part was almost foolhardy. Indeed, but for the fact that the French occupied Vienna with exceptional speed and rescued him, Schulmeister would almost certainly have been arrested. The probability is that the slick Alsatian was relying on using substantial bribes to buy himself out of trouble. He must have been a rich man already, for he boasted afterwards that he had earned almost as much for his services to Austria as for those to France.

At the beginning of 1806 Vienna was occupied by Napoleon's forces and, as a reward from Savary, now a general, Schulmeister was appointed head of the police in Vienna as well as censor of press, publishing and theatres. Savary described Schulmeister to Napoleon as being 'a man who is all brains but with no heart'. This was perhaps not totally fair, for, despite his almost ceaseless espionage work, the ace spy adopted two orphan children and paid for their upbringing. His one big disappointment was that Napoleon could not be persuaded to award him the *Légion d'Honneur*. The Emperor insisted that gold was the proper reward for spies – no more and no less.

During the period Schulmeister was in charge of censorship it must be admitted that he used his powers to extend the Austrians' knowledge of works which had before been denied to them, including those of Voltaire, Diderot and Montesquieu. In many ways he revealed unsuspected traits of bravery and daredevilry, not merely in staying in Austria when he was under suspicion and risking his life in the French cause, but in other escapades and, not least, in applying for a cavalry command in the French Army. This request was granted and he was wounded in an attack on the Russians at Friedland. On another occasion when he was asked to report on a civilian uprising at Strasbourg he resolved the situation by shooting the ringleader of a threatening mob.

Certainly he thoroughly enjoyed the wealth which he won for himself by his activities as a double-agent. He purchased the exquisitely constructed Château le Meinau in Alsace and, much later, another mansion near Paris. It was not unusual in those days for the purchaser of an estate to take on the name of the owner, and this was something which Schulmeister did, being known as M. de Meinau.

Another of Fouché's discoveries was Lazare Carnot, a captain of engineers, a mathematician and one of the creators of modern geometry. Carnot helped to reorganize the Republican Army, being appointed Minister of War in 1793, and was later dubbed the 'Organizer of Victory'. With some encouragement from Fouché Carnot created the *Bureau de la Partie Secrète*, which was yet another useful section of intelligence. But in 1797 he was proscribed by the Vicomte Paul de Barras, who was a senior member of the *Directoire*.

Meanwhile Fouché was beginning to be concerned that Napoleon was unnecessarily adding to the number of his enemies. His detailed and shrewd analysis of the intelligence he received told him not only that Britain had now built up a first-class secret service, military as well as civilian, but that no good purpose could be served in continuing hostilities against the British. For much of this work he depended upon the indefatigable Mingaud. Mingaud, 'my bulldog' as Fouché called him, was sent to Boulogne not merely to organize and control intelligence coming from England, but as a counter-espionage agent to clamp down on the racket of the sale of false passports in that area, something which had been a boon for the British for years.

Fouché believed that to fail to come to terms with Britain would be disastrous, a belief which was strengthened by the knowledge that the secret services of the private banking houses, most notably that of Rothschild, were lukewarm about support for the French Emperor. Indeed, Rothschild's organization was convinced that in the long term Napoleon was bound to lose unless he changed his policy. From this point onwards Fouché's policy was aimed at peace and understanding with Britain and he used secret intermediaries in other nations, including Holland, to bring this about. In adopting this policy, contrary to Napoleon's wishes, the chief of police was not merely acting as a patriot facing the facts of life, but as one who wished to survive himself. He clearly saw the fate which awaited Napoleon if he continued warmongering. It has sometimes been said that governments take risks if and when they allow their policies to be dictated by their secret services, but in this instance the Napoleonic government failed in the long term through neglecting such advice.

Characteristically, Fouché used bankers as some of his most important intermediaries. Yet this was to lead to his downfall for a second time. A Monsieur Ouvrard, one of his banker friends, had set out to carry on negotiations with the British principally through Holland. Napoleon learned of this intrigue and other moves for conciliation with Britain which his police chief had made. When Fouché went to see the Emperor he tried his hardest to persuade him that he had only acted in the national interest.

'Fouché,' roared Napoleon, 'you have deceived me. I should order you to be shot immediately.'

Perhaps it was the influence of the Empress which saved Fouché's life. Certainly she pleaded his cause with Napoleon and so, too, did others in the Emperor's entourage. Nevertheless, Ouvrard the banker was arrested and Fouché dismissed from office, being supplanted in 1814 by General Savary as chief of police. The Emperor, who was subject to almost daily rages of temper at this time, merely sent for Savary and curtly and abruptly informed him that he was to 'take the oath and start work at once'.

Savary had previously been somewhat devious in his dealings with Fouché, and was one of those who had suspected him of having tried to appease the British. But his brief and terse encounter with Napoleon must have made him feel uneasy and insecure. This can be the only explanation of the fact that he sought Fouché's aid in the handover of duties. Savary hated Fouché even though he had worked closely with him for years, but when Fouché actually welcomed him to his new post, he actively sought his help and guidance. There he made a big mistake, for though Fouché was friendly and said he was eager to assist his successor and answer any questions, his aim was, as always, to safeguard his own future. He asked to be allowed a few days' grace in which to put his papers and affairs of his ministry in order.

During those fatal few days Fouché not only created chaos, making the police files thoroughly disordered, but he removed a vast quantity of documents and the names and addresses of many agents. Some files were destroyed, while everything that might aid Fouché's cause in the days ahead was taken away. When Savary discovered what had happened he immediately informed the Emperor, who in turn sent a message to Fouché at his estate at Ferrières demanding the instant return of the documents. Fouché's reply was that certain papers had been burned because they could have been incriminating. He hinted that such material might concern other members of the Bonaparte family and be used for blackmail. Eventually Comte Dubois, who had been serving under Fouché, was sent to put these same papers under seal and remove them. That did not particularly worry Fouché, who had already transferred the most important of these papers to a place of safety. In agreeing to hand back the other papers he even tried to ingratiate himself with Napoleon by offering his apologies. But the Emperor was in no mood for further dealings with Fouché: he ordered him to leave the country within twenty-four hours.

Meanwhile Schulmeister, who had consistently proved his worth in many espionage activities, fell out of favour with Napoleon after the Emperor's second marriage to the Austrian Archduchess Marie-Louise. She viewed Schulmeister's betrayal of the Austrians as something unforgivable and the master-spy was more or less forced to retire to his vast mansion in Alsace. When in 1813 Napoleon was forced to retreat to Paris and surrender territory he had gained that same year, the Austrians took their revenge on Schulmeister. They assigned a whole artillery regiment to demolish his mansion. Fortunately he was able to escape, but from then on his career took a downward path. Though out of favour with the Emperor for some time prior to his abdication in 1814, Schulmeister loyally offered his services again following the Emperor's escape from Elba. But with Napoleon's defeat after Waterloo Schulmeister was arrested and only escaped lengthy imprisonment by paying a huge sum as ransom. Always a fighter and above all an optimist, he tried to recover his fortunes by gambling, but he lost everything.[7]

He lived until well over the age of eighty, spending his latter years running a small tobacconist's shop in Strasbourg but never again earning much more money than was necessary to keep himself alive.

7

The Birth of the Deuxième Bureau

It is exasperating that nobody provides the Army with the means of
knowing what our military neighbours are doing.

General Ducrot, French
commander in Strasbourg in 1868

For the forty years following Napoleon's eclipse in 1815, there
was a gradual decline in France's intelligence services, civilian
and military, and this applied both inside and outside French
territory. For a while, even after the great Fouché was
dismissed from office, all was well, as the celebrated spy chief
had left behind him some extremely efficient operators. Two
such were Desmarest, Fouché's chief lieutenant, and Pierre
François Réal. Both men were specialists in the art of counter-
espionage.

Eventually it was Réal who became Director of Police and
Desmarest was his principal assistant. Both men were highly
skilled in interrogation techniques, handling their prisoners in
such a shrewd and friendly manner that often they completely
disarmed them and obtained all the information they required.
As was usual in many of the police and secret service appointments in those days each man came from an unconventional
background. Desmarest was an unfrocked priest with Jacobin
sympathies; indeed, the discipline and training of the Jacobin
clubs undoubtedly helped him in his interrogation work. An
example of this training can be seen in a method adopted by
Desmarest in recruiting spies. This was to insist that the recruit
to the espionage service commit some offence before taking up
his duties. This crime would then be documented by the police
and held as evidence to be used against the spy, if he should

attempt to double-cross the service. There was in this period a
kind of consensus among the chiefs of police and intelligence
(military as well as civilian) that the best spy or counter-spy
was a criminal, or someone who had at least committed some
misdemeanours earlier in life. This policy was the product of
the pig-headed military viewpoint that espionage was something unseemly and only fit for the criminal classes, and the
civilian view that the police had a tighter control of former
criminals and could exploit and direct them more easily.

Not surprisingly, in the long run, such tactics defeated their
ultimate aim as they put the emphasis on subjection to threat
rather than an appeal to patriotism. One exceptional agent,
employed as a result of these tactics, was Eugène François
Vidocq (1775–1857). Born at Arras, he became a criminal at
an early age, indulging in a number of spectacular coups before
he was caught and sentenced to eight years' imprisonment. In
1809 he escaped from prison and was employed by the secret
police in Paris. His intelligence and wit impressed senior
officers and he was recruited largely because of his extensive
knowledge of the underworld.

From then on 'Detective Vidocq', as he was known, devoted
all his knowledge of the underworld to the service of the police.
He was imaginative, with a disciplined mind, and never missed
a detail. Even more importantly, he became an authority on
secret codes, especially those used by the criminals. In his
Mémoires Vidocq quotes a song which was used to teach young
criminals a code to the special language of the underworld:

> *J'ai fait par comblance*
> *Girond languepé,*
> *Soiffant picton sans lance,*
> *Pivois non maquillé,*
> *Tirants, a passe à la rousee,*
> *Attachés de gratousse*
> *Cambriot galuche.*

> I happily gained
> A lovely mistress
> Dreaming of wine
> And spirits without water,
> Stockings, fine shoes,

A tightly laced waist,
A feathered hat.[1]

Vidocq provided a wealth of information on codes used by criminals, such as the tramps' sign for 'women only here', the crude drawing of a cat, and he also studied the work of Restif de la Bretonne who was so fascinated by the varied sexual habits and fetishes to be observed in Paris that he compiled an exhaustive study of them, taking notes in hieroglyphics only he could understand. Restif recorded all manner of oddities from encounters with prostitutes to his own fetish for women's shoes – the sight of a high-heeled shoe once causing him to follow a girl from Paris to Lyon. Vidocq insisted that such information was invaluable not only in detecting criminals, but also in recruiting spies.

Vidocq was eventually made a chief of police, but he himself became a victim of conspiracy. In 1832 a new and sanctimonious police officer named Delavau decided that it was time to clean up the service, making the ex-convict, Vidocq, the supreme example, despite his excellent record both in criminal cases and in the secret service. Vidocq, having his own spies in the service, was tipped off about Delavau's intentions and he promptly resigned and set up his own detective agency, calling this a *bureau de renseignements*. Yet the man Delavau chose to succeed Vidocq was yet another ex-convict, a man named Coco-Lacour, which seemed to make nonsense of Delavau's hypocritical pretensions. Later Vidocq's *bureau* was suppressed by the police, after which he published his memoirs in four volumes. Therein lies some of the story, since well authenticated, of Vidocq's own personally recruited team of police spies, comprised of reformed felons like himself.

During the regime of the Second Empire in the 1850s Napoleon III complicated matters by running his own team of spies in addition to the official secret police under the command of the Comte d'Hirvoix. As if that were not enough to make any state intelligence service almost unworkable, the Empress had a small spy service of her own, as, too, did the Prime Minister, Rouher, while there were said to be two other unofficial espionage services under the control of two other police agents also claiming to work for the Emperor. Sometimes all each service was doing was spying on its rivals. The moment arrived when it became apparent that none of these organizations was doing its work properly: on 14 January 1858, an attack using explosives, firearms and other weapons was made by an anti-Bonapartist faction on the Emperor's carriage, causing 160 casualties. The Emperor had his hat pierced by a bullet and the Empress had her temple scarred. But this did not lead to much improvement in police or intelligence services.

The disastrous effects of Napoleon III's failure to run efficient intelligence services made themselves felt especially in his aggressive policies towards Prussia. If ever a war was lost through secret service failures it was the Franco-Prussian War of 1870. While the Germans and most other European nations had built up their intelligence organizations and operated them partly at least by taking the methods of Fouché as a model (most notably his insistence on a steady up-to-date stream of intelligence from other countries daily), France had totally lost its lead in this field. French military circles were aware of this lack of intelligence and warned Napoleon III about this neglected branch of the armed forces. It was pointed out that the French lacked maps of Prussia. After a number of such protests Napoleon III in 1855 approved the creation of what was described as 'a uniform and militarily trained police', to be stationed all over France, but with the intention of seeking intelligence outside the borders. This service was set up in a desultory fashion with links to the *gendarmerie* and the Army, but it was far too slow in obtaining results.

The French had tended to imagine that the lead they had in cipher construction and deciphering still remained, but Rossignol's achievements were long past and other nations had overtaken them. Napoleon III's cipher officers usually deciphered any messages they intercepted, but they did not intercept many and those they got hold of were of little value. Other European powers were adopting more cautious methods of communication. Meanwhile the French were suffering from the ineffectiveness of their own ciphers, for up to the time of the Franco-Prussian War they were using methods that had hardly changed since the time of Rossignol and Richelieu. One result was that the ciphers no longer had the vocabulary necessary for modern warfare.

Meanwhile the Germans boasted of having 40,000 spies inside France. As this came from Wilhelm Stieber, Bismarck's master spy, one can regard the claim with some suspicion, though Stieber's biographer, Dr Leopold Auerbach, suggested that, if challenged, Stieber could have produced names and addresses of as many agents. French Intelligence in Paris should have paid more heed to Stieber because their military attaché in Berlin between the years 1866 and 1870, Colonel Baron Stoffel, constantly warned of the dangers posed by the German spy chief. While nothing Stoffel said or wrote suggested there were as many as 40,000 German agents in France, he gave specific details of some of Stieber's plans, yet he was still regarded as an alarmist.[2]

General Ducrot, the commander in Strasbourg, exclaimed in 1868 that 'it is exasperating that nobody provides the Army with the means of knowing what our military neighbours are doing'. On the eve of 1870 France did not have a single agent living in Germany and this failure was repeatedly and bitterly noted during the campaign.[3]

It was a year to remember for the French, 1870: defeat rankled deeply for years and the memory of it was largely responsible for the patriotic response of 1914–18 when France suffered appalling losses in manpower. After defeats at Woerth, Gravelotte and Sedan, Napoleon III surrendered with his army on 2 September 1870, 25,000 being taken prisoner in the Sedan battle, and 83,000 surrendering. Two days later a republic was declared in Paris and Napoleon and his family eventually sought sanctuary in Britain.

Yet in defeat, and with large areas of France occupied by the Germans, the new republic that was set up not only started to rebuild its intelligence services, but accomplished the task so well that it laid the foundations of France's present system. What is more, the new intelligence service it created started to operate in the occupied provinces. All this happened within a year. Police and the military produced reports out of which the new services were developed, and the hard facts were that during the Franco-Prussian War the French had no data on deployment plans, movements or the order of battle for the Prussian forces. Working discreetly, but speedily and urgently, the *Deuxième Bureau* was created in 1871 and run by Commandants Vinson and Samuel, two officers of the former Depot of War. It originally comprised less than a dozen senior Army officers, but, as its budget was set much higher than that of previous intelligence services, it soon expanded in numbers and influence. The first objective of the new service was to obtain intelligence on the German troops in the occupied areas of France. Officially the *Deuxième Bureau* became the Second Department of the Ministry of War in 1874. Since then the duties of the *Bureau* have always been specifically stated and controlled by the government. In 1893 there was a slight alteration to its terms of reference: an important task was to be 'the registering of matters concerning foreign armies and the expected theatres of war'. During the 1880s the *Bureau* also undertook the analysis of political intelligence, something which had never been adequately tackled before.

The founders of the new intelligence services of France looked far into the future. Eventually it was laid down that the *Bureau* should centralize and interpret intelligence for the French High Command and that in the event of war it would come into its own as the supreme arbiter of how that intelligence was used. No longer was it a case of one man doing the analysis, but a whole committee. What was dreaded more than anything was that France should once again face a war for which it was totally unprepared, and it can safely be said that the *Deuxième Bureau* developed into an organization which up to World War I was probably the best of its kind in the whole of Europe, most especially in the analysis of intelligence.

To help achieve this the enterprising Commandant Samuel installed at Nancy a 'bureau of the first line' which operated extremely well after only a few weeks, thanks to a quickly built team of agents. The aim was to get first-hand information on German troops in the area. It was essentially a small bureau at the start, eager to keep itself totally secret, but from this small organization a network of agents was developed. This bureau was equally concerned with espionage and counter-espionage.

It was because of the success of the Nancy bureau that the

Service de Renseignements, sometimes known as the Special Service, or more briefly as the SR, and devoted to gathering intelligence far and wide, was created. The SR was, of course, always answerable to the *Deuxième Bureau* in the last resort, so remained linked to the military.[4]

The SR was a most important development, as the *Deuxième Bureau* ultimately depended upon it totally. The SR built up its network of agents so speedily that in 1880 they were to be found in Berlin, Vienna, Dresden, Leipzig, Frankfurt, Cologne and Mannheim. By that time the SR had already obtained German mobilization plans. By 1884 the headquarters staff of the SR comprised three officers, one secretary, an interpreter and an archivist: all other expenditure was devoted to increasing the number of agents in the field.[5]

Meanwhile tight control by the military was established inside the *Deuxième Bureau*. There were five senior officers in charge of various geographical sections, the most important of which were the German, British and Italian departments. It was clearly laid down that the *Bureau* had to send new material each day to the Minister of War, the Chief of the General Staff and the Minister of Foreign Affairs. Only in the latter case was the civilian side of government involved. All the time, however, Germany was the main target for espionage.

Up until the early 1880s all was well. Then came a devastating scandal. The French War Minister, General de Cissey, while a prisoner of war in Hamburg, had become fond of the much younger Baroness de Kaala. The ruthless Stieber, the German spymaster, had discovered this brief interlude in de Cissey's life and, plying the baroness with cash and promises of more to come, sent her to France. The result was that de Cissey renewed his acquaintance with the baroness and carelessly betrayed to her many vital secrets. De Cissey was dismissed from office when this was discovered by French counter-espionage officers and the baroness was forced to leave France, but what this scandal most unfortunately and inopportunely created in France was a widespread, almost maniacal anti-Semitic crusade, for the baroness was a Jewess. From that date until World War II France was to suffer the consequences of this evil phobia. It led to frequent persecution of Jews in all walks of French life.

Gradually, both the British and the Germans noticed the improvements in the French Intelligence Service and learned of its reorganization. The Germans became sufficiently wary to arrest a French agent who was a senior railway official at Pagny-sur-Moselle in April 1887. He was held for eight days before being released. The British also noted the changes of policy in French Intelligence and especially that a close watch was being kept on territories close to Germany. Some of the British, however, tended to take a chauvinistic and alarmist view of this. Major Arthur Griffiths, a senior British police officer who had studied espionage, wrote that in Paris he found spies in 'all classes of society . . . in drawing-rooms and in the servants' hall, at one's elbow in the theatre . . . in the Army and the best professions'.[6]

It should perhaps finally be stressed that the *Deuxième Bureau* was essentially an organization controlled by the military and that it kept a low profile in peacetime, but emerged as all powerful in the event of war. Similarly the SR also kept a low profile, but on the declaration of war became part of the *Cinquième Bureau* of the French General Staff.

8

The Dreyfus Affair

No better lesson than the Dreyfus affair will ever be shown to the people; they have to make the effort to distinguish between liars and truthful men. They have to read, question, compare, verify, think . . . It will be understood that a country without justice is a mere enclosure of animals designed for the butcher.

Georges Clemenceau

Despite the great steps forward made with the creation of the *Deuxième Bureau*, the intelligence services soon found themselves caught up in the worst political scandal of the century. There had been a few others which disturbed the political and social life of France in the last few years of the century, but none had greater reverberations than the Dreyfus affair. It might possibly be said that this case was one of the most ignominious events in France's modern history: it was undoubtedly the most appalling instance of maladministration of justice ever to affect the nation's intelligence services. For here was a clear-cut case of an intelligence service's senior officers blinding themselves with religious and racial prejudice and actually doing the opposite of what such a service is supposed to do: they ignored vital evidence pointing to the truth and deliberately falsified evidence to convict an innocent man, and thus an innocent man was sentenced to the harshest terms of imprisonment and the guilty man escaped. It was a case of gross inefficiency combined with downright malice.

The affair was first made public in October 1894 by *La Libre Parole*, a Parisian newspaper, which announced that an act of treason had been committed in the General Staff of the French Army, and alleged that one of its officers had been caught selling French military secrets to Germany, Austria and Italy, who were at that time linked by the Triple Alliance. Posing the question of who this traitor was, the newspaper declared: 'Look for him among the Dreyfuses, the Meyers, the Levys – the rich Jewish families who are ruining the nation.'[1]

This was not merely a vicious and highly inflammatory piece of anti-Semitism, but a gross libel on a man who had not yet been tried, let alone found guilty. But it was symptomatic of everything about the Dreyfus affair from beginning to end: lies, libels, criminal conspiracy and a series of unforgivable cover-ups. Within twenty-four hours *La Libre Parole* actually named the alleged culprit as Captain Alfred Dreyfus, and then other papers took up the case with comments of their own, mostly unfavourable to the captain. Yet it was not until several weeks later that the court martial considering the case gave its verdict – guilty. The hearings were entirely in secret, and Captain Dreyfus was kept in solitary confinement for the whole period and not even allowed to write to his wife.

Dreyfus, the youngest of a family of six, was born in 1859 at Mulhausen in Alsace, where his father was in the textile trade. When Bismarck brought in a law which forced the people of Alsace-Lorraine to declare their nationality, all the Dreyfuses except for one brother decided to become French citizens and went to France to live. Alfred Dreyfus attended the *École Polytechnique* in Paris and in 1880 was gazetted with the rank of a cadet second lieutenant in artillery. From then onwards his career was spectacularly impressive, especially in the dedicated, intense enthusiasm which he brought to it. Intellectually, he was the superior of most of his young fellow officers and this may well have been one reason for their being critical and jealous of him. He soon achieved promotion and in 1889 became a captain in the 21st Artillery with a special appointment to the military academy at Bourges to study ballistics.

At the begining of 1893 he was attached to the General Staff, being the first Jewish officer to receive such an honour. This, too, was resented among those senior officers who had anti-Semitic prejudices. On 15 October 1894, Captain Dreyfus was summoned to report to the General Staff HQ in Paris, no indication of what he was wanted for being given. He was surprised when he was taken to the office of the Chief of the

General Staff where he was received by three officers, a major of the General Staff, the Marquis du Paty de Clam, a director of the *Sûreté* (the French Security and Criminal Investigation Department), a member of the Archives Department and a secretary.

'Captain Dreyfus,' said the Marquis du Paty de Clam, 'General de Boisdeffre [Chief of Staff] will be here shortly. Meanwhile I have a request to make of you. My finger is injured and I need to get off a letter. Will you write it for me, as I dictate?'

Dreyfus not unnaturally thought this was an odd request, particularly as there was a secretary in the room, but he immediately agreed to the proposal.

The Marquis then dictated a few sentences which obliquely referred to the crime which was later to be attributed to Dreyfus, but without mentioning him by name. Then suddenly he stopped and tersely barked at the young officer: 'What is the trouble, Dreyfus? Your hand is trembling.'

Dreyfus was baffled, vaguely wondering whether the Marquis was complaining about his handwriting, as in no sense did he feel his hand was trembling.

When he had finished the letter and handed it to the Marquis, the latter stared at him for a moment and then declaimed: 'I shall now order you to be put under instant arrest. The charge against you will be high treason against the Republic of France.'

By this time Dreyfus was even more perplexed. He managed to overcome his shock by protesting his total innocence of 'any such crime' and even offered the keys of his home so it could be searched. Notwithstanding this, he was immediately arrested and taken to the military prison.

The whole affair was based on tainted evidence, hearsay and, above all, anti-Semitic prejudices of the most virulent kind which were all too prevalent among some members of the General Staff of the French Army at that time. The Marquis de Paty de Clam had deliberately made the comment about a trembling hand so that this could be recorded at the trial as 'evidence' of Dreyfus's guilt. The Marquis was given the utmost credence. When asked about how Dreyfus faced up to his

accusations, he replied: 'The Jew turned pale.' Those were his
actual words.

The crucial piece of so-called 'evidence' used to convict
Dreyfus turned upon the opinion of one Alphonse Bertillon, a
handwriting expert, that a certain document which implied that
certain military secrets were being passed on, but which was
neither signed by anyone, nor addressed to anyone, had been
written by Dreyfus. All that could be said for certain by anyone
examining this objectively was that it would appear that military
secrets were possibly being leaked. No evidence against the
captain was turned up in a thorough search of his home and his
military record was totally without blemish. On how the French
authorities had obtained the allegedly incriminating document,
one story conflicted with another. The most widespread version
was that a French Secret Service agent had bribed a domestic
servant of the German military attaché, Colonel Max von
Schwartzkoppen, to pass on any material in her employer's
wastepaper basket (a ploy which often worked in those days
when security was not practised as rigorously as it is today). It
later transpired that this story would not stand up because the
attaché had never seen the document, nor had it in his office.

In fact, although this cover story was both false and stupid,
the document itself was genuine and its discovery a real scoop
for the French Secret Service. In this period French intelligence
practice in counter-espionage was to make use of Alsatians
against the Germans. One such Alsatian, Martin Brucker, in
keeping watch on the German military attaché had proved to
be a first-class agent. He had managed to seduce the wife of
Schwartzkoppen's *concierge*, and thus had access to the
attaché's correspondence. This was how he found the document
which was used to incriminate Dreyfus.

The letter was delivered to the SR and on to the *Deuxième
Bureau* and the General Staff were duly informed. Yet the
extraordinary thing was that when Govert, the handwriting
expert of the General Staff, compared the document with a
sample of Dreyfus's handwriting, he insisted that they were not
the same. It was then that the General Staff requested Bertillon's opinion. In other words, the General Staff had already
decided who was to be the culprit. This was despite a mass of

evidence in favour of Dreyfus. Even the governor of the military prison where the captain was imprisoned gave it as his firm opinion that 'Dreyfus is as innocent as I am'.[2]

At the same time as Dreyfus was convicted a brilliant and outstanding young officer was promoted from the rank of major to lieutenant-colonel and made head of the *Deuxième Bureau*. Colonel Georges Picquart, a native of Strasbourg, had been attached to the War Office staff in 1883 at the early age of twenty-nine. He had already made a name for himself through his practical experience of both espionage and counter-espionage work. Chosen for his new post in preference to other candidates who were several years his senior both in age and rank, Picquart was jealously and in some cases maliciously envied by some of his fellow officers. This partly explained the hostility shown towards him in later life.

Being one of the most diligent of analysts the Secret Service could have, Picquart examined the Service's files in great detail. He noticed that the plan Dreyfus was alleged to have sold to the Triple Alliance had been produced by the Operations Division of the French Army but had not been passed to the General Staff at the time of Dreyfus's arrest. If this was true, Picquart argued to himself, how could Dreyfus have known about it?

Picquart was a superb intelligence chief in that he did not allow Establishment views to dismay or inhibit him. If Dreyfus was innocent after all, then the real culprit was still at large. So Picquart immediately gave orders to his agents to re-examine the whole situation. All this took up a great deal of time, but in the end it resulted in the finding of the original of what Picquart called a *pneumatique* message from Colonel von Schwartzkoppen when he was military attaché in Paris to a Captain Ferdinand Esterhazy of the Army's Operations Division responsible for drawing up the mobilization plans. This message suggested that Esterhazy had been on intimate terms with the German attaché.

Thus Picquart was immediately alerted to the fact that, whatever the verdict on Dreyfus, there was a possible case against Esterhazy. He used his agents to investigate Esterhazy's whole life and their reports provided some astonishing evidence against the real culprit in the Dreyfus affair. Major Esterhazy's background was so doubtful that it seemed incredible that he could ever have been assigned to highly confidential work. He had said he was a member of the Hungarian family of Esterhazy and served in the Roman Legion, and before that had resigned from the Hungarian Army. Then he had joined the French Foreign Legion and, after war with Prussia broke out, he had been transferred to the French Army. Picquart discovered that Esterhazy had an expensive mistress and that he was almost always in debt, while living above his means.

At this stage Picquart felt so certain that he was on to something important that he ordered one of his agents to burgle Esterhazy's apartments. The fact that the German attaché in communicating with Esterhazy had conveyed messages using air-propelled cylinders and a system of pipes was highly suspicious. The result of the burglary was that Esterhazy was found to be in possession of the key for a cipher which was part of a complicated system operated by the Germans.

It was Picquart's hunch which not only threw doubts on the conviction of Dreyfus, but showed that there was a strong case to move against Esterhazy. But when he passed his evidence to the High Command in 1896 and urged that action should be taken, he was astonished at the reaction. He was almost immediately relieved of his post with the *Deuxième Bureau* and sent on a mission to Tunisia and his position was given to Colonel Henry, a close friend of Esterhazy.

The final verdict against Dreyfus had stated that he was guilty of 'having delivered to a foreign power or its agents a certain amount of secret or confidential documents concerning national defence'. Dreyfus was not only sentenced to life imprisonment, but publicly degraded on the parade ground of the *École Militaire* in Paris, where his sword was broken and his insignia of rank were ripped off his uniform, after which he was marched around the square, openly derided and abused by the watching crowd, despite his repeated cries of 'I am innocent. I did not commit this crime.'

So vindictive were the authorities towards Dreyfus that they even passed a law to ensure that he would be imprisoned for life in the French colony of Cayenne in Guiana. Strictly against normal practice, his wife was not allowed to go with him. He was kept in a hut on a small island of some twenty-five acres, notorious for its insects and the fevers they induced and with temperatures of between 77 and 87 degrees throughout the year. It came to be called 'Devil's Island'.

Meantime a few brave people had begun to question the verdict on Dreyfus, even though there was a formidable body of opinion ranging from the senior ranks of the French Army, right-wing and royalist politicians, priests and even some bishops who continued to condemn Dreyfus even after his exile on Devil's Island. Anyone who dared take the opposite view was threatened with legal action, and sometimes with hints of violence. It was almost as though the whole Establishment had decided to take this line, some on anti-Semitic grounds, others solely because there had sprung up a nationwide witch-hunt against traitors, a kind of late nineteenth-century version of McCarthyism.

One man who was not deterred by such threats was Émile Zola, the novelist, then approaching the age of sixty. His works such as *L'Assommoir*, depicting the evils of alcoholism, and *Lourdes*, with its attack on miracle-working stunts, had already marked him out as a forthright and pugnacious propagandist, but it was the Dreyfus affair which brought him into prominence far and wide. He had an ally in another equally brave man, Georges Clemenceau, the future French Premier, but then editor of the newspaper *L'Aurore*. In 1898 Clemenceau published in full Zola's attack on the French military for their treatment of Dreyfus, implying that they were all little better than criminals. Zola's denunciatory letter, *J'accuse*, was in effect a challenge to the French legal system, civil and military, and Zola was brought to trial for libel.

The military hierarchy, perhaps, had begun to worry about the Dreyfus case being brought into the open. Some officers within the hierarchy had obtained from the SR, or so they claimed, 'evidence' which it was hoped would silence their critics. This concocted evidence (for such it turned out to be) was organized with the full knowledge of Colonel Henry, the new head of the *Deuxième Bureau*. It included what were claimed to be communications between Dreyfus and Panizzardi, the Italian military attaché in Paris. These had allegedly been torn up, but carefully put together again by Colonel Henry's personal assistants. There was also a coded telegram from Panizzardi to the authorities in Italy sent in November 1894, which stated: 'Captain Dreyfus has been arrested. The Ministry of War has announced proofs of secrets given to Germany. If Captain Dreyfus has had no direct dealings with you, it would be well to publish a denial. My secret courier has been warned.'

This certainly seemed incriminating, but Colonel Picquart, who had been recalled to France, was not impressed and he resolutely refused to testify in favour of Esterhazy of whose guilt he was still absolutely convinced. He suspected a devious plot inside the Secret Service to cover up regarding Esterhazy and to produce concocted evidence against Dreyfus. Considering that two years earlier Picquart had personally pinpointed the evidence against Esterhazy to the *Bureau* and the General Staff, it seems incredible that they now asked him to help clear Esterhazy's name. When Picquart declined to play their game, he was arrested and found guilty of the trumped-up charge of 'having communicated official documents', and sentenced to sixty days under close arrest. In the same month Esterhazy, who had been publicly accused of treason, demanded that he should be investigated. As a result he was brought before a military court which dismissed all charges against him on the grounds that Dreyfus had been found guilty and there was no case to answer.

Later Esterhazy wrote a book, *Les Dessous de L'Affaire Dreyfus*, which gave his own totally dishonest account of the whole wretched business.[3] Meanwhile Zola was fined and sentenced to a year's imprisonment for libel. He appealed against the sentence and his case went to the highest court in the land. For once the judge resisted pressure to uphold the verdict and reversed the lower court's decision. Even after a new trial, however, Zola was again condemned, though ultimately he won and received a pardon. Life was made so unpleasant for him for a time that he sought temporary refuge in London. Eventually he returned to Paris where, in 1902, he was found dead in his bedroom, having been asphyxiated by the fumes of a charcoal stove. There is no evidence that this was other than an accident.

Picquart's friends, having been given instructions by him before he was put under close arrest, set about finding the evidence which was to clear both him and Dreyfus. One of them, Captain Cuignet, a specialist in checking documents for forgeries, noticed in checking the Panizzardi papers that under artificial light there appeared to be two types of paper, one pale grey, the other blue. Further examination showed that in several instances the lines of writing crossed the tears where two pieces of paper of different types joined, a pen-stroke on a piece of blue paper continuing over on to a piece of grey paper. This could only mean that the two pieces of paper must have been torn up together with one page over the other, the fragments assembled and *the writing placed on them last of all*.[4]

Both Cuignet and Picquart were equally convinced that the coded telegram was also a forgery. It consisted of groups of four figures which French Intelligence had identified as coming from a code made up by one Baravelli. But when the numbers were checked against the deciphered version presented as further evidence against Dreyfus, they made no sense at all. Part of the telegram was correct when checked with the Baravelli code, but the rest was either incorrectly deciphered, or gibberish. Obviously someone was not merely doctoring a telegram, but manipulating the code to suit his purposes. So further checks were made and this time the notorious Panizzardi telegram read as follows: 'Captain Dreyfus has been arrested. The Ministry of War has announced relations with Germany. If Captain Dreyfus had no direct dealings with you, it would be well to publish a denial to prevent unfavourable newspaper comment on us. We do not know him here.'

This version put a totally different aspect on the case against Dreyfus. In effect, this revised translation of the telegram appeared to clear him. Checks were made with the Italians, who co-operated in this instance, and it eventually transpired that behind this mystery lay not two telegrams, but three. The so-called French Black Chamber (in effect a department which originated forgeries and disinformation) had faked a secret message, using exactly the same number of words as the real Panizzardi telegram. This message was supposed to indicate that there was a French spy inside Italy. It stated: 'Monsieur X, now in the city of Y, will leave for Paris within a few days. He will take with him a document relating to Italian mobilization plans which he has obtained from a bureau there. Present address Z street.'

The faked document was, of course, propelled into Panizzardi's hands through what appeared to be a blunder. He acted promptly, relaying the message to Rome. All these messages used the Baravelli code and it was quite clear to Colonel Picquart and his agents that in this devious manner French Intelligence under Colonel Henry had allowed the report that Dreyfus was innocent to go astray, while all that pointed to his guilt had been retained.

Eventually all this evidence was put before Jacques Cavaignac, the French Minister of War, and he immediately interrogated Colonel Henry. Confronted with the evidence, Henry had to admit both to the forgeries and to the concealment of cryptographic evidence. As a result Henry was placed under arrest and, after writing a letter to his mistress explaining his conduct, he cut his throat. Yet even then Cavaignac, while forced to resign after admitting that he had been deceived, insisted that Henry's crimes did not prove the innocence of Dreyfus.[5]

This was the beginning of the end of the Dreyfus case, but even then action to set things right was taken very slowly. The results of the cryptological analysis were accepted slowly, possibly because of their complexity. But when all was fully understood French Intelligence generally was on trial. The morale of the whole service was affected from top to bottom: after what had happened to Dreyfus, how could anyone rely on the service ever again? It seemed that it was unable or unwilling to defend its own officer, or to ensure that it found the right villain. Despite even the new findings regarding the Dreyfus affair, the case against the able and honest Colonel Picquart was continued: he was rearrested, charged with forgery and kept in prison until 1899.

Dreyfus was released from Devil's Island in the same year and was pardoned by President Loubet. However, Dreyfus only agreed to accept this pardon on the understanding that it left him free to establish his innocence. Eventually both Dreyfus and Picquart obtained justice. In 1903 Dreyfus petitioned for a reconsideration of the case and three years later the *Cour de Cassation* not only quashed the former convictions but completely exonerated him. He was accepted back into the army with the rank of major, and, as a bonus, decorated with the Cross of the *Légion d'Honneur*. Colonel Picquart was reinstated and promoted to the rank of General.

But Dreyfus's troubles were not entirely over. In 1908 there was an attempt on his life when a shot was fired at him at a public ceremony, but he escaped with minor wounds. Even then a French court acquitted his would-be assassin. Although Dreyfus's sons wanted to attend military schools, they were compelled by sheer prejudice and harsh treatment to give up all ideas of a military career. Dreyfus himself offered his services again when World War I broke out, and he was made a brigadier and given a command in Paris. He died in Paris in 1935, suffering in his last years from the knowledge that the anti-Semitism he had known in France was now rising with even more venom in Nazi Germany. As to Picquart, when Clemenceau formed his first Cabinet, he took great pleasure in appointing that gallant defender of Dreyfus as his War Minister.

The Dreyfus affair seriously affected French Intelligence for many years afterwards. There still remained within the service anti-Semitic forces, but also the *Dreyfusards* who defended him. In 1899 there was what amounted to a dissolution of the SR, those officers of the anti-Dreyfus camp being relieved of their posts and sent to other units. There was much tighter command from on high in the *Deuxième Bureau* and specialized research into espionage projects was confined to a small section called the *Section de Renseignements*.

But it was not until 3 September 1940 that the Dreyfus affair truly ended. Then all dossiers on the case held by the SR were incinerated following the evacuation of the French Government from Paris.[6]

9

The Demise of the Double Agent

> Set out to lure over to your side all those who are committed to the enemy. Sometimes you may fail, but sometimes you will succeed beyond all expectations. You must win over your enemies.
>
> Desmarest, an agent of Fouché

At the turn of the century espionage in Europe increased on all sides. There were many reasons for this – the gradual change in the alignment of nations in Europe itself, the rivalry in empire-building and colonial development involving France, Britain, Germany and Italy, especially regarding North Africa, and, not least, the expansionist ambitions of Germany.

The SR was rapidly developed between 1890 and 1905, notably in building up frontier posts for intelligence-gathering. There were three such posts (with an officer controlling each) covering Austria and Italy (Chambéry, Briançon and Nice) and four on Germany (Belfort, Epinal, Nancy and Remiremont). What seems to have been neglected – possibly fatally in the long term – was the northern area of Belgium and Holland. In all cases the target for espionage was Germany.

The reason for this was partly a result of the effects of the Franco-Prussian War, but also an uneasiness about Germany's long-term intentions.

Picquart, by now back in the service, was a meticulous and scrupulous operator, and also one of the first intelligence chiefs to make use of the *agent-provocateur* for obtaining military intelligence. The aim was to make better use of enemy agents than the enemy could. An *agent-provocateur* can be described as an agent employed to stir up trouble, create chaos and generally make mischief. Occasionally, an *agent-provocateur* is also a double-agent and it is then that problems can occur. One such agent was a smuggler named Galanti, who was suspected of spying for more than one power, but whom Picquart felt could be a useful ally, if carefully watched and controlled.

Accordingly, Picquart instructed one of his officers to recruit Galanti to the service of the French. The idea was not merely for Galanti to do some spying, but to create mischief among other powers by passing on false information. The *Deuxième Bureau*'s senior officer was well rewarded, as in due course Galanti was able to reveal that an enemy agent had been asked to gain access to the French gun batteries at Fort Bessoncourt to measure the calibre of the guns and obtain photographs of the batteries. Playing the role of a double agent, Galanti got details of the exact time and date when the mission was to be carried out, with the result that an arrest was made. The spy was caught and sent to prison for three years. Meanwhile Picquart had caused a genuine enemy agent to be sacked on account of his false report that the agent was a traitor, information which caused concern in both Berlin and Vienna. Picquart, rightly judging that Galanti could find himself in dire trouble when his part in all this was revealed, sent him off on a long holiday with pay to a remote part of Switzerland.

However, this episode was not typical of *Deuxième Bureau* operations (their job was and is analysis, not espionage): it was simply an example of Picquart's versatility. It should be stressed that this vital branch of French Intelligence was almost solely analytical and depended almost entirely upon what was fed to it by the SR and the counter-espionage section, the SCR.

Nevertheless, there was a disturbing tendency among the senior officers of French Intelligence to employ double agents – agents working for other powers as well. While this tactic can work in some circumstances, as was the case when Picquart used Galanti, it is always dangerous. In playing with double-agents the SR was laying itself open to trouble and exploitation. The double-agent needs as his controller a very cool, shrewd and tough officer: it should be remembered that the double-agent can also be fed with false information by the other side.

One problematic case was that of an agent named Lajoux, a devious and erratic adventurer, but one who provided much intelligence for France. Major Rollin, an SR officer, said of

Lajoux, 'He was a brave, intelligent agent, sometimes difficult to deal with and temperamental. He was invaluable to us and while I was in the Intelligence Service, of fifteen cases of treason and espionage which led to arrest, four were due entirely to Lajoux.'[1]

Lajoux had been in the French Army for ten years and had acquired the rank of a non-commissioned officer. Having completed his term of service he sought work in Belgium rather than in his own country. This suggests that he might well have been seeking some kind of espionage work for another power and this seemed to be confirmed when he was approached by the German Secret Service in Brussels. They knew that Lajoux was short of funds and they were led to believe that he would not be averse to working for them. Shortly afterwards a generous offer of work was made to him and he immediately accepted it.

But the wily Lajoux had ideas of his own. His original motives may have been patriotic, or they may have been to safeguard himself in the future with both the French and the Germans, or he may even have been entirely mercenary. He immediately reported back to French Intelligence about the German offer, not, let it be noted, directly, but through a letter to the War Minister. He gave full details of the German offer, suggesting that he should take this up and report back to the French all that he learned.

What should have made the French suspicious was that he had not sought work from them when he went to Brussels. However, being only too anxious to have a double-agent, the SR agreed to his proposal and forthwith enrolled him in the *Section de Statistique* (Archives Department). From that moment onwards Lajoux was working for the French and the Germans. This was no easy task because the Germans were most demanding, wanting fullest details of French plans at regular intervals, while the French also wanted to have value for their money. What was never satisfactorily cleared up was why, in the first place, the Germans should think an out-of-work ex-NCO of the French Army could help them in Brussels, of all places. Lajoux must have been an extremely competent bluffer.

The material he passed to the Germans was only what the French authorized him to pass on. This bogus intelligence was prepared by a member of the SR in close co-ordination with the French Army and, of course, the *Deuxième Bureau*. It was always cleared with the General Staff beforehand. But here again the SR and the Army were playing a dangerous game, as anything of this nature (especially if it went wrong) could be called treasonable, and in the light of the Dreyfus affair such tactics were even more liable to misinterpretation. Even the Chief of Staff might have been committed to Devil's Island, had he been accused of passing information to the enemy, despite all excuses for doing so. There was the added factor that some of the intelligence Lajoux passed to the Germans had to be accurate, otherwise they would eventually have become highly suspicious.

At this time, of course, French Intelligence was still being rebuilt and was almost desperately eager to have any kind of agent. So Lajoux for four years was vital to them. Difficulties developed when the Germans, believing that Lajoux had closer contacts inside French Intelligence than was actually the case, became more demanding in their thirst for information. The Chief of Staff of the French Army at this time was General de Mirabel, who must have been well aware that the German controlling Lajoux was none other than Herr Ouers, an expert in both espionage and counter-espionage.

Inevitably, as time passes, the task of any double agent becomes more difficult. Probably the French should have withdrawn Lajoux from this double task after about three years and offered him a more remunerative job inside their own organization. What happened was that the Germans began to suspect Lajoux round about 1896, most notably after they discovered that some of their own agents inside France had been arrested. Then almost immediately afterwards came the merest hint from Lajoux that, if he remained an agent of the Germans, his days were numbered. It was then that the French Secret Service took the ruthless and almost incomprehensible decision that Lajoux could be totally discarded and left to suffer his dismissal by the Germans. What apparently the French took objection to was that Lajoux had told the Germans he worked for the *Deuxième Bureau*. Not only was Lajoux discharged by the French, but he was not offered any other post or work.

At this time Colonel Henry was in charge of the *Bureau*, and he not only terminated Lajoux's employment, but attempted to destroy him into the bargain. Meanwhile other French agents were told to keep him under observation. That was to some extent understandable, but when Lajoux was away from his home in Brussels agents of the SR broke into his house and stole his private papers, as well as using their wiles to try to persuade Madame Lajoux to leave her husband and sue for divorce, aparently with the aim of persuading her to name her husband as a traitor. Lajoux's wife, however, paid no heed to such proposals. He himself suffered from continuous persecution until, realizing he had no future in Belgium, France or Germany, he went to Brazil in 1897 to seek a new life there.

The Lajoux case exemplifies what can happen even with a good double agent, if the officers controlling him lose their nerve and fail to back him up. Lajoux had done a good job for France and he was badly let down.

From the early part of the twentieth century French Intelligence gradually became cleansed of the corruption, deceit, anti-Semitism and criminality which emerged during and after the Dreyfus case. Changes in the top ranks of the intelligence services were fairly frequent at this time, partly due to the fact that the hierarchy were still trying to find the right personnel for such posts. Men like Cordier, Rollin and Sandherr came and went. They all seem to have adopted a cynical attitude towards the agents they so eagerly courted with bright promises, regarding them all as easily expendable if necessary. There was the case of an agent named Corninge, an insurance salesman, who was lured into resigning from a pensionable job in order to work for the SR. From 1891 to the end of the century he worked as an agent in Geneva and supplied a considerable amount of information both on German and Italian affairs. Suddenly in 1899 he found his services dispensed with and he was given neither a promise of alternative employment, nor a pension. Treatment of agents was not always so harsh, but it happened far too often. Once carried to excess such a policy can lead to disenchanted agents going over to other powers even in peacetime.

It must be realized that at this time almost all forms of the French Secret Service were linked to the military. There is no doubt that French Intelligence generally suffered from a lack of some vital information as a result of the anti-Semitic bias of its senior officers. Certainly all countries at this time regarded the obtaining of military intelligence as a matter for the Army, but France in this period seems to have lapsed in failing to maintain a strong civilian intelligence service as it had always done in the past. Thus, much political intelligence was lost. Other powers at this time, especially the British, made much greater use of civilians. It is equally interesting to note how in this period the Germans actually gained ground through their employment of Jewish agents, whereas the French lost some worthwhile agents because of their prejudices.

Prior to World War I the *Deuxième Bureau* suffered from inadequate reports from its agent in Berlin, General Serret, the military attaché from 1912 to 1913. The complaint against him was that his reports were mostly politically orientated and gave no details of Germany's military plans, a quite extraordinary tendency in a military attaché. Slowly it was realized that military men rarely make the best intelligence officers, though little was done to act on this fact, except occasionally to give a brilliant civilian military rank. Both Britain and Germany learned the lesson to some extent that one could not rely too much on purely military agents. Yet all this was changed in World War I when the French started to employ female agents and made better use of them than any other nation. This may seem to be an astonishing change in policy, but when the French make up their minds on a problem, they tend to act more swiftly than most other nations and adapt to major changes more easily.

Such faults in the system in the early 1900s have since been fully admitted by the French themselves, though in the main they tend to blame the counter-espionage services for failing to catch German spies. But perhaps the French have not even today paid sufficient tribute to the intelligence they did receive prior to World War I. There is no doubt that the Germans fully hoped to repeat their successes of 1870, but the French were kept fully aware of the military plans being drawn up by the German generals before the war.

The SR had made every attempt to monitor what was going on inside the homes of the German military attachés and this was continued as far as possible after war broke out. In Paris, for example, before World War I when the German military and naval attachés took an apartment outside the German Embassy for conducting private talks, the SR fitted every chimney in the building with listening tubes leading to the floor above where an agent recorded all that was said. There are countless instances of intelligence gathered in this manner, not only on the Schlieffen Plan, but on the numerical strength of the German Army and details of guns and tanks. One of the most important examples of this was when the French acquired in 1908 a report made by one Colonel Ludendorf, then in charge of mobilization plans for the German Chief of Staff. Another report given to the SR revealed that the Germans would not violate Swiss neutrality, and there were details, too, of how in the case of a major French attack the Germans would retreat behind the Rhine.

But in the years 1905–14, as also happened in World War II, the Chiefs of Staff of the French Army neglected a great deal of the intelligence offered to them by the *Deuxième Bureau*. In 1888 French Intelligence had come up with a report from an agent in Essen that the Germans were working on the production of a long-range gun. Nobody paid any heed to this report and it lay neglected in intelligence files until in March 1918 the Germans opened fire on Paris with their long-range cannon which was nicknamed 'Big Bertha'. This was not solely a French failure: with the possible exception of the German, most military services in peacetime slip back into a kind of sloth and tend to think in the past. The modern exception to this is Soviet Russia. That nation knows exactly what SDI means.

A classic example of French failures in military intelligence was when some of the French generals claimed to be totally surprised by Germany's Schlieffen Plan at the beginning of World War I. This was a devastating attack in which the Germans not only deployed almost their entire military force against France, but also ignored all treaty guarantees of neutrality such as that applying to Belgium. The truth was that French agents had known of this plan long beforehand and such information had been passed to the High Command, who had paid scant attention to it. This resulted in French soldiers being outnumbered two to one at the outset of the war. My own view is that the SR did a first-class job before World War I in supplying intelligence and that the *Deuxième Bureau* did include this in their analysis and interpretation. This viewpoint is to some extent confirmed by Henri Navarre, a veteran member of the SR who has stated: 'It has been said that we were badly informed, that we had no knowledge of the German plan of campaign [in World War I] . . . These criticisms are not justified.'[2]

What the French did lamentably fail to predict effectively and strongly enough in terms of intelligence analysis was the terrible weakness of Belgium. The Belgians failed to strengthen their own fortresses on the grounds that such expense would be too costly and too late to have much effect. The Belgian General Staff had in effect capitulated before war broke out.

This was also the era of the cryptographical battle in which all the European powers were struggling for improvements in the cipher systems used. Studies in cryptography were added to the curriculum at military academies, for it was obvious that in any future conflict a great deal would depend upon the skill and speed of the operators. This showed how war was feared long before 1914. In the 1880s at St Cyr, the French military academy, much time was devoted to the study of this subject, and a cryptographical tool was produced which became known as the St Cyr ruler, a kind of slide-rule which made the writing and deciphering work both easier and quicker.[3]

Slowly, the French began to catch up again in the sphere of cryptography. But it was not only the potential enemies' ciphers which the French had to worry about, but to some extent those of the royalists, who, though a small minority, were strong and secretive. During the 1890s there had been a number of major financial scandals in France which on more than one occasion involved Cabinet Ministers. The royalists, linking up with the anti-Semitic lobby which had come to the fore with the Dreyfus case, denounced the republic as a corrupt institution which should be overthrown. There was a powerful underground movement which urged that a monarchy should be reestablished in its place. It was discovered by police agents and one diligent member of the SR that Paul Déroulède, the poet and leader of the League of Patriots, was in possession of a secret code used for communications between the League and other royalists and the Pretender to the throne of France, the Duc d'Orléans. Undercover agents had no difficulty in obtaining copies of these secret messages, but they were unable to decipher them.

The problem was solved by requesting the help of the Army's cryptological section whose head was one Commandant Bazeries, who had a considerable reputation as a cipher-breaking genius. Even he had difficulties in tackling the royalists' code, but by an imaginative guess he realized that the key to the problem was the names of the days of the week, particularly the days on which the messages were written. As a result Bazeries was able to say how the royalists planned to create a revolt against the republic and that this plot even extended to some members of the French Army.

Consequently, in 1900 when the moment for open revolt was scheduled, the authorities were fully prepared. Déroulède made a move to talk with senior officers of the French Army and was immediately arrested on a charge of treason, as were some others. Then came a complete climb-down when the authorities decided not to reveal the details of the secret messages, preferring to keep to themselves the fact that these had been deciphered. In the light of this failure to produce detailed evidence all the defendants were acquitted. Meanwhile the royalists naturally suspected that their cipher had been uncovered and they immediately changed it.

The brilliant Commandant Bazeries was not dismayed. He immediately set to work to break the new cipher, finding that the clue to it this time lay in one of the poems of Alfred de Musset. He was able to report that the royalists planned an armed insurrection. This time the authorities made no mistake. They arrested Déroulède and two of his assistants, and raided the headquarters of the League of Patriots as well as that of the

Anti-Semite League. For a short while the raiders were resisted, but when troops were called in they surrendered. At the subsequent trials Bazeries was a witness and it was his evidence which resulted in the plotters being convicted. Once again Richelieu's constant reiteration of the importance of ciphers was fully appreciated.[4] Meanwhile, though France and Britain had been drawing closer together over the previous twenty years, there had been some setbacks. Joseph Caillaux as Prime Minister had conducted long negotiations with Germany over Morocco behind the back of his Foreign Minister, M de Selves, which led Europe close to war in 1911. But even before the beginning of the war General Dupont, then head of the *Bureau*, had been in close touch with Britain's Secret Intelligence Service. This was done mainly through military attachés, but sometimes by direct relations with London.

In the ten months immediately prior to World War I France unexpectedly and luckily secured the services of a number of new agents. Several foreigners offered their services at the SR post at Belfort, doubtless as a result of careful reconnaissance by French intelligence officers. Slowly, the errors of an earlier generation were being learned from and much more sophisticated tactics were being used in methods of recruitment. No longer was it the mercenary double-agent who was being sought, but the man or woman inspired by patriotism for a nation other than his or her own. One such agent recruited for the Belfort post was Commandant Andlauer, originally an officer of the Haut-Rhin. He started work for the SR in 1913 and after a short period when he was almost entirely on his own, the post was developed into what in effect was a sub-centre of the *Grand Quartier-Général*, the supreme executive authority among the military for overseeing this area.

Belfort, centre of the former department of Haut-Rhin, which had been ceded to Germany in 1871, was a crucial centre for French espionage in the years immediately before World War I and the first year of the war. It was a commercial entrepôt for trade with both Germany and Switzerland and the centre for a vast system of fortifications. Here French Intelligence set up what they called a *Bureau d'exploitation*, employing mainly Alsatians for a whole range of jobs including gathering intelligence, reporting on movements, intercepting deliveries of mail, and even collecting the documents of German prisoners killed in the war so that these could be used as identity papers for their own spies. Out of all this intensive work (and the Alsatians proved among the most diligent and conscientious of such agents) many worthwhile results were obtained. General Dupont declared, 'In our establishment at Belfort the General Staff had a vital ally. The patriotism of the agents we employed was such that they worked far longer hours than could normally be expected of any person. They showed great initiative in using Switzerland as a means of top secret communications when all else was too dangerous. For all of four years this was a force of rare quality.'[5]

Another Alsatian hero of the French Secret Service was David Bloch, who joined the 152nd Infantry Regiment and volunteered for secret work in his native Alsace which was under German occupation. On 22 June 1916, Bloch was given papers in the name of Karl Sprecher, representative of a silk firm in Mulhouse. He was dropped in uniform by parachute behind enemy lines, and told to change into civilian clothes when he landed; if he were caught on arrival, he could be shot as a spy if he were not in uniform. Bloch took with him a basket of carrier pigeons to be used for carrying back his reports. Everything was arranged for bringing him back to safety: he was to make a rendezvous at a certain date, time and location, and to signal the aircraft picking him up with three green flashes from his signal lantern.

For six days Bloch spent his time gathering intelligence with remarkable success. But his mistake was to ignore French orders that on no account was he to visit his home town of Gutweiler. Possibly elated by the amount of information he had gathered (much of it he managed to send back by carrier pigeon), he took this risk. Someone in the town recognized him and denounced him to the German authorities. He was eventually stopped by a German patrol, arrested and shot in August 1916.

One SR report concerning Bloch states, 'Sprecher managed under great difficulties to send back to us reports which may well have saved hundreds if not thousands of lives . . . this was intelligence of the utmost instant value.'

10

How France Learned of the Gas War Threat

At Ypres on 22 April 1915, the German High Command instigated the suffocating novelty of chemical warfare . . . The first gas used was ejected from metal tanks brought up secretly to the front . . .

A contemporary newspaper report

One of the greatest successes of the war for French Intelligence was their success in obtaining copies of a German plan to make a gas attack on the Allied armies. For several months before the first gas attack of the war there had been some concern in all countries involved in the conflict about the possible sudden use by one of the combatants of a deadly gas which could wipe out troops on a large scale. French Intelligence had made this a major target for research.

The discovery of the gas threat itself was partly engineered by the Abbé Vorage, a young Dutch seminarist who became a French citizen in 1914 and joined the French Army at the Consulate of Rotterdam. In January 1915, he obtained full details of the German plan to use gas in an attack at Dixmude. Later he provided the French with the exact formula for the manufacture of the gas. The Germans regarded him as such a serious threat to their campaign that they put a price of 10,000 marks on his head.[1]

Linked to this intelligence success was the setting-up of a Franco-British post at Folkestone, one of the first and best examples of French and British intelligence services co-operating on an organized basis. It was set up to run agents of both nations throughout the war in Belgium, Holland and those parts of France occupied by the enemy. On the French side it was run by Commandant Zopff and on the British side by Major Cecil Cameron.

As a result of Vorage's information the Folkestone organization, which was generally known as the Anglo-French Bureau, directed French Intelligence to pursue inquiries into possible German plans for developing gas warfare. However, although the Abbé was the initiator of such inquiries and the first to realize the importance of this new and hideous threat, it was Charles Lucieto, one of the most successful of France's wartime secret agents, who must take the credit for the final discovery.

Skilled both as a collector of intelligence and as a counter-espionage agent – a rarer combination than most people think – Lucieto used his counter-espionage techniques and ability to disguise himself as a German to obtain information. He was something of an all-rounder: he had considerable scientific knowledge, had worked in industrial plants, understood the techniques of the manufacture of high explosive shells and guns and was also a commercial traveller.

Early warnings of gas attacks by the Germans had been obtained by the French long before the chlorine gas attack launched by the Germans at Ypres in 1915. Astonishingly, only one French military leader, General Ferry, had taken these warnings seriously: both on the British and French sides there had been scepticism and even scoffing about this intelligence. Ferry, in command of the Eleventh Division, was convinced there would be gas attacks and warned his British colleagues. The astonishing fact is that, despite improving co-operation between Britain and France, General Ferry was not only criticized for warning the British directly instead of passing the information through his superiors in the French Army, but actually punished by being removed from his command.

The original method of gas warfare used by the Germans was to release gas from cylinders when a favourable wind was blowing. Then came an occasion when the course of the wind changed suddenly and German troops had the gas blown into their own faces. Reports showed that this had caused deaths and hundreds of casualties among German soliders, but French Military Intelligence (as distinct from the French Army) felt certain that the Germans would not cease gas warfare on this account. So Lucieto was asked to find out about the production of the gas. Posing as a salesman in Mannheim, he learned that there was a considerable stepping-up of activity at the Badische Anilin and Soda Frabril, a chemical factory that was working day and night. Lucieto discovered that the Germans' new secret weapon was shells filled with gas. He passed the news to his superiors, but found that they were sceptical and demanded detailed proof. This was asking a great deal of a valuable agent; indeed, it was almost an invitation to commit suicide as any attempts to get more details could have meant arrest and execution for Lucieto.

This resourceful agent, however, possessed courage, charm and cunning and he acted with consummate skill. He had made friends with various people inside the factory, and his technique was to pretend not to believe in what they told him. It is a technique which works one way or another: either the agent becomes convinced he is being fooled, or those in the know offer him full proof. Lucieto played the role of a patriotic German who would like to believe that gas shells were feasible, but was extremely doubtful about the whole project. To induce one key person at the chemical works to come up with more evidence that gas shells could be manufactured, he made a bet. 'If you can convince me that this can be done, I'll give you two thousand marks. Take this as a bet: if you lose, you give me five hundred marks, and if I win I'll give you two thousand.'

The bet was taken up and, of course, Lucieto lost, as he hoped he would. He was eventually allowed into the plant to watch experiments at which not only the Kaiser, but senior German generals were present, and saw the cloud of green-yellow smoke released after a shell was fired. As he paid his bet, he said, 'That's a lot of money to lose, but I'm not sorry. As a patriotic German I know this weapon is going to kill lots of French and English and so win the war.'[2]

Finally, he managed to obtain a fragment of one of the gas shells as positive evidence. Without delay, though at much risk to himself, he made his way back to Paris with the shell fragment in his possession. At last the SR were convinced and this intelligence led to the manufacture of gas masks for Allied troops.[3]

That fragment of shell which Lucieto took back to Paris was of enormous value. It was sent to a research laboratory presided over by Edmond Boyle, a chemist of great distinction. He found that the gas used in the shell was a combination of phosgene and trichloromethane, a far deadlier gas than any used before. As a result of this discovery the Allies not only ordered gas masks to be provided for the troops, but manufactured gas shells of their own, even though this was banned by the Hague conventions on warfare. This decision finally made the Germans abandon gas warfare.

The need for swiftly obtained factual evidence of this kind was vital throughout World War I and the Allies might easily have lost hundreds of thousands more lives, but for much of this intelligence. Yet if Lucieto was the supreme artist in this field, credit must also go to those agents even in neutral countries who helped to gather information from the enemy. Typical of this type of agent was Jacques Mougeot, the son of a former French Minister of Posts. He served in the French Army, was wounded early on in the war and, being unfit for active service, volunteered to go to Switzerland to organize an information service spying on German agents and operatives in that territory. He set up his undercover office at the Château de Bellegarde on Lake Geneva, and obtained a steady stream of intelligence reports from his sub-agents, quite often including material secured from the office of the German military attaché.[4]

The French had a spy situated inside the German *Oberste Heeres-Leitung* (German GHQ) for the whole of the war. No other Allied secret service managed to achieve so much. His name was Waegele and he was commissioner of field police, but what made him so important for French Intelligence was that every time the OHL moved, he went with them – from Charleville, Stenay, Kreuznach to Pless. His principal mission was to protect the Germans from the attention of enemy agents!

To survive throughout the war in such a capacity was in itself an extraordinary achievement for Waegele, who was passionately devoted to France. As a counter-espionage officer for the Germans he would always have been watched for any mistake, any small hint of his real sympathies. His whole past would have been subjected to a close examination, especially his links with France or French people. At the same time Waegele had to prove himself to his masters as a ruthless questor for spies and troublemakers. Unfortunately, even a careful examination of documents of the period does not reveal how useful Waegele was to the French, except that it is recorded that early in May 1918, he reported that the Germans were planning a major attack on the Chemin-des-Dames, a battlefield near Laon, but that this message reached Chantilly ten days too late.

Waegele was given various code-names, sometimes even that of another French agent, which makes one wonder who was covering up for whom. It may be that in some of the records of intelligence there has been a confusion about names and code-names. However, it seems more likely that the spymasters sometimes substituted one code-name for another either to mask the real source, or to protect one agent, or a combination of both.

There was one agent who operated under a number of different pseudonyms, though he was best known under the code-name of 'Carlos'. An Alsatian mobilized in 1914 in the German Army, he was wounded in the early days of the war and then switched into the customs service. His main job was supervising the supply of wines and spirits for the officers' mess at the German GHQ on the Western front. As a result of what he overheard and saw he was able to pass invaluable intelligence to the SR. He did this through the intermediary of a chemist in Basle who had links with the Belfort network of agents.

'Carlos' passed on warnings of various German movements and plans of attack throughout the war. He signalled the attack on Verdun in February 1916, and gave news of the last German offensive of July 1918. Yet time after time the French High Command were sceptical about his information and sometimes failed to act on it. His report about Verdun was as follows:

The Germans are to launch a serious offensive in the region of Verdun. The troops charged with this offensive will be placed under the orders of the Crown Prince . . . an important concentration of troops – which forms part of the XV CA – will operate from the moment it arrives in the German lines, notably in the sector of the 10 DR, to the east of Damvillers-Chémilly . . . Numerous guns have been installed in the forest of Gremilly . . .[5]

One of the reasons for the High Command's scepticism about some SR reports is said to have been that the Germans had managed to pass on false intelligence about military movements to them by roundabout routes. But in the last year of the war there was much greater enthusiasm for accepting SR reports. Even the High Command had to admit that they had been negligent in the past. The tragedy was that after the war ended once again there was a tendency to play down intelligence reports as being scaremongering.

One of the major headaches for the *Deuxième Bureau* and the SR in World War I was the secret plans of some of the defeatists in high places to make deals for ending the war. In 1917 the Prime Minister, Painlevé, concerned about the various mutinies in the French Army, gave to Major le Comte Armand an assignment to conduct secret negotiations with Austria following reports that Austria-Hungary was beginning to regret being involved in the war.

Armand, the son of a former French Ambassador to the Vatican and a member of the board of Schneider-Creusot with a fortune estimated at four million pounds, was working in the *Deuxième Bureau*. The theory was that the Emperor Karl might be interested in a separate peace. The Austrian involved in the talks was Prince Sixte de Bourbon-Parma, and it was tacitly understood that Lloyd George (then British Prime Minister) supported the idea and felt it was well worth exploring. Though ultimately hailed as the 'great war-winner' of World War I, Lloyd George always possessed defeatist tendencies, as was exemplified by his attitude towards Hitler's Germany in World War II. Armand was a close friend of the Count Nicolas Rovertera, adviser to the Austrian Government, and meetings took place between the two men in Armand's Swiss residence at Fribourg on 7 August 1917.

The situation changed when the French Government fell and Clemenceau became both Prime Minister and War Minister. Clemenceau was made aware of Armand's secret mission and at first approved of it, or at least so it seemed. 'Tiger' Clemenceau was no defeatist: he probably wanted to see how far things had developed and if there was a chance for a

favourable deal for France. But shortly afterwards, undoubt-
edly wisely in retrospect, he had Armand transferred from the
Deuxième Bureau to the staff of the general commanding
Orleans.

No doubt Armand had acted rashly in agreeing to conduct
secret negotiations without any guarantees of protection from
misrepresentation, but he was shocked when one day he found
officers of the *Sûreté* searching his rooms. He was himself
forcibly stripped and searched on the excuse that he had with
him 'documents to prove his treason'. Armand demanded to
see the War Minister in Paris, but this plea was refused and he
was questioned by *Deuxième Bureau* officers. One of his former
colleagues had made allegations against him, saying he was
communicating with the enemy. Armand committed suicide by
shooting himself, though to avoid an immediate scandal his
family were at first officially informed that he had died of
influenza.[6]

This story even today remains obscure on many points. These
were, of course, tense days for France and the merest hint of
dealings with the enemy could quite easily create panic. On the
other hand it does seem that the *Deuxième Bureau* took very
high-handed action in dealing with Armand in this manner,
even if his suicide suggests there was an element of foolishness
in his conduct. But after Armand's death there was no more
talk about secret deals with any of the enemy and the action of
the *Bureau*, however ruthless, certainly strengthened its own
position which otherwise might have been totally undermined.

11

Women Who Helped Win World War I

Behind the enemy lines many people followed the honourable profession of a spy . . . Marthe McKenna was one . . . she was brave, wise, virtuous and patriotic.

Sir Winston Churchill'

When World War I broke out it was still very much a man's world in most European countries. There had been sporadic demonstrations by suffragists and the cry of 'votes for women', but on the whole these had made very little impact. Yet, as the war progressed, the role of women became of paramount importance. The sheer scale of the appalling losses in manpower gave women roles to play in many spheres where previously only men had been employed. In France, more perhaps than in any other nation, there were many heroines in the field of espionage. It is not so much that France had more women agents than other nations, but that so many of them were first-class. Their versatility, adaptability and talents were quite outstanding.

Previously France had been over-reliant on military men in espionage and counter-espionage, and often these men were not merely rigidly militaristic, but chauvinistic too. One proved to be the exception – Captain Ladoux, who even made himself unpopular with his colleagues by recruiting female spies. It was he who found such outstanding women as the flier, Marthe Richer, who proved to be the equal of any man in the field of espionage.

It is ironical that the one woman spy in World War I whose name has gone down in history is Mata Hari, who was not only not French, but was executed by the French and was highly incompetent in her efforts at espionage. Born as Gertrud

Margarete Zelle in Leeuwarden in Holland, where her father kept a hat shop, she displayed her ultimately fatal zest for adventure when at the age of seventeen she answered an advertisement placed by an officer on leave from the Dutch East Indies who was looking for a wife. She married John MacLeod, of Scottish ancestry, who was serving in the Dutch Colonial Forces, and went out to Java with him. There she became fascinated by the arts of Javanese dancing which she studied and practised.

Margarete was divorced in 1902 and returned to Holland. She never received any alimony from her husband and, finding herself without funds, went to Paris in 1904 and secured work first in a circus and later in her self-conceived role as an exotic oriental dancer known as Mata Hari. The glamour surrounding both her name and her dancing were such that soon she was a much sought after figure in society. She had male friends in high positions, but seemed to prefer a life of adventure to a sound and secure marriage. Constantly moving around, she was in Berlin when World War I broke out, and here she made friends in police circles, and was engaged as an agent by Colonel Nicolai, Chief of Staff of the German Secret Service.

It is, however, doubtful if any secret service would ever have taken her seriously except perhaps for any bedroom chats she might report, and such are rarely all that informative, at least in a military sense. Whatever she earned she seemed to spend freely with no eye to the future. The publicity she was given provided her with an air of mystery and romance. London's *Tatler* described her as 'Lady MacLeod, who dances in the light of the moon to her friends . . . the dances she performed were most suggestive of religious rites and love and passion and were brilliantly executed'. Sometimes Mata Hari pretended to be Javanese, sometimes Dutch, occasionally Russian, French or German. During the war she was constantly on the move, travelling backwards and forwards in Germany, Holland, France, Spain and Portugal. Then in the spring of 1916, having obtained a new Dutch passport, she applied to both the French and British for visas. The French visa was quickly granted, but the British visa was refused. Already she was regarded as a possible enemy agent by the British.

In Paris she had several lovers, one of whom, Jean Hallaure, a French cavalry officer, sent her to see the SR. She was confronted by 'a certain Captain Georges Ladoux, a short, rather squat man of forty, with hair *en brousse*, steel-rimmed spectacles and a short, rather straggly moustache'.[2]

Ladoux was chief of the counter-espionage section of French Intelligence, at that time probably the worst funded of all its sections. But he was an exceptionally able commandant, and he had noticed certain discrepancies in Mata Hari's papers: in one of these she had wrongly described herself as 'born in Belgium'.[3] But the truth was that Mata Hari had attracted so much publicity to herself all over Europe that she was inevitably doomed once she entered the world of espionage. The *Servizio degli Informazioni Militari*, the Italian equivalent of the French SR, had already notified the various intelligence services of the Allies in 1915 that Mata Hari had 'renounced her claim to Indian birth and become Berlinoise. She speaks German with a slight Eastern accent.'[4]

Without doubt it had been suggested to Ladoux that he might usefully interview the wandering dancer and form his own opinion on whether she was a German agent, or if she could be persuaded to work for the French. If he was taken aback when she asked him why police spies appeared to be watching her movements and why her hotel room had been searched in her absence, he expressed no surprise. But he had heard rumours that the British were doubtful of her motives, though he assured her that he did not share their suspicions. He asked her to come and see him again, hinting in an oblique fashion that he might well be glad of her services on some future occasion.

Sure enough she did return to see Ladoux and said that she had many useful contacts in Germany and Holland, casually mentioning that she knew the German Crown Prince: '*si je devenais la maîtresse du Kronprinz, vous me le donneriez . . . mon million?*' It was a playful remark, but Ladoux decided to try her out. He informed her that she was to go to Holland, travelling via Spain, and gave her certain instructions. There is no firm evidence of what those instructions were. It is rumoured that she had a brief love affair with the spymaster.

All the time she was playing off the Germans against the

French and vice versa: it is also clear that Ladoux believed she was a German agent and wanted to find out more. Certainly she was shadowed by the French from the very moment she entered Spain. The shadowing cannot have been very effectively carried out on this occasion as she confronted the agent concerned in the foyer of her hotel and said she was proposing to stay in Madrid another day, and told him her subsequent plans. Then there was a pause and Mata Hari with a sweet smile asked: 'This afternoon between two and four o'clock I have a meeting with a very dear friend. Will you please not follow me during this period? After that I do not mind, but I beg this one favour of you.'

This was, of course, a singularly fatuous request of an agent of French Intelligence, but possibly Mata Hari felt her personal charms and an appeal to French chivalry would make it work. The agent smiled, bowed low, kissed her hand and assured her he would be glad to grant her this wish. Immediately, however, he arranged for another agent to do the shadowing. This time the French took no chances: the agent selected was a man approaching the age of seventy who followed her on a bicycle.

It may well have been that Mata Hari half suspected she would still be shadowed, as she did not meet anyone that afternoon, merely going to a small café from which she made two telephone calls. But her shadower was very astute: he traced the calls she made, ascertaining that they were to the Deutsche Bank in Madrid and the German Consul in Vigo.

The net was closing in on the dancer. On her way from Spain to Holland on the ship *Hollandia*, she was questioned in transit at the British port of Falmouth. A police inspector from Scotland Yard arrested her and took her to London on the grounds that she was Clara Benedict, a German agent. She was also alleged to have made contact with German agents in Spain and was eventually interviewed by Sir Basil Thomson, head of the Special Branch at the Yard. It had also been suggested that she had sent one British agent to his death.

This was probably her last chance to mend her ways and to give up her blundering, amateurish approach to espionage. Thomson warned her that if she valued her life, she would in future avoid the kind of contacts she had made. She had the audacity to suggest that she really wanted to spy for the Allies, the British as well as the French, and that if she had made friends among German officers it was only to learn what they were doing.

By this time, having exchanged information on Mata Hari, the British, the French, and especially Captain Ladoux, were convinced she was a German agent. Only the proof was lacking. Gradually Ladoux gathered the information which eventually led to her arrest. First there was a report of her clandestine affair with the German military attaché in Spain, though the dancer maintained this had nothing to do with espionage. Ladoux suggested she should go to Brussels and, in an effort to test her reactions, gave her a list of six French agents in Belgium. 'Any one of these you can safely co-operate with,' Ladoux told her, 'and report back to me how they are operating.'

Then came news that one of the six had been arrested by the Germans and executed. This one man was suspected of being a German agent and acting mainly in their interests, though nominally he was on the French payroll. He had been of practically no use to the French and Ladoux felt sure that the Germans would not have executed him unless someone had named him as a French agent. Information from the British suggested that the person who had named him was a woman. Everything pointed to Mata Hari.

On her return to France the dancer was arrested and after a court-martial at which she was charged with espionage, she was convicted and shot by a firing squad on 15 October 1917. Yet she had never given any really important intelligence to either side, and had it not been for the fact that France had suffered such appalling casualties in the war, she might well have escaped with a prison sentence.

Setting aside Mata Hari as an exception, Captain Ladoux proved remarkably successful in attracting several top-quality women agents. One of the best of these was Marthe Richer, the widow of Henri Richer, who was killed in action in May 1916, on the Western Front. Born at Blamont, Marthe Richer had learned to fly as a young girl, and was fluent in several languages. Ladoux had already noted her down as a highly desirable agent, and, within three weeks of her husband's death, he had recruited her.

Marthe Richer's first assignment was to keep watch on the German colony in San Sebastian in Spain. As a counter-espionage agent, her job was to infiltrate the enemy ranks. Her charm and intelligence were such that she made sufficiently strong an impression on one German agent, Dr Stephan, for him to invite her to become an *Abwehr* (German Secret Service) agent like himself. Richer asked if she could meet Stephan's chief in the area, Captain Hans von Krohn, who was not only naval attaché in Madrid, but head of German espionage in Spain. When eventually she met von Krohn he immediately became infatuated with her and she became his mistress. While in Madrid she met Mata Hari, then living with the German military attaché, von Kalle, though Ladoux, probably wisely, had not told her that the Javanese dancer was one of his agents.

Ladoux had undoubtedly made a shrewd estimate of Richer's capabilities, for she was to prove as reliable and useful as Mata Hari was incompetent. She provided Ladoux with intelligence on German submarine refuelling at points along the Spanish coast and on the routes and contacts used by German agents crossing Southern France into Spain. Von Krohn asked her to provide the Germans with production figures of the Schneider arms factories in France. When Richer returned to France and reported what the Germans had asked her to do, the counter-espionage service expressed doubts at first, even though Ladoux himself believed in her patriotism. Eventually she was sent back to Spain with misleading information to pass on to the Germans.

Without doubt Richer had one of the most difficult jobs in espionage in the whole war, especially as she was being used as a double-agent and therefore was always vulnerable to accusations of disloyalty from French or Germans. In view of the criticisms made of the misuse of double-agents in the years leading up to the war, it should perhaps be stressed that in the case of Richer the double-agent technique was invaluable and fully justified.

On one occasion her German controller sent Marthe to

Buenos Aires to pass on detailed instructions for German agents in South America. He also gave her a number of phials containing chemicals to destroy stocks of wheat desperately needed by the Allies, which she disposed of on her voyage across the Atlantic.

Because of her prowess as a flier, Richer was nicknamed '*L'Alouette*' (The Lark) by her Secret Service colleagues. One of the more outrageous plans which she submitted to the French was to get von Krohn aboard a plane and to fly him into France where he could be taken as a prisoner-of-war. Ladoux personally rejected this scheme as creating a dangerous precedent and also on the grounds that it would blow Richer's cover as an agent in Spain, where she was invaluable.

This decision by Ladoux proved to be fully justified when she obtained from von Krohn all manner of secret documents, secret codes and even the key to his private safe. All the money she was given by von Krohn for the missions he assigned to her she scrupulously passed on to Ladoux. These funds were especially welcome to his bureau which had been forced to exist on the meagrest of resources.[5]

Probably Richer's pleas to be given permission to fly her German lover out of Spain was a sign that she could no longer tolerate this relationship with an enemy agent. This seems to be the likeliest explanation of why eventually she told von Krohn what her true mission was – an action which must have required some courage – and then returned to France. In doing so she took the risk of putting herself in the wrong with both the French and the Germans. Von Krohn was from all accounts visibly upset by what she told him and poor Richer on her return to Paris was greeted with stern disapproval by senior members of the *Deuxième Bureau*. Unlike Ladoux, they regarded a sexual liaison with the enemy as being quite disgraceful whatever the reasons for it.

Richer was given no official honours for her services, invaluable though they were. She went to live in England where she married a man named Crompton. After her full story was published years later the French belatedly acknowledged her patriotic service by awarding her the *Légion d'Honneur*.

Another heroine recruited and controlled by the French was

Louise de Bettiquies, who became better known later by her cover name of Alice Dubois. In 1914, when war broke out, she was working as a governess in Lille, and, as the Germans pushed forward into this territory, she joined the refugees going to England. Immediately she offered her services to the British and, being duly impressed with her personality and eagerness to serve the cause, they took her on. Louise was enrolled as an Allied agent, being linked to French Intelligence through the Anglo-French Bureau at Folkestone.

It was as Alice Dubois that she eventually returned to Lille, by then a key centre of enemy activity. Her channel for passing back information was through Holland, and once she was installed in Lille she organized a network of agents, usually choosing travelling saleswomen: she trusted women more than men. One of these was Marie-Léonie Vanhoutte, whose cover name was Charlotte. While Alice travelled to sell lace, Charlotte's goods were cheese. It was through moving around that they and the other agents in the network obtained so much information about German plans and movements, often little more than a hint here and there, but sometimes much more positive. There was a total ban on anyone crossing from Belgium into Holland, but these courageous agents managed it despite electric fences, guards and all other hazards. On some occasions where there was a stretch of water to cross, Alice swam to the other side to avoid the Germans. Charlotte couldn't swim and sometimes it was vital that she should be interviewed and questioned on the other side, so Alice kept a wooden trough hidden in the bushes and Charlotte crouched down on it and Alice pushed it in front of her as she swam across.

Also in Alice's team were Paul Bernard, who was a cartographer and therefore invaluable in pinpointing vital areas, and de Geyer, a chemist who was also a competent forger. She developed her network to include children as couriers, mainly boys of about ten or eleven who would not be suspected and who could carry forged passes between agents. Possibly this was too great a risk, as in due course the Germans closed in on the network, eventually searching Charlotte's home and arresting her. Following this arrest suspicion descended upon Alice, who was shadowed for several weeks before being arrested. Both Alice and Charlotte were condemned to death, but their sentences were reduced to imprisonment. Charlotte lived on, but Alice died in prison in September 1918. It was a tragic end to a brilliantly conceived local network.

It was again and again the young, intensely patriotic woman spy who became outstanding in French Intelligence in World War I. Marie Birckel in 1914 was a young schoolmistress living with a family in Lorraine. When war broke out she decided to return to her parents' home at Variscourt near Château-Thierry when the Germans invaded Lorraine. It was a very small community and her mother, who was the village school mistress, was in charge when the men were called up for service. Even the Germans had to consult her on local problems. Marie helped her mother in this task and largely handled the consultations with the Germans.

Then early in 1915 the civilians of Variscourt were ordered by the Germans to go to unoccupied areas of France, Marie among them. She had an astonishing talent for swiftly assimilating and understanding haphazard information and sorting out fact from fiction, and as a result made detailed notes of what she discovered the Germans were doing and passed them on to French Intelligence. The SR were very impressed and invited her to Paris for talks. There she was enrolled as an agent on the understanding that she returned to Variscourt as a spy. Once again the French linked up with the Folkestone Bureau and Marie was first ordered to travel there.

After further briefings in Folkestone she was ordered to travel to Variscourt via Holland, a lengthy, dangerous and difficult journey. Marie came up against the same problems as Louise de Bettiquies in crossing over between Belgium and Holland to pass on information. On the first occasion when she tried to get into Belgium from Holland she was nearly drowned in trying to cross a canal. Some might have given up after such a mishap, but not Marie. On her second attempt in company with a young French agent, Emile Fauquenot, she succeeded. Fauquenot, when he was only seventeen, had escaped from Belgium to France where he joined the infantry. However, he soon became an agent for the SR.

For a while the Birckel–Fauquenot combination worked admirably and provided highly useful intelligence. But eventually Marie was betrayed, arrested by the Germans and put in prison. She refused to answer any questions, but this did not save Emile, with whom she had fallen in love. He too was arrested and they were court-martialled together, sitting side by side in the dock. Each was sentenced to life imprisonment.

Somehow Emile managed to escape and the Germans, afraid that he might try to organize the rescue of Marie, swiftly changed her prison. There was a happy ending to this story: after the Armistice Marie was released from prison and they married. Both received OBEs from the British and the *Croix de Guerre* from the French.[6]

Yet another heroic agent of a different calibre was Marthe Cnockaert, who was born at Roulers in Belgium in 1893. Though usually considered to be primarily an agent of the British, she did in fact also serve the French and was one of the Folkestone Bureau team. 'I served British and French with total impartiality,' she once told me. 'I needed to be believed by both nations otherwise my work for the Allies would have remained in doubt and I should always have been under suspicion.' Her comment shows only too well that it is not only the double-agent who gets into trouble, but the spy for a single cause supported by more than one nation. In the case of Marthe Cnockaert one of her problems was to convince Allied intelligence officers that she was genuinely and voluntarily offering her services to them while she was also a nurse at the German military hospital in Roulers. How she enticed secrets out of German senior officers while still preserving her virtue, though often precariously, she described in two books, *I Was a Spy* and *Spies I Knew*. Relating how churches were rendezvous places for spies in Flanders, she wrote that 'no celebration of divine service took place without a Secret Service agent being present'. Eventually she was caught, court-martialled and condemned to death. Fortunately execution of the sentence was delayed, and when the war ended in 1918 she was still in prison.

She was mentioned in a dispatch by Field-Marshal Haig 'for gallant and distinguished services in the field'. And after the war she married a young British officer, Jack McKenna. Following the success of her two non-fiction books she launched out as a spy fiction writer in later years.

Captain Ladoux had problems with a few women traitors apart from the case of Mata Hari. One was Marussa Destrelles, Romanian by birth but French through adoption, who became an actress in Paris. It was her frequent visits to Switzerland which aroused Ladoux's interest in her. He suspected she was in the pay of the Germans and employed much the same technique as he had with Mata Hari: he let it be known that he might find work for her. Destrelles, not wishing to give cause for suspicion by turning down this indirect approach, agreed to be interviewed by an intelligence officer. During the interview the officer made an excuse and left her alone in the room for a brief period. Lying on his desk was a list of agents. Three weeks later the man whose name was first on that list was shot by the Germans. Ladoux was convinced he must have been betrayed by Destrelles.

It is still not altogether clear whether the man at the top of the list was a double agent, but one suspects that Ladoux would not have risked sending one of his best or most faithful agents to his death. As Destrelles was then spending most of her time in Switzerland Ladoux decided to liquidate her by passing information to the Germans that she had offered her services to the French. A young German officer was ordered to take her out to dinner and dispose of her. He furtively slipped a dose of Veronal into her coffee after he had persuaded her to take him up to her room. She died almost instantly, and the Swiss assumed it was a case of suicide.[7]

Ladoux was to some extent a victim of the jealousy of his colleagues and he suffered because of this. This was mainly a reaction to his talent for recruiting women to the service and the allegations of some of his colleagues that he mixed pleasure with business. After the war there were attempts by these people in the SR to vent their spleen against him. This took the form of laying technical charges against him for allowing his agents to break certain rules of passport control. Nevertheless, Ladoux's example in using female talent was accepted from then on and increasingly women were regarded as the equal of men in the sphere of espionage.

12
Between the Wars

I hear – rumour
I see – reliable source
I know – absolute truth
                SR code-rules in the 1930s

After the armistice of 1918 there were some slight changes in French Intelligence, as usually happens when war ends. One such change was that the SR became known as the *SR Guerre* to distinguish it from the *SR Marine*, which developed its own intelligence-gathering on the naval side. Hitherto, naval intelligence on a broad scale had been somewhat neglected, and the French had taken the hint from the tremendous successes of British Naval Intelligence in World War I.

Still closely linked to the *Deuxième Bureau*, the Central Office of the SR was located at 75 Rue de l'Université, Paris, in an annexe of the War Ministry. At that time it consisted of some seventeen officers, two civilians (one a lawyer), two orderlies, four typists, a secretary and a caretaker. Its budget was estimated at between nine and ten million francs a year. However, this figure only shows part of the picture, and it compares much more favourably with Britain's total budget for the SIS which was slightly below £90,000 a year right around the world.

Sections of the SR after World War I were expanded to include an administrative department and specific German, Russian and Italian sections (the last-named covering the Mediterranean area generally), the Near and Middle East, a British section (covering the whole British Empire and the rest of the world) and a *Matériel de Guerre* department concerned with research into armaments world-wide. Only several years later was an *SR Air* unostentatiously created to be solely concerned with aviation.

The SR also developed a new system for the presentation of reports by its officers. There was an attempt to obtain greater accuracy and to make assessment easier through the rules laid down by this system. The quotation at the beginning of this chapter illustrates the simplicity and commonsense of some of these rules. By using 'hear', 'see' and 'know' the officer had to be categoric. Woe betide him if he said 'I know' when he should have said 'I hear'!

When agents' reports were being assessed for the *Deuxième Bureau*, or even for internal appraisal, very much the same practice was adopted, this time using a combination of letters and numbers to signify the view the assessor took. A1 indicated that the report was 'quite outstandingly good', while at the bottom end of the list D3 suggested it was 'unreservedly suspect'. In between were such assessments as C1 which could be translated into the somewhat ambiguous phrase 'nearly good' and C2, 'above middling'. The last two must have given those who read the final reports some misgivings.

Three senior officers of the central office of the SR also worked permanently in close collaboration with the *Sûreté* (highest branch of the police) which had formed a banch specializing in counter-espionage rather along the lines of Scotland Yard's Special Branch. The French had been greatly impressed by this British section in World War I. Sir Basil Thomson, its creator, became well known in French intelligence and security circles after his part in the Mata Hari affair.

There were now two main sections of the SR, the one, as before, devoted to intelligence-gathering (*Section de Recherche*), still mainly concerned with military matters, and the second section solely concerned with counter-espionage, *Section de Centralisation des Renseignements* (SCR). The title hardly suggests what its activities essentially were, but then Britain's MI5 (Military Intelligence 5) does not indicate counter-espionage.

In the early 1920s both the SR and the SCR became convinced from reports reaching them from Russia, where they still maintained a useful spy network, that the Soviet Union was concentrating on forming a vast nationwide espionage organization of its own inside France. This was, of course, part of the Comintern's campaign to recruit spies in foreign factories and scientists in the universities. But it was not until about 1926–7 that the French Intelligence Service began to find out details of this. France was regarded as the USSR's chief enemy in the early twenties, being not only the greatest military power in Europe, but also the country which had most actively supported the counter-revolutionaries and the war of intervention of 1918–22. As communism had far more adherents in France than in Britain, the first major espionage drive was against France, seeking the French Communist Party as an ally. Jean Cremet, a leading member of the French Communist Party's central committee, became chief of the Soviet intelligence network in France.

Stalin, though he mistrusted most of the French Communist leaders, had a high opinion of Cremet, who was secretary of the St Nazaire branch of the Shipbuilders' Union as well as being secretary of the Metalworkers' Union. In 1926 he was given the official title of head of the French Section of Soviet Intelligence, a rare honour for a foreigner. This appointment was, however, kept secret from the French Communist Party. Cremet organized a huge network of informants inside the French armaments industry. From then on there was a steady flow from France to Russia of intelligence on factory work, arsenals, ship and aircraft construction and all else of a military character.

Eventually, as Stalin had always feared, Cremet was betrayed by one of his fellow Communists, a man named Cochelin. Cremet had asked Cochelin for information and he reported the matter to the French War Ministry. From then on the SCR worked hard and fast to wind up the network. They discovered that each leading spy, such as Cremet, had been given detailed lists of questions concerning armaments, explosives and plans for new weapons. These questions had been drawn up by engineers and scientists. Information was required on 'the armour and construction and the tactical results of the new tanks now on trial and under construction, particularly the new heavy C2 tanks, the light C and the middle-weight Vickers tanks'. The questionnaire continued, 'We know all about the

tanks used during the war. We want details as to dimensions
and weight of the new tanks, the motor, its system and horse-
power, armament and armour, speed and climbing capacity,
fuel and radius of action.'[1]

The counter-espionage service followed Cremet everywhere
he went and this led them on to the trail of Uzdanski-Yelenski,
a Soviet military intelligence officer, and from him to his
intermediary, a man named Grodnicki. It was soon obvious
that copies of the questionnaire had been circulated to factories
and shipyards all over France. For some while after this the
French fed masses of false information on armaments to the
Russians. Only belatedly did the Soviets realize what had been
happening. When the French closed in and made arrests
l'affaire Cremet was a major blow to Franco-Soviet relations
for a long time. When sentences were passed at the trial of the
Soviet agents this statement was made in the summing up:

Since at least 1924 an espionage system has been set up in France
under the direction and for the benefit of a foreign power, the seat of
which is in Moscow. A foreign government sent to us its agents and
money to obtain from the workers, even from Government workers,
the most complete and secret data on the production and operations
of our important defence machinery.[2]

After 1925 the SR extended the number of its posts. The rise
of Mussolini was partly responsible for the creation of posts at
Nice and Chambéry, while others at Algiers, Oran, Rabat,
Tangier and Tunis were set up to keep watch on Italian and
Spanish affairs. Yet probably the wisest move made by the SR
was to concentrate on Poland, and this was largely due to the
advice of Colonel Rivet, who became one of the outstanding
figures in French Intelligence. The SR post in Warsaw concentrated on technical research which proved valuable in eventually obtaining some of the secrets of the Enigma deciphering
machine which proved of such value to the Allies in World War
II. Apart from Warsaw the SR had cells in Danzig, Katowice
and Poznań.

For eight years after the Treaty of Versailles the German
Army was subject to inspection by the Allies' Control Commission, established to ensure that Germany did not exceed the

military limitations laid down after the armistice. From the expiration of that deadline the *Deuxième Bureau* was kept fully informed about German clandestine rearmament. The archives of the *Bureau* at Vincennes provided detailed and accurate information on this.[3] Even in 1930 General Gauché, the head of the *Deuxième Bureau* at that time, reported that, 'Theoretical studies and discussions show to what extent the problem of reorganization [of the German Army] excites and preoccupies their minds. They also show the extent to which the German Command is determined not to be an hour or an idea behind in anticipating the day when it will be possible to reorganize its army again to measure its ambitions.'[4]

A watch on Germany was kept from SR posts at Aix-la-Chapelle with sub-posts at Essen and Dortmund during the occupation of the Ruhr in 1923 by French troops under the orders of Prime Minister Poincaré. The French occupation of the Ruhr was an attempt to enforce reparations payments by Germany. The Essen and Dortmund sub-posts disappeared in 1925 when the occupation ended. In 1933 a new post was established at Lille under Lieutenant-Colonel Louis Rivet. He had been wounded and taken prisoner in 1914 and, during his imprisonment, had acquired some knowledge of German techniques and methods. He was a most astute observer. He had also served as an attaché in Berlin and Warsaw.

In 1932 *La Centrale*, the headquarters of the SR, left 75 Rue de l'Université for larger and better premises at 2 bis Avenue de Tourville near the Invalides. Colonel Laurent had been succeeded by Colonel Roux as head of the SR, and then in 1936 Colonel Rivet became chief. It was in this year that the SR became an organization attached to the *État Major de l'Armée*, quite distinct from the *Deuxième Bureau*, though closely linked to it both for preparing reports and giving guidance. In effect this gave the SR quite a boost and made it that much more prestigious, in being within the domain of the French Chief of Staff.

Under Colonel Rivet's administration a much tighter control of all fields of intelligence was achieved and considerable improvements in day-to-day work were made. A grave, serious man, Rivet was always looking ahead, frequently interested in what the problems of the following year were likely to be. It was a trait which proved invaluable. It was agreed that in time of war there would be a merging of intelligence sections so that both the SR and the SCR (counter-espionage) came directly under the *Deuxième Bureau*. By this time the SCR had acquired quite a high reputation. If there was a fault at this time, it probably was that the SR paid considerably less attention to political and economic intelligence than to military and aviation matters. This was probably due to the domination of the military inside the service.

'I had heard of the *Deuxième Bureau*, of course, but never of the SR until I was told to report to them at the Avenue de Tourville in 1937,' declared Captain Paul Paillole, who in that year was attached to the counter-espionage section.[5] This newcomer, who was to play such a major role later on, admitted that in his younger days 'the *Deuxième Bureau* was a legend . . . especially in films of espionage and fiction'. Paillole was made chief of the German section of counter-espionage. This was a formidable task in that he had to liaise with the *Sûreté* and the *Préfecture de Police* as well as the SR. To some extent he also had to keep some contact with the newly created DST (*Direction de la Surveillance du Territoire*), which had been formed within the Ministry of the Interior and given the task of combating foreign intelligence operations inside France. To some extent this had been an official response to the Cremet affair.

It may seem extraordinary that Paillole had not heard of the SR before 1937, but it shows what a low profile this service kept. Much the same would apply in Britain in that period: while many people had heard of what was vaguely termed the British Secret Service, few had then heard of MI6.

The SR made some major advances in the late 1930s. A new technical section of the SR, entitled *Service NEMO*, was created to deal with the interception of highly technical secret messages, controlled by Captain Cazin d'Honicthun. By 1938 the post at Metz had actually managed to infiltrate the *Abwehr* and a mere three years after he had first been welcomed at SR headquarters Captain Paillole was able delightedly to report to his masters that nearly four hundred *Abwehr* agents had been traced and either liquidated or at least put out of action.

There had also been an intensive, one might almost say feverish, drive to recruit agents and informants on a large scale. In 1938 small discreetly-phrased advertisements were inserted in *Paris-Soir* and candidates were interviewed by the French police. This was done as much to seek out possible subversives as to gain agents, as the Ministry of the Interior had been worried at reports of Frenchmen being used by the Germans to spy on the Maginot Line. Such cases were, however, relatively rare and the SR could take great pride in its regional post at Metz where Colonel Mangès managed to retain in his team old hands in the espionage game who had served France well for twenty years or more.

On Saturday 8 March 1936 German troops entered the demilitarized zone of the Rhineland and repudiated the Locarno Treaty. This was a non-aggression pact signed in London in 1925 between France, Germany and Belgium, and guaranteed by two supposedly impartial powers, Britain and Italy. French radio broadcast a message from Sarraut which mentioned that the German military attaché in Paris had asked to be received by the chief of the *Deuxième Bureau*. By this time the SR post at Metz had given the fullest details of the German penetration of the Saar and the units deployed there. Unquestionably, without support from all France's allies, France had no choice other than to declare war on Germany or to make a formal protest. Invariably Germany took provocative actions, political or military, at weekends, when diplomats everywhere were on leave, especially those of Britain and France, and this tended to work in favour of Germany. Consultation over weekends between Britain and France was minimal at the best.

The *Deuxième Bureau*'s view was that merely to protest was futile and could be disastrous. General Gauché, then head of the *Bureau*, stressed to the High Command that Germany had some thirty divisions against twenty French divisions, some of which were incomplete. But during that fatal weekend there were insufficient ministers available to take decisions and so nothing was done. General Gauché continued to warn his compatriots and the British, too, about the harsh facts of German rearmament, but little heed was paid to him. As early as 1934 the SR had reported that Germany had ninety-three flights of first-line aircraft which amounted to more than 1,400 planes. In 1937 Gauché warned that there was 'no slowing down in the manufacture of armaments. The firm Rheinmetall, for example, has continued to feed the arsenals at the same rate. In artillery material alone its 1937 deliveries represent almost seventeen divisional artilleries.'[6]

One major reason why such categorical intelligence was not taken seriously was the view of the bankers and politicians that the German economy was in too parlous a state to make war a possibility. Little allowance was made for what slowly, if steadily, became the German economic miracle of recovery from the financial and economic disasters of the late 1920s. Had agents paid more heed to the manner in which Germany had recovered financially and economically, the message might have got across sooner. Yet French agents continued to supply ample proof of German intentions both before and after Hitler came to power. Some five French agents actually acquired jobs as labourers working on German defence posts and provided maps of these.

The practice of using women agents was continued after World War I, as it was fully realized that sometimes the female agent had the advantage, not least in the deployment of charm. An example of such recruitment is provided by the case of Edita Zukermanova, a Czech who left Vienna when the Nazis marched in and who, through a friend of her father's, volunteered for secret service with the French. In many countries this would have been managed through a formal interview in an office, with possibly half a dozen people sitting in on the cross-examination. But Edita was seen informally. Had it been done otherwise a valuable agent might quite easily have been lost, because she was the type of volunteer who responded much better to an informal interview in a bar than the kind conducted with pomposity and ultra-seriousness in the atmosphere of a court room. Edita Zukermanova was duly enrolled as an agent in the naval division. She was trained in how to use a camera and in the techniques of invisible ink. 'The ink was either lemon juice or powdered aspirin mixed with water. You wrote on a very rough sort of paper and held it slanting to the light so that you could see what you were writing. In seconds it would dry and become invisible. To make it legible, all that was needed was to heat it with an iron or toast it in front of the fire.'[7]

Given the code-name of 'Marianne', she set about her task with enthusiasm and intelligence, photographing gun emplace-ments and pill-boxes. In Sicily she persuaded her boyfriend, an Italian lieutenant, to drive into the forbidden zone as 'a dare'. When she wanted to use her camera she always began to sing. When she stopped, he begged her to go on, but she claimed she was shy and could not bear anyone watching her. So she moved into the back of the car, and once she was sure he could not see her in the mirror, she could take pictures unobserved while she sang. She apparently 'swung to the time of the music as I took the pictures'.[8]

Yet, as Edita herself admitted, 'memory was a secret agent's most important piece of equipment'. This is one of the eternal truths of secret service activities. After the war Edita became a French citizen and was decorated by General de Gaulle in 1945, and awarded a citation which said that she 'accomplished without a break during four years several very fruitful missions on foreign and enemy territory. She displayed in the course of these missions wonderful qualities of courage, coolness and intelligence as well as technical ability.' Her award carried with it the *Croix de Guerre*.

Help often came to the intelligence services from unexpected sources. In 1937 a young German opposed to the Nazi regime offered his services to the French in Berne. He claimed to be attached to the *Forschungsamt*, the German deciphering sec-tion of intelligence, and that his elder brother was on the staff of General Keitel of the *Oberkommando* of the Wehrmacht. Though regarded with suspicion at first, 'D', as he was coded, was carefully listened to and contact was maintained through a system of dead-letter boxes in Belgium and Switzerland. These included such hiding-places as crevices in walls and flowers on a grave. Eventually Colonel Rivet in Paris ordered one of his ablest officers, Captain Henri Navarre, to go to Switzerland to talk to D. He was able to provide detailed information on a new deciphering machine, of which the French duly made a replica. As a result many German messages could be read.

By this time the menace of Nazism had extended far beyond the occupation of the Rhine and Austria and begun to threaten Czechoslovakia and Poland. Yet still the High Command of the French Army expressed optimism and continued to talk non-sense about the 'invincibility of the Maginot Line'. It was the purely defensive role of committing themselves entirely to that line which so alarmed the chief of the SR. By this time Colonel Rivet had ample proof of the total military superiority of Germany both on land and in the air. 'If we do not take action regarding Czechoslovakia, we run the risk of passing over our last chance,' he said. Meanwhile, General Vuillemin, a General Staff intelligence analyst, visited Berlin in August 1938, and returned in a pessimistic mood: 'I discovered a new world, about which I had had reports from the SR, yet in which I did not believe until now.' This was yet another instance of how, regardless of the efficient reports French Intelligence had provided, the French military and politicians so often ignored what they were told. In such circumstances the finest secret service in the world would be at a disadvantage.

Already Commandant Perruche and Captain Navarre of the German section of the SR had obtained a copy of a document entitled *Kriegsspiel*, which set out in detail German plans for taking over Czechoslovakia. This document was secured from someone who was quite unaware he was working for the French. Co-operation with the British SIS was stepped up and some idea of the success of this is shown by the assessment of Major-General Sir Kenneth Strong, who had been a military attaché in Berlin, that the French gave 'extraordinarily accurate analyses of Germany's war plans'.

But for many years while espionage on Germany was good, counter-espionage was poor. Possibly all sections dealing with counter-espionage had concentrated too much on Russia. Security in French consulates in Germany was inadequate. Even as late as 1937 there were nearly 17,000 Germans in Paris and less than 500 French in Berlin, statistics which surely screamed out loud for some attention. French consulates quite often employed Germans for such work as typing and secretarial duties and nobody then seemed to have heard of the 'Fifth Column'.

Cremet had left France for Moscow and in 1937 he was sent to Shanghai on a secret mission, being reported 'missing' shortly afterwards. He had been killed by Soviet agents in Macao because it was suspected that his mistress, Louise Clarac, had subverted him: she had returned to France two years earlier. For some few years after the smashing of Cremet's network the SCR failed to discover that there was a small group of Soviet spies inside the printing-works of the College of Military Studies in Versailles. Typesetters in this works handled masses of confidential material about which they were supposed to maintain total silence. But ten Communists were employed there and they passed on material to Soviet agents and were well paid for doing so. Eventually the cell was detected as a result of information received on the Soviets' intermediary, a man named Rougaeyres. He and ten others were rounded up and they received sentences ranging from six months to five years.[9]

Another major failure for counter-espionage was the affair of General Muraille. 'General Muraille' was the cover name for a Soviet commissar who had built up a new espionage network on armaments production with agents in Le Havre, Lyon, Marseille and Toulon, acquiring information on new types of naval vessels, torpedoes, guns and aircraft. What alarmed the French was that he was not caught through the diligence of the SCR or any other agency, but because he was betrayed by one of his own agents. Yet he only received a sentence of three years' imprisonment, after which he was sent back to Russia.

However, after this, co-operation between the SCR and the Ministry of the Interior's DST improved and greater attention was paid to the vast number of Germans living in Paris. The SCR also strengthened co-operation with the Ministry of the Interior and a surveillance team from the Ministry was established to cover all the military regions. This team comprised ten senior officers and twenty inspectors. By this time both the DST and the SCR were working together in relative harmony.

The achievements of the counter-espionage services in the years just prior to World War II were remarkable by any standards. Until the mid-1930s the SCR had consisted only of five officers at headquarters, one of whom, Commandant de Robien, had been responsible for the German section. It was when he was moved to the Balkans as a military attaché that Paillole took his place and began to work miracles. By the end of 1937 he had not only supplied a lengthy list of suspects, but a detailed plan of German intelligence-gathering in France. Yet many obstacles were put in his way, despite the support of his chief, General Schlesser. Very little help was given to the SCR by the Ministry of Foreign Affairs, whose various chiefs all refused to agree to Paillole's demand that foreign employees in key positions in embassies and consulates abroad should be replaced by French personnel. The astute Captain Paillole, aided by General Schlesser, even got the backing of the Prime Minister on this point, but the Foreign Ministry still would not budge on the issue.

Some idea of the great improvement in counter-espionage work can be seen in the official figures of arrests made through the SCR between 1935 and 1940. In 1935 only twenty arrests had been made, whereas in 1937 the number was 150, and in 1938 400. Even in 1940 one thousand arrests were made.

The problems General Gauché encountered over espionage in Germany had caused him to seek close co-operation with the British Secret Service. Their budget was still ridiculously small and the merest hint of possible co-operation seemed to be a bonus to the head of the SIS, Admiral Sinclair. He relied heavily upon reports from both the *Deuxième Bureau* and the SR. By the end of the 1930s the SIS depended upon the help they gained from French Intelligence to an extent which they could never have hoped for in the 1920s. One vital result of this was the systematic photographing of the entire length of the frontiers with Germany – a minor bonus in one sense, but this led to Anglo-French exchanges of information, with the British getting the secrets of the German Enigma coding machine. In the end this was a greater boon for the British than the French.

That Anglo-French co-operation was good in this period is also demonstrated by Captain Paillole. In his memoirs of those days he speaks enthusiastically of 'resurrecting our relations with the British', making a special mention of help from Colonel Menzies (who succeeded Admiral Sinclair as head of MI6), Commander Dunderdale and Tom Greene. Paillole said: 'A veritable camaraderie was established between us: it was strengthened to the point of making Dunderdale and Greene, whom we called Bill and Uncle Tom, collaborators in our own organization and also friends.'[10]

But even in the 1930s there were limits to the extent of such cooperation, as in the case of John Leather, which ended with three Britons, who had been acting on behalf of British Intelligence, being sentenced to varying terms of imprisonment. The general rule for any organizer of an espionage service is that he resides outside the country upon which he is spying. But Leather set himself up in Paris as the manager of a wireless business while devoting his time to organizing the collection of intelligence on French military, air, naval and secret communications. Phillips, one of his agents, in quest of intelligence, sought out a Frenchman who had been losing heavily on the tables at Monte Carlo. But the latter, after seeming to agree to provide information, informed the French authorities. Despite this tip-off, the SCR took a long time to track down the network, eventually finding a major clue through a French artists' model named Marthe Moreuil who had seduced a number of officers in the Services.[11]

Thus even in the period between the wars there were occasions when British were spying on French and French spying on British. Nevertheless, to have achieved such close co-operation by the late 1930s, though in part due to the Nazi threat to each nation, was also a tribute to the senior intelligence officers of both Britain and France. In short, intelligence people found it easier to get together than did the politicians, many of whom ignored the findings of their intelligence services.

13
'Kléber' for Survival

'*Kléber*' was the code-name for the French Secret Service entered into clandestinely after the armistice of 1940. It was then announced that '*un SR camouflé est constitué immédiatement avec un personnel de qualité* . . . [A camouflaged SR with a highly specialized personnel is being set up immediately]'

From documents on *Projet de Réorganisation du SR après l'Armistice*, 27 June 1940

Anglo-French relations which had gradually warmed in the late 1930s dramatically improved at the beginning of World War II. Co-operation on intelligence was to prove vital to both parties throughout the war. The SR in particular gave to the British SIS all the information on German territorial forces which the British themselves lacked. There was also much closer collaboration between the two nations on counter-espionage, and lists of suspects were exchanged. Said one French senior intelligence officer of this period: 'It became easier to work with the British than with our own Chiefs of Staff. The latter continued to ignore us and all our warnings.'

One result of this was the arrest of a young French naval officer who was found to have been working for the *Abwehr*. This was the result of a tip-off from the British. He was caught and condemned some days before war broke out. Another traitor in the French services was Captain Masson, who had been given the task of penetrating French Intelligence by the *Abwehr*. Again there was valuable information from the British and Masson was finally identified by Commandant Sérot, and arrested after a trap was laid for him in Tunis.

On the diplomatic side, though, the story was rather different. On 13 July 1939, Sir Eric Phipps, the British Ambassador in Paris, sent to Lord Halifax, the British Foreign Secretary, a list (with details and comments on each) of 198 supposedly important French personalities, yet he did not include in this a single intelligence chief or officer. One would have thought that this was a grave error of judgement, as such information would have been valuable as a check on what the SIS were receiving and reporting on. Equally there was not nearly enough reassurance coming from Britain on the diplomatic front to discourage the view frequently expressed in France that in the event of war Britain would 'fight to the last Frenchman' and that, even if the war could be won, Britain would encourage a beaten Germany to regain its former position in the world. Centuries of Anglo-French hostility die hard.

The *Deuxième Bureau* had warned the High Command on 11 January 1939 about the probability of German operations against Belgium and Holland. But this warning had come at a time when the High Command was still hoping either for a miracle from outside the country or for some kind of deal with Germany. The politicians, not getting much sound advice from the military, remained largely in the dark and intent on seeking their own way out of engaging in a seemingly unwinnable war. Germany had intended that the so-called 'Phoney War' period should fully demoralize the Allies, and in France this is what happened.

French Intelligence was not helped very much by the Venlo disaster, a brilliantly conceived German gambit in which two key British Secret Service operators, Stevens and Best, were lured across the border from Holland in 1939 and taken prisoner. 'That was our most mortal blow,' says a French intelligence operator of this period, who shall be named *Le Bon et Vrai*, at his own suggestion.

I cannot say much more because indirectly I was involved. But from all we knew from our links with the British it became instantly clear that the British Secret Service in Europe had been virtually wiped out in one day. The Germans made sure they got all the names and addresses from those they captured. Only by degrees did we in Paris realize this, and it came as a mortal shock. We also felt we had been partly betrayed as a result. While SR relations with the British Secret Service were extremely good, we were always worrying as to whether

British politicians, like our own, were playing a game which ran counter to our own efforts. Information coming to us from Germany about such matters was not encouraging. Before Menzies became head of MI6, though we got on well with our SIS colleagues in Paris, we always had some doubts about his predecessor, Sinclair. We thought the old admiral was somewhat out of touch on occasions, not least when we heard that he had had an approach suggesting that Goering should come over to London to see the Prime Minister towards the end of August 1939, shortly before war was declared. We had full details of this – how Goering was to come over to England secretly on 23 August, land at a deserted aerodrome and from there be taken to Chequers. Luckily, this plan never seemed to get off the ground.

That *Le Bon et Vrai* is extremely accurate and reliable is amply demonstrated by British official papers of the period. Lord Halifax, who was British Foreign Secretary at this time, wrote his own record, *Events Before the War, 1939*, in diary form. This states that on 21 August:

'C' [Admiral Sinclair] tells us that he has received an approach suggesting that Goering should come over to London if he can be assured that he will be able to see the Prime Minister. It was decided to send an affirmative answer to this curious suggestion, and arrangements were accordingly set in hand for Goering to come over secretly on Wednesday the 23rd. The regular household at Chequers is to be given *congé* and the telephone is to be disconnected. It looks as if it is going to be a dramatic interlude, and, having laid the plans, we await confirmation from Germany.[1]

But, as Lord Halifax shortly afterwards recorded, 'The Goering idea has, temporarily at least, faded out.'[2]

But another report just before the war in 1939 gave the SR much greater cause for anxiety. It was well known in France that both the Duke and Duchess of Windsor had shown sympathy towards Nazi Germany and had a number of friends with Nazi connections, including some in France. It was also well known that Josef Goebbels, Hitler's propaganda chief, had repeatedly praised the Duke. This new report was that the British Foreign Office – or someone claiming to be in that Office – had asked a Dutch interior decorator named Herman Schrijver, who had done work for the Duchess of Windsor in London, to go to Paris and tell the Duke of Windsor that he must go to Hanover to have himself declared Emperor of the German Reich. The suggestion was that everything would be ready for this *coup d'état* and that because of the Duke's popularity in Germany he was bound to succeed.

This story was so fantastic that it could not easily be accepted. Schrijver was supposed to have been contacted by Lord Halifax himself. There was absolutely no confirmation of this and one can only draw the conclusion that somebody in some secret service was trying to make mischief. Nevertheless Herman Schrijver's sister, Elka Schrijver, was staying with her brother in London in 1939 in his South Audley Street flat. She stated, 'A telephone call came through from the Foreign Office. You know how one sometimes can hear what is said and in this instance I heard a loud man's voice asking my brother to hold the line and saying, "I'll put you through to the Foreign Secretary." A very short conversation followed with a much softer voice and I could not hear, but from my brother's replies it was clear that an appointment was made for him to go and see Lord Halifax next day.'[3]

When her brother returned Elka Schrijver confirmed that he said Lord Halifax had asked him to see the Duke of Windsor to ask him to go to Hanover to be declared Emperor of the 'German Reich'. 'It seemed to both of us a mad story,' said Miss Schrijver. 'My brother very wisely refused this extraordinary mission on the grounds that he was a foreigner living in England, that he was completely apolitical . . . He said that he had been told not to mention this matter to anyone . . . and he told me and made me promise never to mention this to anyone as long as he was alive.'[4]

The whole story is almost totally incredible, yet it is carefully documented by Miss Schrijver, who worked for the Dutch Resistance during the war (incidentally, her brother seems to have been opposed to the Resistance and to his sister working in it). Equally the story about Lord Halifax seems totally preposterous and there is nothing in Foreign Office records to support it. The incident to which Miss Schrijver refers, according to her, took place on 26 or 27 August 1939. There is nothing in Lord Halifax's detailed diary of those two days which even hints at a meeting with Herman Schrijver.

Yet the fact that someone in the SR knew about this quite fantastic story lends some credence to what Miss Schrijver says, and *Le Bon et Vrai* is quite positive on the subject.

This could have been a plot to create mischief and dissension, even Nazi-inspired, but we felt at the time, and I have had no reason to change my views, that there was something behind it. Herman Schrijver was a highly intelligent man and we kept a dossier on him just in case we ever needed one. He was a regular visitor to the Duke and Duchess of Windsor over many years, even until a short time before his death. He had a big and successful business in Duke Street, London, right up until World War II. He was called up to serve in the Dutch Army in late 1940 in a camp in North Wales, but he was soon invalided out.

From what we knew about him it is almost certain that, not wishing to put a foot wrong with any nation while living in a foreign country, he would have notified MI5 or someone in authority about such a project if he had suspected a hoax or a trap. But we had no information as to whether he did.

Nevertheless, there is evidence that in France, especially among high-up defeatists and some right-wing politicians, this story was not only circulated but taken as a warning to watch out for trickery from the British. If this was a clever propaganda plot to foment Anglo-French hostility, it was certainly effectively exploited in France. However, by early 1940 the collapse of French resistance to Germany looked imminent, and such suspicions had little significance beside the fight for survival itself.

On 10 May 1940, Colonel Rivet ordered the burning of some of the archives of the *Deuxième Bureau* and the evacuation of the most vital papers. Even during these last days of war with Germany the *Deuxième Bureau* and the *Cinquième Bureau* (as the SR services became in time of war) were working together, still hoping France would be saved, but all the time taking steps to ensure that an intelligence service would survive even after defeat.

After the Armistice between France and Germany in June 1940, General Schlesser, head of the SCR, was able to claim, '[The Germans], though all-powerful, did not succeed in smash-

ing the tool we had forged. Supple and strong, in the hands of
a marvellously dynamic team, it was to be used with sufficient
skill, despite so many difficulties, for a pitiless struggle to be
carried on against the activities of the enemy until the long-
awaited moment when our bright land of France was to be set
free.'[5]

After the fall of France and the installation of a new French
government at Vichy under Marshal Henri-Philippe Pétain,
Colonel Rivet made valiant efforts to hold the SR together, as
did Captain Paillole with his German section of the SCR. Paris,
the French capital, was firmly under the control of the Germans, as were territories facing the English Channel and areas
in the West and the South: it was for this reason that the
government was set up in Vichy, an unoccupied area. In theory
the French were in control of their own unoccupied territories,
but this was always subject to the influence the Germans had in
the occupied territories, and the pressures they brought to bear
on the government in Vichy. The SR and the SCR were in a
quandary on all fronts. There was the feeling that Pétain, head
of the Vichy government and venerated still as the hero of the
Verdun victory in 1916, would find it difficult to resist all the
German demands. At this stage it was much too risky to
establish any liaison with the military officers led by Charles de
Gaulle, who had moved to London, determined on setting up
a Resistance organization. And there was a need, secretly at
least, to keep some contacts with the British SIS and rather
more openly with the Americans such as Colonel Schow, the
US military attaché at Vichy.

Just before the Armistice Captain Paillole got away to
Bordeaux and immediately set about building up a clandestine
network of agents for the future. On 25 June 1940 Colonel
Rivet was telling his staff, 'The mission of the Service is not
ended.' Two days later, at Rivet's instigation, a project for the
reorganization of the SR after the Armistice was drawn up.
This stated that:

The *Cinquième Bureau* will cease to exist on 27 June. Its officers and
other ranks are reinstated in their original corps of the Army. Its civil
personnel are disbanded.
A camouflaged SR is immediately established with personnel of
quality specially chosen from the former *Cinquième Bureau* . . . This

will have two principal missions: 1. the gathering of intelligence; 2. protection of military secrets and action against anti-national plots.[6]

Various tasks were set down for the undercover service. These included obtaining full details of the German troops in occupied France, building up SR posts around the world and reorganizing communications. It was then arranged that *Kléber* should be the code-name for the *SR Guerre* that was clandestinely set up after the Armistice.

The *Deuxième Bureau* also managed to survive in an emaciated form. It was reconstituted in the Seminary of Bon Encontre. Surprisingly, the Germans accepted arguments that the *Bureau* should continue to exist. Probably they thought they could collaborate militarily and so control it, so they sanctioned the continuation of the *Bureau* with a peacetime size staff under Lieutenant-Colonel Baril who took over from General Gauché. Meanwhile the *Cinquième Bureau*, whose headquarters had had to be moved from Gretz to Paris as the Germans advanced, was abolished as part of the armistice agreements. It was at the same time understood that the *Deuxième Bureau* would only be sanctioned in the Vichy-controlled part of France. Colonel Baril continued his work as a secret opponent of the Germans and, indeed, was within a year forecasting their ultimate defeat.

The Vichy Government and its servants were split between those who were eager for collaboration with the Germans and those who accepted the armistice as unavoidable, but wished secretly to conduct an anti-German campaign. Colonel Groussard was ordered to dissolve his counter-espionage organization by Peyrouton, the Vichy Minister of the Interior. Groussard obeyed, but this did not stop him from secretly forming intelligence cells of his own which later became part of the network known as *Gilbert*. He chose his personnel carefully from former members of the auxiliary police service, directing them to keep watch on German movements and to track down collaborators. This organization of Groussard's had links inside Italy, Switzerland, Alsace-Lorraine, Spain and in the Occupied Zone of France under Colonel Heurteaux, who was eventually caught, arrested in Paris and deported to Buchenwald.

Colonel Rivet was, however, the supreme planner responsible for a continuing and effective clandestine intelligence service, though he was permanently in fear of some order from above which would ruin his plans. Money to keep the organization functioning came from diverse sources, sometimes being drawn from Army accounts under some innocent-sounding heading with connivance from someone in the military hierarchy. Much money came from well-wishers, while some even came from captured enemy agents.

The espionage service operated under the official title of BMA (*Bureaux des Menées Anti-Nationales*). It was supposed to deal with anti-national intrigues, to stamp out subversion against the Vichy regime and also to stamp out espionage (a nicely ironic touch, this).

One of the prime achievements of the BMA was to protect the Free Zones of France from German penetration in one form or another. It had branches everywhere, but its prime command post was at the Villa Eole on the Promenade de la Plage in Marseille. Colonel Rivet could operate from Vichy, knowing that he had secret posts in the Occupied as well as the Free Zones, while the closest links were kept with Captain Paillole. A key man in the BMA was Colonel Sérot, who had had wide experience in Air Force counter-espionage for more than a decade. He was killed in Jerusalem in 1948 after having served as an assistant director in counter-espionage at Algiers following the Allied occupation.

Paillole's energy was boundless. His speed of action and the amount of work he could get through in a day were prodigious. He was as well informed on Soviet intrigues as he was on those of the Germans.

Paillole managed to camouflage the equivalent of the old SCR under the title of *L'Entreprise des Travaux Ruraux* (Office of Rural Works), known as TR for short. It was registered as a commercial firm specializing in setting up various rural works projects using as its slogan the Vichy cry of 'Back to the Land'. Its code-name was *Cambronne*, which was extremely cleverly chosen. The name *Cambronne* was a reference to General Pierre Cambronne, who took part in the Battle of Waterloo. When told by the British to surrender, tradition has it that he

replied in one word: '*Merde!*' Ever since, this word has been
referred to as '*le mot de Cambronne*', and Cambronne has
symbolized France's hatred for its ancient hereditary enemy,
Britain. The use of such a word as a code was intended to
reassure the Germans that TR regarded the British as their
enemy once again!

Colonel Rivet gave Paillole every encouragement to develop
TR and to expand it from its original sixty members. These
people were dispersed over a wide area, forming some five
cells. Despite the risks of being discovered by some collaborator in the Vichy Government, or even by the Gestapo, literally
thousands of reports were made on individuals suspected of
working for the Axis services, or collaborating with the Germans or Italians. Once these reports were sifted and vetted,
they were passed on to the *Deuxième Bureau* in Vichy. A few
highly confidential reports were passed through a French Canadian diplomatic source for transmission to the Allies.

An example of the risks some of these patriotic intelligence
officers took is best shown by the daring of Commandant
Thibaud, head of TR in Vichy. He actually put a microphone
in the office of Geissler, the Gestapo chief in Vichy. The
microphone was discovered, but the Germans had no proof of
who had put it there. Commandant Thibaud was assisted in this
instance by Commandant de Cazin d'Honicthun, another astute
secret service operator who had warned again and again of
German infiltration into influential French circles long before
the Armistice.

Successes eventually came the BMA's way. In February
1942, for example, BMA officers arrested Henri Devillers, an
ex-prisoner of war who had been used as an agent by the
Germans. He had become a major threat to the very existence
of the BMA and thus was dealt with speedily by a military
tribunal who found him guilty. He was executed by a firing
squad in Lyon only hours before an order signed by Pierre
Laval, the Prime Minister and arch collaborator of the Vichy
Government, demanded that the man should be freed.[7]

The TR managed to infiltrate some of its own people into the
Abwehr's spy network in Algeria and Morocco as well as into
an *Abwehr* network in the Côte d'Or through which they were

able to trace nearly all the collaborators in the area. At one stage it became necessary to avoid conventional codes using numbers and letters which could quicky arouse suspicion. Instead the names of flowers for TR posts and German towns for French towns were introduced. Thus the chief centre was *Camélia*, Lyon was *Lys*, Vichy was *Violette*, Bourg was *Bégonia* and Lille was *Narcisse*. Similarly, Limoges was *Munich*.

The SR's pre-war high-level source, 'T', the anti-Nazi Austrian, continued to send in reports mainly through Budapest. The clandestine services had a good friend in General Huntziger, the Vichy War Minister, though he was never informed that these services were orientated against the Germans and would help the Allied cause whenever they could safely do so. Admiral Darlan, a key Minister under Pétain and no lover of the British, aimed to bring all the intelligence services under strict War Ministry control, but Huntziger opposed this. There was, therefore, a real anxiety in these services when it was announced that General Huntziger had been killed in an air crash when returning from Africa.

Soon after this Darlan became Minister of War and coincidentally within a few weeks the *Abwehr* arrested two key men attached to the TR, one of whom was also linked to the *Deuxième Bureau*. These were crisis days for the French Intelligence Services, as Darlan was still insisting on a unified Secret Service entirely under his control, while Laval went further than this: he wanted such a service to collaborate with the *Abwehr*. Colonel Rivet, who bore the brunt of this jostling for power and control in the intelligence world, was fortunate in gaining support from General Revers, Chief of Staff, and Admiral Battet, in opposing such moves. There was also substantial backing from Colonel Baril, the new head of the *Deuxième Bureau*, who did his utmost to convince other senior serving Army and Navy officers that in the long run the Germans could not win the war. He took grave risks personally in saying so. In the end Marshal Pétain heeded the Service officers rather than the collaborators even if the support he gave was somewhat feeble.

Meanwhile the camouflaged version of the SR had extended

its posts far beyond France and French North Africa to Syria, Lebanon, Berne, Budapest, Bucharest, Belgrade, Sofia, Istanbul, Riga, Moscow, Stockholm and Madrid. The number of personnel used in these places was relatively small, sometimes confined only to members of French consulates, and altogether probably never exceeded twenty persons. It is interesting to note how well Paillole, whose very name would have alerted the *Abwehr*, if not the Gestapo, concealed his identity as head of the TR. The Germans believed that the head of the TR was a man named Perrier. After August 1942, Paillole became chief of all the counter-espionage services.

In due course the Germans found out about both the BMA and the TR. A Gestapo report of 18 July 1943 stated:

The *Cinquième Bureau* was officially dissolved, but the personnel stayed where they were, devoting their energies to pursuing the struggle. From 25 August 1940, an organization called the BMA was created on the official pretext of combating anti-nationalist intrigues. The activity of espionage was pursued beneath its cover in the same anti-German spirit. The real activity of the BMA was known to the Reich Services: for these reasons this organization was dissolved.[8]

But after the BMA was dissolved in August 1942, it was secretly replaced by a new organization, the SSM (Service of Military Security). The SSM only had authority to cope with disorganization and subversion in the French Army, but under cover it still worked as a counter-espionage service for the French. The SSM was another brain-child of Paillole.

14

De Gaulle's Wartime Secret Service

It was necessary for British policy-makers to understand that, at Vichy, the sound element of the Ministry wanted to aid the anti-German struggle . . . In the event of my succeeding in my mission the British could no longer be tempted to treat the Vichy state as a kind of secondary enemy; they would regard it as a trump-card . . . without any the less giving their support to General de Gaulle's Committee, which I would make every effort to contact.

Colonel Groussard, who went to
London as a secret envoy from Vichy[1]

Charles de Gaulle had been a critic of the French military hierarchy during his years as an officer of the French Army before World War II. He had repeatedly urged the creation of more armoured divisions, giving added weight to this in his book, *The Army of the Future*. Disgusted with the French Army hierarchy, he escaped to Britain after the defeat of France in 1940 and through the strength of his own personality set up an organization which became known as the Free French, dedicated to restoring France to its status as an individual nation and to the defeat of Nazi Germany. It was no easy task because his contacts in Britain were few and from the very beginning he had a hard fight to convince the British that he was one of the staunchest allies in the war against Germany.

Perhaps Colonel Groussard's statement, quoted at the head of this chapter, shows better than anything else how many inside the Vichy government and its various services were not only prepared to support the British secretly, but also the cause of General de Gaulle. Groussard and de Gaulle had served together at the Defence Ministry in 1935–6 and had been on good terms. Because of this Groussard took the bold step of consulting General Huntziger on his idea of paying a secret visit to London after 1940.

De Gaulle had to establish his credentials as a Resistance leader almost from scratch in Britain, where there was only a small contingent of French troops, and very few French territories overseas were willing to acknowledge his authority. Some mischief had been done by some members of the SIS in claiming that the British had been totally misled by French Intelligence about the Maginot Line. They said they had been led to believe it was impregnable. Certainly this was not the view of the SR, nor did they make any such suggestions. It might possibly have been partly the result of Admiral Sinclair, then a very sick man, relying on certain reassurances from the *Deuxième Bureau*. Shortly before the war began the SIS claimed that it was short of funds and that this was hampering its work. 'The Cabinet reluctantly approved a further interim grant to SIS, but the sum involved was too small to make any difference,' states Nigel West. 'Throughout the crisis [i.e. immediately before the war] Sinclair relied almost entirely on the Paris station, which in turn depended heavily on the *Deuxième Bureau* and the *Services de Renseignements*.'[2]

Le Bon et Vrai is convinced that at this time many stories were circulated by certain people in France to discredit the British and to make mischief inside General de Gaulle's Free French Forces. 'I refer to the same people whose smear tactics led to the arrrest of Admiral Muselier on the instigation of your MI5,' he said. 'Look into that story carefully and you may find a clue to the Schrijver mystery indirectly.'

The extraordinary case of Vice-Admiral Pierre Muselier of the French Navy, who joined the Free French in London at its inception, has never been satisfactorily cleared up. De Gaulle wanted to liberate the islands of St Pierre and Miquelon off the coast of Newfoundland which were held by a pro-Vichy governor. 'The Free French Naval Forces were capable of doing this and the Foreign Office saw no objection,' stated Sir Winston Churchill, 'but the US State Department wished the occupation to be carried out by a Canadian expedition. We asked de Gaulle to refrain and he said he would do so. But he ordered Muselier to take the islands. The Free French were welcomed. Cordell Hull [US Secretary of State] wanted the Free French turned out, but public opinion was against him.'[3]

Then in 1941 a security officer at Free French headquarters in Carlton Gardens, London, informed MI5 that Muselier was not only a Vichy agent but that he was in touch with German sources. The alleged proof was a number of letters which later turned out to be forged. There had been rumours for some time that there might be double-agents in de Gaulle's service, some alleging they were pro-German, others that they were pro-Soviet. Muselier was not the only name that was mentioned. As a result of the duping of MI5 into believing the letters were genuine, Churchill ordered the arrest of the Admiral and one other Frenchman.

Muselier spent some time in Pentonville and Brixton prisons until General de Gaulle, outraged that he had not been consulted, satisfied the authorities and the British Premier that the evidence against Muselier was false. The Admiral was not only set free, but received a letter of apology from Anthony Eden, the Foreign Secretary, dined with Churchill and was received by King George VI. Afterwards Muselier claimed that the information lodged against him came from agents of de Gaulle's secret service who were anxious to get him out of the way. However, it is by no means certain that this was the case, and the mischief in the first place may well have come from American sources. Later there was a disagreement between de Gaulle and Muselier and the admiral resigned his post on the National Committee of the Free French Forces. This affair did a great deal of damage to Anglo-French relations, and, unfortunately, it was not the only case of its kind to cause ructions during the war.

The Gaullist intelligence service was set up at the end of July 1940, in modest premises at St Stephen's House, near the Houses of Parliament, with Commandant André Dewavrin as chief. At first glance Dewavrin looked an unlikely figure to be an intelligence chief. He was in his late twenties, with fair wispy hair and a pouting, puzzled look about him. Yet he was a superbly qualified candidate for such a post. He had already had some experience of espionage, having co-operated in collecting intelligence with the backing of Colonel Claude Dansey of MI6, whom he always referred to as *'l'Oncle Claude'*.[4]

As Captain Dewavrin he had been one of the last French

officers to escape to England from Brest. Later he was awarded the *Croix de Guerre* for his service with the French forces at Narvik in the Norwegian campaign against the Germans. He spoke English fluently.

When he left de Gaulle's office after his appointment as intelligence chief of the Free French he noticed that their interview had taken less than a minute and a half. It is a tribute to de Gaulle's judgement that Dewavrin took this in his stride and immediately set about finding staff. He chose as his principal aides Alexander Berenskoff and Maurice Duclos, two friends who had served with him in Norway early in the war. The trio decided to disguise themselves as Englishmen to avoid detection, wearing bowler hats and striped trousers. Later, laughed Dewavrin ruefully, 'We realized we were overdoing it and that in wartime such clothes seemed out of place, so we bought something more informal.'

The senior officers all took aliases mainly to protect their families at home. Dewavrin and Duclos both chose the names of Paris Métro stations, Passy and St Jacques. Dewavrin was offered some assistance by the British SIS, including facilities for the training of agents, transport and communications. But SIS were still cautious in their dealings with the Gaullists: the truth was that some of them missed the excellent relations they had had with French Intelligence officers previously, people who were now serving the Vichy Government. Some also took the view that more could be usefully learned from the so-called network which had been set up inside France and was linked to the Polish Intelligence Bureau in exile, a somewhat tenuous and indisciplined organization which was finally betrayed to the *Abwehr* through one of its own members, Mathilde Carré, who became the mistress of one of the *Abwehr* officers. But the more experienced members of the SIS hierarchy took the view that Groussard was their man. Just to complicate matters still further, though with the best intentions in the world, Dunderdale, the SIS's previous man in Paris, built up his own organization with a Catholic network run by a Jesuit priest, Father Arnould, based on Bordeaux. This was Amicol, which had its headquarters in the convent of the sisters of St Agonie in Paris, and provided splendid information towards the end of the war.

Dewavrin had a revolutionary idea for collecting intelligence which must have impressed de Gaulle, even though he realized it might take years to organize. Working on the theory that if the Germans did not invade Britain, eventually the Allies would have to invade France, he knew that such an expedition would require in advance detailed information on German defences in France. He planned to obtain this not by any conventional secret service methods, but through organizing hundreds if not thousands of informants from all over France – ordinary people such as farmers, farm labourers, housewives, railwaymen and especially fishermen. How to do this from a cramped office in London was a major problem.

Luckily, there was co-operation from Churchill at Downing Street, as he himself wanted detailed intelligence on German movements in Normandy and Brittany. Dewavrin proposed to send Berenskoff and Duclos to France to undertake this mission and was delighted when the British Prime Minister gave the go-ahead. On 4 August 1940, the two men set off with strict instructions that they were to return within five days. This really was asking too much: Dewavrin felt it allowed too little time for his own scheme of organizing a network of agents. From a naval speedboat the men were transferred to a rubber dinghy not much more than two miles from St Aubin. In the early morning mist they managed to get safely ashore after narrowly escaping detection by a German patrol boat. Duclos, who had been a stockbroker, had a deserted chalet belonging to him at Langrune not far away and it was to this building that, against all the rules of orthodox intelligence-gathering, they made their way. They obtained quite a lot of information as there was ample evidence of the barges which had been brought up to the coastal harbours for 'Operation Sealion', Hitler's plan for invading Britain, but all arrangements for their return were ruined by fog as their signals to the naval craft scheduled to pick them up could not be seen.

Dewavrin felt desolate: his one big gamble seemed to have failed. Yet his two agents used their own initiative: Berenskoff set off alone to Vichy to get himself demobilized and to find out what was happening, while Duclos took the risk of going to Paris to try to set up a network of agents there. By the autumn of 1940 Dewavrin began to assume he had lost both his key men. Nevertheless he continued to try to organize his plan for a vast network of informants in France, though it took a long time to achieve.[5]

One of the greatest Free French heroes in the intelligence battle of this period was Gilbert Renault-Roulier, a man of many aliases. It was his habit of changing his name that made it difficult for the Gestapo to track him down. But he was also a former film producer with an appreciation of the value of playing a variety of roles. He gave up his film production work when the Germans invaded France and he escaped to Britain to join de Gaulle. Much later Dewavrin was to describe Renault-Roulier as 'one of the most extraordinary agents of all time, contributing by his efforts to our ultimate success in returning to France in 1944'.

His own ideas of obtaining intelligence were almost identical with those of Dewavrin, so it was not surprising that so soon after being recruited Renault-Roulier returned to France secretly, operating under the alias of 'Colonel Remy', with the sole object of setting up a Resistance network inside occupied territory. This network was named *La Confrérie Notre-Dame* and apart from gathering intelligence it also recruited agents from France and Belgium. 'I was talked into this job,' he said. 'With no experience or contacts I had to build up an espionage network all over France. I did it with pure amateurs. Those amateurs were tortured and some died. But they never let me down.'[6]

He helped to smuggle hundreds of people out of France during the war. To the people of occupied France he was 'Colonel Roulier' and few suspected him. He built up what Dewavrin had wanted most, a network of ordinary people who gave him details of what went on at various ports around France. One of these was a French naval commander working in the naval base at Brest. From this source Renault-Roulier learned that the port authorities were preparing to receive the German battleship, *Bismarck*, after its raids on Allied shipping in the Atlantic. Renault-Roulier radioed London and as a result British warships were able to chase the *Bismarck* and sink her.

The British paratroop raid on Bruneval was also a result of one of his intelligence tips.

It is a striking tribute to the outstanding ability of both Dewavrin and Renault-Roulier that they had a small, well-organized intelligence network established inside France before the end of 1940, but that as early as 17 July 1940, the first Free French agent was landed in France from Britain, using a combination of fast motor-craft and a fishing boat to achieve this. Eventually Renault-Roulier had to leave France when the Gestapo got on his track. He escaped from Lorient in a fishing boat with his wife and five children. In retaliation the Gestapo arrested his mother and five sisters and deported his brother and an uncle, both of whom died in concentration camps. The Gestapo's anger was fed by their knowledge that most RAF raids on French Atlantic ports appeared to be based on intelligence from Renault-Roulier's agents.

Meanwhile Groussard's plan for going to London secretly to make contact with de Gaulle was agreed by General Huntziger, but he warned that Groussard was taking a grave risk and insisted that Marshal Pétain must not be told, although Groussard believed that deep down in his heart the Marshal still had the will to resist the Germans. Arrangements for the visit were made by Pierre Fourcaud, who was a Gaullist agent. But even with this co-operation the trip was not easy. First, plans for going to London via Spain failed, and on a second occasion Colonel Groussard was unable to locate a plane sent to pick him up. Finally he made his way with a false passport via Spain and Portugal, travelling as 'George Gilbert' with help from the British Consulate in Lisbon. Yet another of his code-names was 'Georges Guèrin'. His contacts included Churchill, Eden and Winant, the US Ambassador to Britain.[7]

Groussard was met in London by Dewavrin. During the same visit he met both Churchill and the head of MI6. It must have been a bewildering interview with Churchill indulging in his usual pontificating, but at least Groussard got the message that Churchill realized how valuable it was for Britain that Pétain and not some collaborator such as Laval was governing France. Undoubtedly, too, Churchill was interested in the possible collaboration of General Huntziger.

Dewavrin's plan of building up resistance and agents every-where was bold and brave, but also realistic. He was trying to achieve the impossible, but this was what de Gaulle believed could eventually be done. This was a secret service of a new kind which embraced a whole people. In 1941 Dewavrin entered into an agreement with the British Special Operations Executive, SOE, over active operations inside France. This liaison never worked too well as Maurice Buckmaster of SOE tended to prefer his own French section of support to those of the Gaullists. Each began to mistrust the other, and if anything this tended to encourage the Gaullists to develop their own service. Slowly, Dewavrin's own intelligence inside France was built up. On 17 January 1942, the Gaullist secret service was named the *Bureau Central de Renseignements et d'Action Militaire* (BCRAM), comprising five sections: liaison com-mand, liaison with MI6, military action in liaison with SOE, counter-intelligence (liaison with MI5) and a technical section dealing with ciphers and accounts. This last section was a nicely cynical creation: to link up ciphers and expenses was perhaps not a bad way of operating!

Later the word *militaire* was dropped from the title and the organization became simply BCRA. In March 1942 it moved from its premises in St James's Square to a larger headquarters at 10 Duke Street. At the same time BCRA established relations with the American Office of Strategic Services (OSS), which had just opened an office in London.

Thus there were two French intelligence services operating: the camouflaged SR controlled by Vichy and the Gaullist BCRA in London. Unquestionably, the skilful use made of both of these organizations by the British and Americans paved the way to the successful invasion of North Africa in November 1942. It was this operation, entitled 'Torch', which ultimately brought the two services into closer contact. De Gaulle's organization eventually acquired a military liaison officer, first General Petit and afterwards Colonel Billotte, and on the political side another liaison officer in André Philip.

Prior to Operation 'Torch' both BMA and TR were extremely wary of Admiral Darlan, Vichy's vice-premier, who, though anti-German at heart, was viciously anti-British. He suspected that Colonel Rivet and the special services, as they were then called, were working against him, and he ordered the police to search the offices of Colonel Ronin, officer in charge of air intelligence. This affair came to a climax when General Huntziger, the war minister, ordered his staff not to submit to police search warrants unless under orders from him to do so. Darlan then tried to find out who was blocking his policy of collaboration. Pucheu, the Vichy Minister of the Interior, ordered that special services men were to be 'hunted down pitilessly'.[8]

One of the men Admiral Darlan suspected was Colonel Baril, head of the *Deuxième Bureau*, who was later killed in a plane crash at Beirut in 1943. Baril was much too pro-British for Darlan's liking and consequently he was switched away from the *Deuxième Bureau* to a post in North Africa. Baril had indeed obtained some excellent up-to-date intelligence as head of the *Bureau*. On 22 June 1941 he commented:

It is customary to say that the Red Army is an unknown quantity. We do, however, know the essential thing about the Red Army. The high command, the higher formations, the staffs undoubtedly lack science, but at least they have the will to fight. The lower formations know their job. The soldier is brave and fanatical . . . The Red Army is better equipped than the Tsarist Army of 1914 . . . English resistance is enabling the United States to prepare. One thousand and five planes left the American factories in May. Next spring this figure will be more than doubled.[9]

In North Africa Baril helped to build up a secret network of agents which was extremely useful when the Allied landings took place. It was perhaps ironic that Admiral Darlan should be in North Africa when the landings occurred, and that his presence there should lead to this anti-British officer becoming High Commissioner after the invasion by the Allies. At that time Darlan was not only the senior French naval officer in Algiers, but also French Foreign Minister. Immediately he set about co-operating, however unwillingly, with the Allies. It was his assassination on Christmas Eve 1942 by a young man named Bonnier de la Chapelle, who claimed he was fulfilling a patriotic mission that left the path open for the appointment of General

Henri Giraud as Commander-in-Chief of the French forces in North Africa. It was a confusing situation, with the Americans strongly backing Giraud, and the Gaullists antagonistic to him, and things became even more complicated when Colonel Rivet seized the opportunity to go to Algiers and make contact with Giraud.

After the Allied invasion of North Africa it was inevitable that remnants of Vichy and the new forces of de Gaulle had to operate together. One factor which historians have sometimes failed to emphasize is that government under the Vichy rulers was extremely efficient, and this showed as much in North Africa as in France itself. Despite France's defeat by the Germans, there had been no revolt by any of the various Arab factions in Morocco, Algeria or Tunisia. General Giraud nominated Colonel Rivet as the head of the new SR in Algeria while General de Gaulle opened a mission in Algiers under General Catroux, who was backed by Commander Pelabon as the BCRA representative. But for a long time SR and BCRA were antagonistic to one another. Matters were not helped by de Gaulle's appointment of General Cochet as an intermediary to try to fuse the two services together. Cochet alleged that a number of individuals had been guilty of collaboration. The result was that each service tended to spy upon the other instead of concentrating on joint action against the enemy.

General Giraud had been taken prisoner by the Germans in 1940, but had escaped and returned to Vichy. He had held secret talks with the Americans and, with the collaboration of the British, was smuggled by submarine first to Gibraltar and then to North Africa. Naturally, perhaps, the Gaullists felt he should have come over to their side and they suspected that he still favoured the Vichy Government.

A statement by Dewavrin tends to balance up the arguments which raged against anyone tainted with association with Vichy at this time.

It is known that certain members of the SR at Vichy worked against the Germans and passed intelligence to the British in the period between 1940 and 1942. But during the same period they brought about the arrest of many Resistance people. When, in November

1942, the SR chiefs from Vichy went to Algiers and put themselves under the orders of Admiral Darlan and then General Giraud, they forgot before departing to open the gates of the prisons where, on their account, were held our comrades who had been 'resisting' for two-and-a-half years. The Gestapo found its victims all prepared, with dossiers in order. One will understand our lack of enthusiasm for these *nouveaux venus*.[10]

This is a churlish admission that Vichy's intelligence chiefs passed information to the Allies, but it does confirm what actually happened. Coming from a Gaullist, it was a substantial tribute. In the end some kind of compromise was arrived at in North Africa with BCRA building up a network of reliable agents after making careful checks on their backgrounds and the other services linked to Vichy concentrating on who had relations with the Gestapo and the *Abwehr*. But there was still conflict between the Giraudists and the Gaullists. In December 1942 the British had discovered a plot to capture Dewavrin and liquidate him. This was at a time when Giraud was trying to ban all contact between his allies and the Gaullists. Then in January 1943 the *Abwehr* decided to take action against the *Deuxième Bureau* and the Gestapo's *Hauptsturmführer* Geissler went from Paris to Vichy to make arrests.

General de Gaulle managed to outwit the ever awkward General Giraud. He agreed that Giraud should retain command of the military while he became the leader of what was really the Provisional Government of France and chairman of the *Comité Français de Libération Nationale* (CFLN). Early in 1943 de Gaulle succeeded in the unification of the various Resistance groups in Occupied France under his own representative, Jean Moulin, and the CFLN.

Meanwhile the intelligence services argued about whether they should be attached to the army or the CFLN. Giraud tried desperately to keep his own military intelligence service, but de Gaulle won the day when he decided to replace Cochet with Jacques Soustelle. In November 1943 the *Direction Générale des Services Spéciaux* was established with Soustelle as its chief. This set a new pattern, unifying intelligence, counter-intelligence and special operations under one body and backed by the authority of the CFLN. It was, of course, a break from tradition in that it took the special services away from the army to which they had always been attached, and put them under political control. It was a move which, though bitterly attacked at the time, resulted in great improvements in French intelligence-gathering and a more imaginative approach to the subject.

Soustelle was anything but a typical intelligence chief when he was appointed and he had had very little experience in this sphere. He was a scholar, an ethnologist, a distinguished writer and an imaginative interpreter of the life of the ancient Aztec Indians in Mexico. But he was and remained all his life a passionate French patriot who believed that France had much to give to the world. His first book, *Mexique, Terre Indienne*, was published when he was only twenty-three. Prior to this he had, while living in Paris, edited a Fourier anthology and written some detective stories to supplement his scholarship money. He was in Mexico when war broke out. He immediately took a Dutch ship to Ramsgate and from there made his way to France to join the regiment in which he had done his national service in 1936. For some months he had nothing to do, and then he was suddenly recruited into the Ministry of Information which the Daladier government was setting up. The Ministry sent him back to Mexico and there he was when France fell.

His first thought had been to go to Canada to serve in a French Canadian regiment, but a friend in the British Consulate told him there was a French general in London who was setting up an organization to carry on the fight against Hitler's Germany. Soustelle sent a cable to London and within a few days had a reply from one of de Gaulle's aides. He was asked first of all to organize support for the Free French among the local French community, but eventually he went to Britain by sea and met de Gaulle. From that moment Soustelle's progress was phenomenal. From the Free French's foreign service section he became Commissioner for Information with the Liberation Committee.

It was in many ways a brilliant choice on the part of de Gaulle to select Soustelle for this role, but not altogether surprising because the whole team of the CFLN was made up of first-class brains. Soustelle dealt with the difficulties that confronted him with superb aplomb. At first he had problems with people such as Colonel Rivet and Paillole, both men in the military tradition. They insisted on having precise orders as Giraud was still Commander-in-Chief. Each actually talked about resigning, even though they were devoted to the defeat of Germany.

In his memoirs Soustelle admitted that Vichy's Special Services were strong where those of the BCRA were weak:

The real bastion of the Special Services in Algiers was Paillole's counter-espionage. Gifted with great capacity for work, with a real talent for organization and with unequalled powers of leadership, Paillole had been able to reconstruct in Algiers an organization which was not content to seek out enemy agents and guard our military secrets, but also placed in France itself intelligence agents with transmitters to keep contact with North Africa.[11]

Soustelle succeeded because he was not concerned with personalities, but with what was good for France. Undoubtedly it was this trait which originally recommended him to de Gaulle. Obviously opinions tended to differ as to what was good and what was bad, but on the whole the Gaullist view seemed to be fully justified in that period.

There were, of course, many mistakes made in this exceptionally difficult time. The former Vichy intelligence chiefs tended to believe they had rather better relations with the British SIS than had General de Gaulle. This was partly true. Colonel Rivet believed he had a remarkably good working understanding with Menzies, the head of MI6.

In April 1944, shortly before the invasion of France by the Allies, de Gaulle dissolved the post of Commander-in-Chief and Giraud was thereby retired. Colonel Rivet, unfortunately, declined to work with Soustelle and also retired, though he was promoted to Brigadier-General. Captain Paillole, now promoted to Commandant, remained as chief of the counter-intelligence service, though even he was pushed out of office in November 1944, no doubt saddened to think that the courageous clandestine SR had lost out to the BCRA.

On 24 April 1944, de Gaulle signed an order confirming that

he accepted the soundness and efficiency of the Special Services he had inherited from the Third Republic. After August 1944, and the liberation of Paris, Soustelle moved his intelligence service from Algiers to London and then to Paris where its overall name was changed to *Direction Générale des Études et Recherches* (DGER).

15
Heroes of the Resistance

T managed to be employed as an agent of the Gestapo, in which capacity he was assigned to pursue a terrorist called Ricardo and his band. In fact Ricardo was a pseudonym of T's: the band was his [intelligence] network.

Sacrifice du Matin, Guillain de Bénouville[1]

Tales of the heroism of the French Resistance, both of those working officially for French intelligence services and those operating independently for some local group, are many and varied. Many, like the above quotation from *Sacrifice du Matin*, sound more like fiction than fact, but it is possible all these years later to assert that most can be fully substantiated as narratives of almost incredible heroism and ingenuity. Yet this is something which is typical of the outstanding individualism of French secret service work down the ages. Often the individual proves more important than the service: this is perhaps more true of the French than of any other secret service in the world.

'T' had nothing whatsoever to do with that other 'Source T', the pre-war Austrian agent of the SR. This 'T' was a member of the TR counter-espionage group. A competent but modest soldier in the French Army, he had risen through the ranks from sergeant-major to commandant. His name was Marcel Taillandier and he had been recruited into the *Cinquième Bureau* before the fall of France in 1940. He continued to carry out undercover operations, these being mainly concerned with the collection and concealment of arms and ammunition. Under orders from the *Troisième Bureau* he kept such collections of arms hidden as far as possible from the Armistice Commission, but when the Germans entered the Free Zone of France they located many of the hidden dumps.

Frustrated by this, Taillandier volunteered to work with 'TR', making his headquarters in the Café Frascati in Toulouse. On one occasion the Gestapo raided the café, though they found nothing incriminating. Forming a group of his own known under the code-name of *Morhange* (a Franco-German battle in August 1914), he was daring enough to put himself forward as an informant for the Gestapo and to be employed by them as an agent.

Even more daring was the special mission which he and his small group gave themselves: they told the Germans of a terrorist band run by a man called Ricardo, and set out to track it down on behalf of the German Reich. In fact, this was a fictitious band, but for the Germans it was in effect the very unit which Taillandier was running himself. Using German petrol, Taillandier and his men travelled around the country, easily getting themselves through German roadblocks and collecting intelligence all the time, while passing on disinformation to the Germans. Such a situation could not last for long and eventually the Germans realized who Taillandier really was, but he still eluded them.

By the autumn of 1943 the *Morhange* group had become an invaluable aid to the Resistance movement, not only helping to link this up with various TR posts in France, but even managing to keep in touch with TR in Barcelona and North Africa. This unit's talent for counter-espionage was such that it not only continued to infiltrate the Gestapo, but also discovered the identity of some Germans who had infiltrated the Resistance movement. *Morhange* killed a major in the *Abwehr* who had found out too much about their activities, and also kidnapped a colonel of the German Intelligence Service, closely interrogated him and were thus able to warn other Resistance members that they were being investigated.

On the whole *Morhange* was a highly disciplined unit, taking the minimum of risks when operating, however daring may have been its missions. At the end of 1943 one of their agents who had got himself a job in one of the Gestapo HQs reported that a Gestapo detachment was being sent to Nice to assist the Italian Intelligence Service in putting down Resistance organizations in the southern part of France. As the Gestapo convoy was taking vital information files with them to Nice, including details of alleged Resistance arms dumps, *Morhange* members disguised themselves as *gendarmes* and not only halted the armed convoy, but captured the files. This was Taillandier's most brilliant coup.

Inevitably, *Morhange* suffered severe losses. Twenty-four of its eighty-two members died or were killed, seven managed to return from concentration camps, while three were crippled for life. Taillandier was caught by the Gestapo in the summer of 1944 and long afterwards his mutilated body was recovered.

An outstanding individual intelligence-gathering organization existing at about the same time in 1944 was the Century network in Normandy. Its mission was to obtain detailed information on what was called Germany's 'Atlantic Wall'. The Century network consisted of hundreds of French civilians who collected data on enemy beach fortifications and underwater defences. This was the kind of information which was vital to the Allies before they attempted to land in France.

Chief of the Century organization was Marcel Girard, who showed a remarkable talent for recruiting the right people. Long afterwards he declared that, 'It is easier to find good, observant spies in the remoter parts of the country and the coastline than in the towns. Such people exist by being observant.' One of his recruits was a house-painter named René Duchez who managed to get himself employment at the German headquarters in Caen. Here he found plans of various coastal fortifications and escaped with them.

There was one ploy used by Duchez which strikes me as being in some ways typical of the swift mental processes of the French and their ability to improvise brilliantly at a moment's notice, a trait which is revealed again and again in the stories of French agents. The Gestapo were hunting for the plans and mounted a search of the whole area. Duchez was drinking in a bar with the plans in his pocket. When the Gestapo broke in he avoided arrest by stealthily slipping the plans into the overcoat pocket of a German soldier who stood drinking with a French girl. When the Gestapo departed Duchez managed successfully to retrieve the plans, thus giving Century one of their major successes.

It is notable that during the war some of the French Arabs, especially those who had served in the forces, gallantly aided the intelligence services. Not even France's defeat killed their patriotism. One such was Chouali ben Larbi, who had been taken prisoner by the Germans while serving in the Tirailleurs, a French colonial regiment. Deciding that he would make an admirable spy against the French, the Germans sent him to Naples on an espionage course and then to an *Abwehr* radio operators' school. In 1943 they had him parachuted into Algeria at a point south of Blida, giving him a radio transmission set and some gold coins.

Chouali had long before decided he would never work for the Germans and as soon as he landed he buried his radio in the sand, carefully memorizing the exact spot, and gave himself up to the *gendarmes*. He told them his story, showed them where the radio was buried and they referred his case to TR. As a result TR was able to feed him with considerable disinformation to radio back to the Germans, including some details of bogus troop movements just before the end of the Tunisian campaign.

One of the youngest agents operating in the war was Anne-Marie Walters, who was only fifteen when war broke out. Her father was English and her mother French, and she had been educated on the Continent. Young as she was, she acted as a courier to the French Resistance in Guyenne and Gascony for more than a year. In 1943 she made contact with Britain's SOE and, after brief training, in December of that year she was parachuted into Gascony with a young medical student, twenty-year-old Jean-Claude Arnault. Later she was compromised and in August 1944 escaped into Spain over the Pyrenees.[2]

The story of SOE does not come into this book's frame of reference, as it was essentially a British-controlled organization. There were, of course, occasions in which SOE, French Intelligence Services and Resistance groups linked up, the case of Anne-Marie Walters being one of them. There was also an example of co-operation when that gallant officer, Wing-Commander Forest Frederick Yeo-Thomas, one of the heroes of the SOE, was given the mission, which he was unable to fulfil successfully, of attempting to rescue the BCRA officer, Major

Pierre Brosselet, who had been caught by the Gestapo and put in Rennes Prison. However, some mention must be made of SOE, if only to show how it was viewed by the French Intelligence Services. One of the problems for historians in assessing SOE's achievements has always been the lack of vital documentation. The official history, *SOE in France*, by M. R. D. Foot, reflected a good deal of the antagonism of the heads of the SOE towards General de Gaulle and his followers. Its publication revealed such widespread evidence of inaccuracies in the official version of events that the author found it necessary to reply to his critics:

> SOE's own archives are of course in many respects sadly incomplete . . . There have been heavy losses by accident and by ill-advised intent . . . *All* the files of AMF, the section that worked into southern France from Algiers, were burned at – or even before – the end of the war; and almost all the messages exchanged between Colonel Maurice Buckmaster's F section and France by wireless have disappeared.[3]

There were many reasons why files disappeared and few of them were creditable. Apart from many blunders in planning operations SOE had also been infiltrated by Soviet and German agents inside the British Intelligence Services and this was to lead to a massive cover-up. One theory was that the Germans had an agent on de Gaulle's staff. Even M. R. D. Foot admitted that he had not found proof for or against this. Latterly it would seem that Soviet agents through the influence of such people as Anthony Blunt and others did the greatest harm, not only through passing on information, but also through the manipulation of double agents in the Double-Cross network which was at least partially controlled by Britain's MI5. Dewavrin's verdict on SOE cannot be ignored: he said that it had 'accumulated the errors of others and added others to them'. In Foot's book it was alleged that every message the French sent out in their own code could be read by the Germans as late as March 1944. 'If this were true,' commented Dewavrin, 'then it was surely criminal of the British to go on using them.'[4]

Compared with either French undercover operations or those of the Resistance inside France, SOE still appears as a totally amateurish organization, groping in the dark, and wide open to anyone who wished to sabotage it. One of the things which caused most trouble to the Gaullists in London was a guerrilla army of French politicians whose only war aim was to smear the Gaullists and to restore the discredited Third Republic. These were the people who passed on anti-Gaullist propaganda to British Intelligence, which sometimes accepted this information rather than that given by the undercover SR and SCR of Vichy.

Even Jean Moulin, who was not hostile to the idea of SOE, warned close friends that he suspected that not all the blunders of British agents were accidental and that it sometimes seemed as though someone in London had links with the enemy, or was deliberately sabotaging the Resistance movement, or those within it who wished for swifter action. Moulin, hailed by M. R. D. Foot as 'a piece as powerful as the queen at chess',[5] was a man of fearless integrity in the field of action. At the age of forty-one he was the youngest Prefect of Police in France, in Chartres. The Vichy authorities dismissed him for disobeying orders, but the truth is that he tried to cut his throat in an attempt at suicide rather than obey what he considered to be a dishonourable order. After this he escaped to England where he demanded to see General de Gaulle. At that time the Germans were sending agents into Britain disguised as refugees and few could be taken on trust.

De Gaulle demanded that Moulin should prove his identity, and the ex-Prefect did so by removing the scarf which hid the scar on his throat. De Gaulle immediately appointed Moulin as his personal delegate and sent him back to France with the dangerous mission of unifying Resistance groups into a national force. Moulin sometimes appears to have been all things to all people, having made a favourable impression on de Gaulle, Dewavrin and, not least, on Buckmaster, head of SOE's F section. Moulin was a genius as an organizer, but he had no easy task in bringing cohesion into the diverse Resistance groups. Yet he seemed to have achieved this when he arranged the first plenary session of the National Council of the Resistance in France on 27 May 1943, at which all pledged full allegiance to de Gaulle. But only a few weeks later he was betrayed to the Germans. He was tortured and killed without having given anything away, as far as can be ascertained. His body was cremated and the ashes secretly buried without a name. Only in 1964 was it established that the ashes of No. 10137 were those of Moulin.

Moulin, totally courageous and dedicated as he may have been to the defeat of the Germans, hailed as the mastermind who organized Resistance groups into one cohesive unit under de Gaulle, has more recently been accused of being a fellow-traveller, sympathetic to the Communists who worked against de Gaulle.

Henri Frenay, head of the former Secret Army and founder of *Combat*, one of four groups – Gaullist and Communist – which Moulin co-ordinated as head of the National Resistance Council on de Gaulle's orders, alleges that Moulin laid plans for the French Communists to overthrow de Gaulle and take power in the aftermath of war. Frenay also states that Moulin could be 'directly or indirectly blamed for all the troubles after the liberation and right up to the present time . . . All his closest advisers in the National Resistance Council were Communists . . . in all probability he was what is called a fellow-traveller.'[6]

There is some support for this view: Moulin was directly influenced by a former Popular Front minister, Pierre Cot, who was closely associated with the Communist Party after the war and who was militantly anti-Gaullist. Moulin's sister said that there was 'a complete identity of views' between the two men.

Much evidence suggests that Moulin had laid the Resistance movement open to Communist manoeuvers, but he could, of course, have replied that Communist cells were among the most efficient in the Resistance. When Moulin's ashes were enshrined in the Pantheon in a ceremony in December 1964, André Malraux, an ardent Gaullist, described him as 'the poor king tortured in the shadows' and 5,000 torch-bearing children followed the coffin as heroes of the Resistance gathered to salute him.

Possibly de Gaulle's greatest error was his hostility to contact between his secret service and those in Vichy under Colonel Rivet. This meant that the British SIS always had to deal separately with the Army of the Armistice of the Vichy

Government and the Gaullists. In effect this meant that Dewa-
vrin's men were kept out of French North Africa by both the
British and Americans, who kept in touch with Vichy and
Colonel Rivet. But the fact was that security was tighter when
in contact with Vichy than it was with either Gaullists or
Resistance groups.

But the Gaullists would, on some occasions, have been in
great difficulty but for help from those still nominally under
Vichy, such as TR. There was the case of Maurice Duclos
(code-name *Saint-Jacques*) who was the main Gaullist link with
Free French networks in France. He parachuted into France on
one occasion, and broke his leg as he landed near Périgueux.
After being taken to hospital he only escaped through help
from TR. From then on he and his networks exchanged
intelligence with TR in Paris.

It was TR again and again which managed to help other anti-
German organizations without compromising themselves or the
people they were helping. Another of de Gaulle's men,
Renault-Roulier, acquired considerable help from TR. Madelin, an industrialist who was chief of the counter-intelligence
network in Saumur, took Renault-Roulier to Paris and introduced him to TR.

One of the most intelligent and perceptive of all commentators on espionage in this period was Jacques Bergier, a scientist,
experimenter in the paranormal and one of the founders of the
highly successful *Rote Kapelle* spy network in pre-war days
when such an underground movement seemed to be the only
effective means of combating fascism and Nazism. Bergier told
me in a long letter about the *Comité des Intellectuels Antifascistes de France*, which was founded during the Spanish Civil
War. 'I was in it, concerned with gun-running – arms to the
Republicans,' wrote Bergier. 'Two members, Malraux and
Soustelle, told me at the time of a "big English intellectual, an
Oxford professor", helping the Committee. This in my opinion
was the fourth man, the man who was helping Philby, Burgess
and Maclean.'[7]

Another clue to the identity of this man came from a former
member of the pre-war Soviet *apparat* in Switzerland who

stated: 'André Malraux, who, as you know, was organizer of foreign aviation for the Republican forces, had his communications links with us at this time via "*Zoologiste*", who was living in Málaga, and, according to Malraux, was an invaluable and ingenious director of courier operations.'[8]

'*Zoologiste*', it would seem, was one and the same as Bergier's Oxford professor: that was the code-name of none other than Sir Peter Chalmers Mitchell, the eminent zoologist of Christ Church College, Oxford. He had been knighted in 1929 and was indeed a friend of Malraux when he was living in retirement at Málaga. Chalmers Mitchell was not the 'Fourth Man', that is to say he was not the man who recruited Philby, Blunt *et al*, but he certainly furthered the Soviet cause both in Britain and Spain far more than was generally realized. Mitchell worked in Military Intelligence for Britain and for a time was responsible for the distribution of propaganda on the German fronts. One of his innovations was the *Courier de l'Air*, messages sent by balloon to occupied territories. Sir Peter organized a small Soviet cell inside the Fortress of Gibraltar, one which was maintained with the help of civilian contacts undetected throughout the war and which some still link to the plane disaster in July 1943, when the Polish Commander-in-Chief, General Sikorski, was killed. Chalmers Mitchell died somewhat mysteriously as a result of a motor accident in London in 1945.

Bergier was not only a keen student of the world of intelligence and a diligent collector of information concerning it, but quite an able agent himself. If confirmation of this is needed, it is given in this letter from General de Gaulle long after the war: 'My dear Bergier, you have the gift of relating the story of your network, already magnificent in itself, in a captivating manner. This is to say that I thank you and send you my warmest regards.'[9]

Bergier had his fingers in all manner of anti-fascist and anti-Nazi networks before World War II and was associated with the *Marco Polo Promontoire* network, founded to help the French Resistance towards the end of 1940. His principal aim at this time was to find out what the Germans were doing in trying to develop a super-bomb through nuclear research.

Bergier himself says that this task was made even more difficult because there were 'few if any' British Secret Intelligence agents in France at that time. 'This undoubted fact,' he asserts, 'was then put down to a secret agreement allegedly come to between Hore Belisha [then British War Minister] and Daladier in 1938 and amounting to a full military alliance between Britain and France, as a result of which all British agents were, it is said, withdrawn in 1939 from France, and vice versa. Not that we have ever been able to obtain any official confirmation of this alleged agreement.'[10]

Bergier operated under the cover name of Verne. He was eventually caught by the Germans and put in the Mauthausen concentration camp, and was liberated by the Americans in May 1945. Prior to this his French Resistance network had discovered valuable data on the German flying bomb weapons. He complained that:

An essential point of the information sent to Britain by the Marco Polo organization was completely ignored, namely that the V1 would fly at low altitude – between 2,250 and 3,000 feet – thus making it difficult for anti-aircraft guns to hit them since the latter were designed for much greater operational heights. In consequence, it became necessary to improvise, after the battle had begun, special mobile platforms for the guns. And as for the information sent over concerning the V2, it seems that at the time not a soul took any of it seriously.[11]

Bergier would have made an admirable senior intelligence officer for he possessed imagination and a sense of humour. He told me of a certain Pierre Laval (no relation to the pro-German Vichy Minister) who had volunteered for service in the network, adding that, 'We sent off the following message to the controller: "Pierre Laval engaged for Marco Polo. Code-name Judas. Awaiting instructions."'

There were, of course, blunders on the French side in espionage operations during the war just as there were with the SOE. Renault-Roulier, Dewavrin's key man in organizing the Gaullist network in Normandy, was horrified in March 1942 to be handed a secret message which tersely stated, 'Five radio operators arrested.' This dread news meant that five out of his six key men in the whole area had been taken prisoner. Soon afterwards, when he landed secretly in France, he learned the truth. One of his radio operators had disobeyed instructions by transmitting several times in one week from the same place: a villa in the suburb of Chatou, in Paris. The Gestapo used a detector van and soon traced him. In his pocket they found he had – again against all the rules – kept the names and addresses of the other operators in a notebook. It was after this disaster that Renault-Roulier found Marcel Girard and persuaded him to set up a fresh network of agents.

It took courage to undertake such work, because the penalties could be drastic and they were well advertised by the Gestapo. The legal penalty for spying against the Germans was beheading by the axe, with the person's head strapped to a board, face up. Apart from this threat there was always the danger of interrogation coupled with such tortures as electric shocks and immersion in ice-filled baths.

There is one story of Resistance activities which seems more than any other to illustrate the courageous ingenuity of these people. Two years after the war ended I met a white-haired and prematurely aged man of twenty-seven named Fernand Dalbreux in Algeria, then a part of Metropolitan France. His wife was in her own way one of the great uncelebrated heroines of World War II. Her husband had been working for the Resistance when he was caught by the Gestapo, tortured unmercifully, and sentenced to death. At that time his wife was in Algiers.

Madame Dalbreux smuggled herself out of Algiers into occupied France to try to save her husband's life. She heard the death sentence had been passed on him and immediately went to see the German commandant responsible for carrying it out. She told him she was about to have a baby (which was true), and that she was unmarried (which was untrue) and that though Fernand was a scoundrel and she hated him, she wanted to go through with the marriage ceremony to give her unborn child a name. If the commandant would do this, she promised to give him information about the Resistance.

Hoping for results in the form of unexpected intelligence, the commandant agreed to a marriage before the execution. Fernand was put in a truck to be taken to the police station for the ceremony. On the way his wife, who had organized a rescue party, ambushed the truck with fellow *Maquis*. Together they escaped and only a few weeks later their baby was born. When I talked with him, Fernand gave me a toast in anisette: 'To the women of France,' he said. 'In the underground movement the women outnumbered the men, and some of them did the shooting, too.'

16

The Trials of André Dewavrin

What might be called human secrets are by far the most interesting and at the same time the most difficult to discover. The existence of such secrets proliferates from a specific characteristic of our time, namely the increase of intolerance.

Jacques Bergier

After World War II the first major problem in the sphere of French Intelligence was ironing out the differences between the various factions which made up the new services – those who had remained loyal to Vichy, the Gaullists' BCRA and the various factions of the Resistance, many of which made efficiency nearly impossible because of their constant bickering with one another. Added to this problem was the fact that de Gaulle's own service at Duke Street had suffered from a series of scandals, as, too, had the SOE and to a lesser extent MI6 and the service controlled by Soustelle from Algiers.

After the liberation of France in August 1944, Jacques Soustelle moved his DGSS service from its offices in Algiers to Paris and its name was changed to DGER (*Direction Générale des Études et Récherches*). Many who had been, or claimed to have been, in the Resistance (and there were many whose claims were unsubstantiated), rushed to join the *Services Spéciaux* for a variety of reasons. Some merely wanted office, others hoped to acquire decorations and many had ulterior motives for seeking membership. The result was that very quickly the DGER became too large. Its canteen in the Boulevard Suchet was described at the time as the lushest black market restaurant in Paris. It was also alleged that it had become the centre of many scandals over requisitioning and evasion of rationing restrictions.

General de Gaulle quickly became aware of this and in 1945 he called in Dewavrin to take over DGER and work out plans for a reorganized and streamlined service. Dewavrin was horrified at what he found and immediately decided to act ruthlessly: 'I made the decision which was put into effect on a single day in July 1945 – to dismiss 10,500 people who were being subsidized by the DGER budget; to remove the requisitions on more than one hundred buildings and to retain temporarily only three; to find over four hundred vehicles requisitioned at the liberation and to retain only twenty needed for the service.'[1]

Not surprisingly, in carrying out such drastic reforms and getting rid of so many hangers-on and interlopers Dewavrin made enemies who swore to make life difficult for him. Meanwhile, however, he succeeded in his reorganization and out of all the muddle created the *Service de Documentation Extérieure et de Contre-Espionnage* (SDECE), which came to be known as 'S-Deck' for short.

The battle for power in Paris was confused and confusing for long after the Liberation and the end of the war. It is now generally accepted that in the void which was left by the ending of the highly efficient administration of the Vichy Government the Communists might well have seized power but for de Gaulle acting like a temporary dictator, albeit one who was forced to some extent to work with the Communists. There was a mixture of suspicion, hatred and demoralization in this battle for power. Rightly or wrongly, Soustelle thought much of this could be attributed to the agonies of the winter of 1943–4 in France, just prior to the Allied invasion: 'So many people one knew disappeared, were killed or committed suicide. Such a waste of life. I don't think the underground in France would have lasted another year.'[2]

This particular winter was one in which many people were betrayed to the enemy, and this had created an atmosphere of mistrust which lasted long after the war. Soustelle's job in 1943–4 had been to pool the resources of the Free French Intelligence with those of Vichy, who had moved to North Africa, and to supply the French Resistance. 'We ran short of French banknotes and in the end we were dropping little pieces of paper signed by Mendès-France, promising to pay after the Liberation.'[3]

Pierre Mendès-France, who later became French Prime Minister, was then helping the Free French while serving in their air force.

Dewavrin's experience in clearing up and cleaning up the DGER illustrates how secret services can expand not only beyond their capacity, but beyond any true purpose, if not carefully monitored. The story of the rehabilitation of the French Intelligence Services after World War II provides a stark contrast to the British Intelligence and Security Services which remained more or less in their pre-war format. But it should be added that the French Intelligence Services had a much greater need to be reorganized than their British counterparts, and that the comparison is not entirely justified. On the other hand it can safely be said that the benefits to be gained from reorganization, learned in such drastic fashion in 1945, have been taken to heart by successive French governments, and as a result the Intelligence Services, including the SDECE, have been frequently reorganized since then.

As the SDECE eventually had for its headquarters a disused barracks near a swimming pool in the Boulevard Mortier in Paris, it came to be nicknamed the '*Piscine*', partly in joking fashion, but also with a touch of irony. Cynical French intelligence officers sometimes talk of 'taking a jump into the pool', or comment that it is 'time to drain the pool'. It has not been so much the small staffs and budgets which worried its members, but the frequent recurrence of political interference which has plagued the service ever since the Liberation.

Whereas the SR had been firmly under military control, after the Liberation and the setting-up of a French government, the administration, first of the DGER, then of the SDECE, had been hindered by members of the Socialist and Communist parties who were constantly sniping at the leadership, especially at Dewavrin. There was frequent governmental interference and there were also sections of the SDECE who were divided into right-wing and left-wing and pro-American and anti-American factions. Many on the right were extremely concerned about the open support given by some American intelligence officers in North Africa to various Arab nationalist groups in Morocco, Algeria and Tunisia.

Dewavrin had pruned the old DGER budget for the new service by authorizing only 1,300 personnel with an official budget of some twelve million dollars, at the same time setting up an Operations Service which had four sections: foreign intelligence, counter-intelligence, studies and action. He was eager for SDECE to come under the Foreign Office, as was the case with Britain's MI6, but he was overruled and it was decided that it must come under the direct control of the Prime Minister of the day. Dewavrin had his close colleague of BCRA days, André Manuel, as his deputy, but many of the other senior posts were held by military officers who had been in or associated with the old SR.

Matters were not helped when in late January 1946 General de Gaulle resigned office a month after the French franc had been devalued. Immediately, left-wing attacks on the SDECE were launched, some openly, but others more damaging in undercover moves. The situation was not helped when the SDECE wanted to make its own interpretative analyses of intelligence through its studies section and the Foreign Ministry promptly insisted on doing its own analysis, not only for the Foreign Minister, but also for the Prime Minister. Laughlin A. Campbell, a former United States intelligence officer with extensive European experience, has summed up the problem as follows:

The SDECE had to undergo its development during the Fourth Republic under Third Force governments (neither Gaullist nor Communist), followed by the return to power of de Gaulle in 1958 and the establishment of the Fifth Republic . . . the new SDECE was formed by the unhappy marriage of SR and BCRA. Yet this service spent its first twelve years without the support of the military leaders who had established SR or the Gaullists who had established BCRA.[4]

Once de Gaulle left office trouble started for Dewavrin, who was denounced in the most extravagant and outrageously inaccurate language by the left wing. He was even described as 'de Gaulle's Himmler' and of 'being the brains of a would-be neo-fascist putsch'.[5] Information coming from Britain – no doubt from such sources as Philby, Blunt, Maclean and Burgess, all of whom had French connections – suggested that he had upset the British authorities in connection with a suicide and a secret inquest at Marylebone. Yet Dewavrin had been awarded the DSO and MC for 'special service missions', including visits to German-occupied France.

In February 1946, Dewavrin was removed from the secret service and Félix Gouin, head of the new administration, announced that the organization was to be purged of elements hostile to the government to avoid the risk of a *coup d'état*. Not that there was any evidence of such a development. The excuse for Dewavrin's removal was that he was connected with highly-placed officers of the French Army who were considering seizing power by force in the event of either political unrest or a left-wing victory. The Communists accused him of being mainly anti-communist in his views.

But the campaign against Dewavrin went on long after he resigned. In May 1946, it was reported that he and fifty other members of the Resistance movement had been arrested and Dewavrin had been taken from his Paris apartment by *gendarmerie* and placed in a military fortress. The only explanation given for the arrest was that it was 'the result of an administrative inquiry'.

For days after this there were vague hints about why he had been arrested. It was said that there was a general belief that attempts were being made by or for Colonel Dewavrin to allot secret funds for political purposes. This was based on previous allegations made in the French Assembly on 30 December 1945 by d'Astier de la Vigerie, a former Commissioner of the Interior, who had alleged that the service was misusing its funds.

In September 1946 it was announced that Dewavrin had been discharged from the French Army and stripped of his decorations for 'grave errors in financial management' of the secret service bureau – this, despite all his efforts to cut the costs of the bureau. Teitgen, the Minister of Justice, alleged that following an official inquiry, Colonel Dewavrin admitted to having failed to account for between £80,000 and £100,000 which had been deposited abroad since August 1944. It was stated that Dewavrin had been found guilty after a military inquiry into alleged misappropriation of secret funds placed under his control. Almost immediately Dewavrin issued a detailed statement in which he asserted that the secret deposits of funds which he had placed abroad were to finance the activities of his organization and nothing else. He declared himself as being innocent and demanded a public trial.[6]

L'Affaire Passy, as the case against Dewavrin was called in the media, dragged on until 1948. One story was that Dewavrin felt that France could suddenly have a Communist government, or at least one in which Communists dominated, and that he should set aside funds to counter such an eventuality, and if necessary finance another government-in-exile. What needs to be made absolutely clear is that Dewavrin made no personal use whatsoever of intelligence funds which, in any case, were not under his direct control. As has been seen, many of his troubles had been due to his stamping out corruption and misuse of secret funds. But it would seem that Dewavrin had not told his successor, Ribière, about the purpose of this secret allocation. When he took his case to the civil courts it became clear that the funds had been accounted for and that there was no point in pursuing the matter further, and Dewavrin was reinstated in his rank in the Army and given all his entitlements. He resigned from the Army a year later.

L'Affaire Passy dragged on in various forms for some few years. There was no let-up for Dewavrin. It is said that when he divorced and married a beautiful blonde Frenchwoman, he found the austere General de Gaulle less friendly towards him. In 1948 allegations were made in France about Dewavrin having been involved in torture tactics in London. Maurice Henri Dufour, a Free French soldier, claimed that he had been tortured by members of the Free French Intelligence Service in a cellar at their headquarters in 10 Duke Street, Manchester Square, London. During the war Dufour took action in the London courts (at the time unreported because of censorship), naming General de Gaulle and seven of his leading officers as having interfered with his rights under English law. The case was never heard, but it caused a furore in the intelligence community.

Dufour had come to Britain from occupied France in March 1942, claiming to be a cavalry lieutenant in the French Army and to have been awarded the *Croix de Guerre* as a result of action against the Germans in which he was wounded. He had also claimed to have been in touch with a British agent called O'Leary, who was in fact a Belgian Army doctor named Albert Guérisse. British Intelligence had cleared him when he arrived in Britain and he had been duly signed up by the Free French in their Intelligence Service on the authority of General Pierre Billotte.

Dewavrin and his officers had not, however, been satisfied with the newcomer and had started to make inquiries of their own. Their checks allegedly revealed that Dufour was a sergeant and that he had not been awarded the *Croix de Guerre*. According to French records, he had been held for fifteen days, at the end of which he signed a declaration retracting his claim to 'the decorations and uniform of an officer'.[7]

Dufour, who insisted that he wanted to continue to serve in the Free French Intelligence Service, had been taken to the French barracks at Camberley and committed for trial by a French military court. His case had also been referred to MI5, and it was the British who had suggested that the French should undertake this court action. After all, it was the British who had blundered in not fully checking his record.

On the night of 16 July 1942, Dufour escaped. Next day he was arrested by the British authorities, but was not given back to the French until 17 August. It is what happened during this whole month that puzzled the Free French and Dewavrin in particular.

According to agreements between the Free French and the British, Dufour should have been handed back to the French at once. Inside French Intelligence (and this suspicion was shared by General de Gaulle himself) there was a belief that for some unknown reason Dufour had during this period been allowed to contact the American Embassy in London. But the record shows that Dufour escaped again before his trial in

December 1942, and was not seen again by the French. In his absence he was sentenced to six months' imprisonment.

Then in February 1943, the Dufour case became a major irritation between the Allies. A Lieutenant Johnson of the British mission to de Gaulle informed the Free French that Dufour was bringing an action in the High Court in London contesting the validity of the judgment passed by the Free French military court. The writ was served on 6 August 1943. In bringing this action Dufour not only repeated his previous claims to have been a lieutenant and wounded in action, but alleged that during his fifteen-day stay at the Duke Street HQ of FFI he had been taken into a cellar by Captain Roger Wybot (subsequently head of the French counter-intelligence service) and, after being kept without food for a long period, had been made to stand under a bright light from 8.30 P.M. to 10.30 P.M. The writ also claimed that he had been 'stripped to the waist and beaten in the small of the back with a steel rod bound in leather on his old wound'. (These allegations are not generally regarded as being true.)

Renault-Roulier in his own account of this affair refers to a meeting with General de Gaulle when he brought up the name of Dufour.

'There is no *affaire* Dufour,' angrily replied the General.
'I beg your pardon, General, but the problem exists,' replied Renault-Roulier.
'I forbid you to speak of it.'
'I regret, General, but I have promised to do so.'
'Promised? To whom?'
'My English friends.'
'Ah! Your *English* friends!' The General pronounced the word English in a certain tone.[8]

Dewavrin admitted at the time that it was 'only on the word of the two officers named, Wybot and a Captain François Girard, that "torture" charges could be dismissed'. He added: 'I had my office on the second floor of that building. As far as I know the interrogations were carried out in a room on the third floor. Since the building was right on a busy street it would seem odd that the shouts of a tortured man would go unheard. I personally do not believe these tales.'[9]

Ultimately the Dufour case never reached a judge and the writ was somewhat mysteriously withdrawn. Major General Sir Edward Spears, head of the wartime mission to de Gaulle, stated: 'I understand he was awarded £3,000 by the Free French and £10,000 by Britain not to go ahead with the action. It would have caused too much scandal between Allies if it had come into the open.'[10]

This in itself seems a most extraordinary statement. One would have thought that what with censorship and wartime security regulations the matter could easily have been hushed up without such payments. Could there have been some kind of American involvement after all? Eventually Dufour emigrated to Canada, but the mystery surrounding his case remains. Much of it, undoubtedly, can be put down to hostility to de Gaulle by the US administration of that period. The whole Roosevelt lobby had been infiltrated by anti-Gaullists and Communists, most of whom were not unmasked until the 1950s and some of whose true intentions were never revealed. This de Gaulle fully realized from his own reports, though the full significance of this was not appreciated until long after. The cases of Admiral Muselier and Dufour both helped to make the General permanently prejudiced against the Americans, and this hostility showed itself again after the North African landings when the USA backed Giraud.

Though the Dufour case was publicized in France in 1948 and Dewavrin's name was dragged into the controversy because he was head of de Gaulle's intelligence service at the time, it did him no real harm and was quickly forgotten. In 1956 he was awarded the cravat of Commander of the *Légion d'Honneur* and felt he had been vindicated. Meanwhile the militant socialist, Henri Ribière, who was appointed head of the SDECE after Dewavrin, began to run it almost as if the service was an operational wing of the Socialist Party. To say this does not exaggerate Ribière's intentions, because he actually created a section which was intended to link up with various international socialist groups, some of them extremely left-wing. Ribière used the SDECE as a political activist service to support Latin American revolutionaries, to spy on Franco's

Spain and to conduct all manner of trade deals with Soviet Russia.

Such deals, including that of shipping bauxite to the USSR in a manner which eluded the American embargo on such trade, brought Ribière into conflict with some of his colleagues in the SDECE. Prominent among Ribière opponents inside the service were Colonel Verneuil (sometimes known as Roger Lafont, a former SR officer) and Henri Fourcaud, a one-time member of the right-wing organization, the *Cagoulards*, who had later joined the Free French and become a technical director of the new intelligence service. Both men opposed some of Ribière's decisions and tried to co-operate with the Americans in parachute raids behind the Iron Curtain at a time when there were also attempts to support guerrilla activities inside the Eastern bloc, notably Albania and Hungary. Certainly in this period SDECE suffered to some extent from conflicting policies within its own ranks. There was an almost total lack of firm political control at the top, largely because during the Fourth Republic governments changed with such rapidity that SDECE was left to its own devices: one of the main problems was that there was no continuity of direction in the service.

Ribière brought Socialist colleagues of his own into SDECE, including Pierre Sudreau, an old Resistance friend, as his chief of the administration department, and Louis Fauvert as his financial director. But it was Colonel Pierre Fourcaud who kept things under control and checked some of Ribière's left-wing activities. Fourcaud had joined BCRA in London in 1940 and had been with the former DGER in Paris in the latter part of the war, so he was an experienced operator. Indeed, some felt that he rather than Dewavrin should have been made head of the new service in 1946. Though he had been a member of the right-wing *Cagoulards*, he had latterly made contacts with French Socialists, including Gouin, the Prime Minister. This relationship between Gouin and Fourcaud, however, did not make Ribière any happier. In a move destined to increase his own political influence he appointed a special link-man in his office, Louis Kastenbaum, who was assigned the task of keeping closely in touch with various Socialist parties and groups.

One of the issues with which Fourcaud was deeply concerned was that of Soviet activities in North Africa and Algeria in particular. In late 1946 Algiers had become the headquarters of Russian espionage in North Africa, with the USSR Consulate-General there having a radio station which was in constant touch with Moscow. The French were also worried because Soviet agents in Algeria had been contacting Italians and Arabs in the area, making promises of support for Italy getting back Tripolitania (Libya), if Palmiro Togliatti, the Italian Communist leader, came to power. What made things more difficult at this time was that Algiers had a pro-Communist mayor who had refused to allow General de Gaulle to speak in the municipal forum. Later de Gaulle spoke at a local open-air sports stadium and outrightly condemned Soviet 'expansionist techniques' which, he said, 'menaced France once again', adding that the French Communists were, 'Separatists, overcome with insolence, who have just publicized that they are nothing but delegates to the foreign enterprise hoping to absorb France'.

Another case which concerned the French Intelligence Service in North Africa was the mysterious disappearance in late 1948 of the Comtesse Marguerite (Marga) d'Andurain from her yacht, *Djeilan*, in the waters of Tangier bay. At the age of seventeen Marga, daughter of a magistrate, had married Comte Pierre d'Andurain, a French aristocrat with a passion for the Middle East. In 1918 they had travelled to the Lebanon and started trading in pearls. Marga had learned Arabic and loved to dress in Arab garb. She had led a queer, enigmatic existence. A British major who fell in love with her during a trip to Cairo committed suicide after she left him, and in 1925 she divorced the count and married an Arab admirer, Sheik Suleiman, who took her to Mecca disguised as a boy where she gratified her wish to see the *Kaaba*, the sacred black stone in the mosque.

But when Suleiman locked her up in his harem at Jeddah she rebelled. Within a few days her husband had died of poisoning. Arraigned before a Muslim court, Marga was sentenced to death, from which French intervention and King Ibn Saud's clemency saved her. In Syria she remarried Comte d'Andurain who by now owned a hotel in Palmyra. She named it the 'Queen Zenobia' after an ancient Roman queen who ruled over large parts of the Eastern Empire from her capital at Palmyra. Her Arab friends nicknamed her 'Queen of the Desert'.

Within two months of the remarriage the Comte was found in the hotel grounds with seventeen knife wounds in his back. Two men were arrested, one of whom was stabbed to death in prison before he could speak. The widowed Comtesse started a roaming career. She smuggled gold into France, dabbled in forged passports and frequented the best hotels from Nice to Alexandria. It was also believed that she was a secret agent for more than one European power. At the outbreak of World War II she was in Paris, rather impoverished, but still as mysterious as ever and a sparkling conversationalist. The SR discovered that she had done some petty spying for the Nazis, but that they had paid her badly. No action was taken against her and it is possible that she worked for Vichy Intelligence, too.

By 1945 she was living in an apartment which her nephew, a young lawyer named Raymond Clérisse, had lent her. When Clérisse wanted his apartment back there was a quarrel. Later this was patched up and Clérisse was invited for a meal with the Comtesse. Shortly after the meal he died, writhing in agony, but before this he had accused Marga in the presence of a servant of having poisoned him. Marga fled, but a few months later was arrested in Nice and brought back to Paris under a heavy escort. Clad in a red dressing-gown, she appeared in court charged with twenty-two crimes, including two murders, those of her first husband and Raymond Clérisse. Yet, astonishingly, she was released because of lack of evidence, after which she returned to Nice where, after having some luck at a casino, she bought the yacht, *Djeilan*. It was then she sailed on her last voyage to Tangier bay.

Then in November 1948 coastguards, police and fishermen started searching the sea around the Moroccan coast between Tangier and Gibraltar for the body of the Comtesse, whose disappearance from the yacht had been reported a few weeks previously. This time the search was made after police in Casablanca had taken a statement from a German named Hans

Abel which suggested she had been murdered. The Comtesse had, on arrival in Tangier, made an application for a visa to visit Gibraltar. This had been refused on the grounds of her association with former Axis agents, including Hans Abel, an ex-Gestapo man who had entered Tangier illegally on a Swiss passport under the name of Renato Poncini.

Immediately a number of secret services began to take an interest in Marga's disappearance. It was said that when she came to Tangier she had received anonymous telephone calls from Paris, threatening her with death. Matters became even more complicated when French agents investigating the affair in collaboration with the Tangier police force (Tangier was then an international zone) discovered letters among the Comtesse's papers aboard the yacht. These letters were 'alleged to have been written to her by Britain's Lieutenant-General Sir John Glubb [more popularly known as Glubb Pasha, commander of the Arab Legion in Transjordan] and King Abdullah of Transjordan'.[11]

At the same time French Intelligence investigated the possibility that the Comtesse had been involved in large-scale smuggling of funds out of Europe by former Axis war criminals. As this smuggling involved the illegal leakage of vast sums of money from various European countries to Tangier (then a free money market for all currencies) all the powers concerned in the administration of Tangier were anxious for a full investigation. It was partly as a result of this that Hans Abel and his friend Helen Kulz, who were caretakers aboard the yacht, were arrested.

The story which emerged from Hans Abel's confession was that he had killed the Comtesse, put her body in a sack and disposed of it in Tangier bay, after which he sold the yacht's sails and fixtures and fled to Casablanca with Helen Kulz. Gradually something of the Comtesse's new activities was discovered: not only was she involved in currency smuggling, but in helping ex-Nazis to escape from Europe to Latin America and in trafficking in Congo gold. But apart from the fact that the Comtesse's body was never recovered (which gave rise to the question of whether she was really dead), there were other unanswered questions: Who was the Soviet agent who had been following her for many months? Who telephoned her from Paris with death threats? For how many secret services had she worked? The mystery remained unsolved officially, though a French Intelligence officer told me in 1948: 'We have got most of the answers we most needed. From that point of view the case is satisfactorily closed, especially as it led to our discovering the identity of some agents hostile to French interests.'

Some other remarkable successes were scored by the SDECE in the late 1940s and 1950s. In 1948 SDECE agents kidnapped the German commando ace, Otto Skorzeny, from an United States prison camp in Darmstadt in an effort to get information on Russia. They were anxious to learn the truth about a Soviet story that Ilya Svetlov, a Soviet agent, had joined the Nazi Party and became a storm trooper under the name of Walter Schultz. Eventually, according to Soviet sources, he joined the *Abwehr* and was selected as the leading man in Operation Long Jump, a German plot to fly two planeloads of their specialist troops into Tehran to kill the three Allied leaders, Churchill, Roosevelt and Stalin. Svetlov went ahead into Tehran, warned his Soviet masters and the German plot failed. My own information from Paris is that the French were able totally to destroy the story of Svetlov–Schultz as a Russian swindle and invention.

It is somewhat unfair to allege, as some have done, that France's secret service became 'a troubled and a troubling organization'.[12] It is true that from the Socialist government of Félix Gouin onwards, the SDECE was desperately trying to create a proper role for itself. Yet even in those difficult years of the late 1940s and early 1950s it managed to escape from its purely military role of pre-war years and to develop imaginatively into the technological age. In technical and scientific intelligence it achieved far more than it has ever been given credit for, especially in the fields of aviation and marine intelligence-gathering which went far beyond the requirements of the respective military and naval services. Some of this intelligence proved absolutely vital for NATO in the early days of that organization. In the decryption of communications France's pre-war lead in such matters was well sustained.

French Intelligence probably led the way in realizing the importance of the underwater detection of nuclear-armed submarines. Some of their experts also felt that from a purely economic viewpoint underseas exploration was important. The French were the first to detect that there was a Soviet interest in this subject. In the late 1940s Professor Piccard's deep-sea diving bathyscaphe experiments made from Dakar aroused considerable controversy. Professor Piccard planned to attempt to break the ocean-diving record in his self-propelled fifteen-ton metal observation diving bell off Dakar in 1948, but the experiment was abandoned owing to faulty equipment. The original attempt was sponsored by the Belgian government, after which a new attempt was to be made in the Mediterranean under joint French and Belgian naval sponsorship. But a complication arose because Piccard's chief assistant, Professor Max Cosyns, who was a director of the Belgian centre of nuclear research, attended the Communist-sponsored World Peace Congress in Paris. In Dakar it was suggested that Cosyns should be asked to withdraw from the new experiment if the French Navy was sponsoring it. Later French Intelligence benefited greatly from the underwater researches of Jacques-Yves Cousteau, the archaeologist and former captain in the French Navy who established the Underseas Research Group as early as 1945 and in 1950 formed and became president of the *Campagnes Océanographiques Françaises*. In his ship, *Calypso*, he made annual oceanographic expeditions and took part in the making of the bathyscaphe, first with Piccard and then with the French Navy, though he declined to be in charge of it.

After France's surrender Cousteau had stayed in the Navy in Occupied France, but had also worked for the Underground Services. Once, posing as an Italian officer, he had led a party into the Italian headquarters at Sète and spent four tense hours photographing a code-book and top-secret papers. Yet he has little to say about such experiences. 'I have always hated espionage and secret service work, and I still do. I think it is unfair,' he told *Time* in March 1960. He maintains to this day that his main aim is to obtain information from the depths of the sea, not to interpret it. This, over the years, he has certainly carried out with great persistence all around the world and with commendable results.

A great deal of data on nuclear developments was obtained by French Intelligence in this period, using a skilled team of assessors to make the most of information that came in from all parts of the world, not least from what was then the Belgian Congo where uranium had become almost a second currency. All this intelligence certainly helped the French to gain that lead in the use of nuclear power for peaceful purposes which they have held for so many years. This led very swiftly to the experimentation at Fort Châtillon, France's first atomic research station. Some slight, but quite valuable, intelligence on the nuclear side was also provided by Chinese physics students who had been educated in France. It was through such intelligence that French military scientists as long ago as 1947 developed the idea of a system of planetary satellites acting as 'watchtowers', perpetually armed, ever vigilant against a possible invasion. Even at that early date the French visualized the 'watchtowers' being used for such peaceful purposes as the manufacture of artificial rain over the barren Sahara and even for 'burning' the ice-caps around the Poles.

17
Service 7 and Other Developments

Seven is a mystic or sacred number, composed of three and four, which among the Pythagoreans were, and from time immemorial have been, accounted lucky numbers.

I am told that when Guy Marienne proposed setting up a new clandestine section of intelligence in the 1950s, aimed at gathering foreign intelligence from sources within France, another intelligence officer commented, 'If we really expect to do that, we are pushing our luck.' The reply he got was that for this reason the new service should be given a lucky number as its title. 'What about seven? The old astrologers recognized seven planets each having its own heaven. There are seven sciences and seven joys of the Virgin Mary, so let us call it Service 7.'

The reason for creating this service was that as such it could operate more safely and more cheaply and in some ways was likelier to be more accurate. There was some logic in this, and the idea of obtaining accurate intelligence on foreign countries in one's own homeland is not quite as naïve as it may seem. Service 7 had its own typically French techniques to provide the right kind of intelligence by obtaining documents or recorded conversations from targeted foreigners, while some of its work involved opening diplomatic pouches in transit at Orly airport, clandestine and illegal entry into foreign embassies and various bugging activities. These things are sometimes done by other secret services, but are exceptionally well directed in France.

Service 7 was, of course, subsidiary to the SDECE and therefore linked to it in every way, but at the same time it was allowed far greater freedom of action than almost any other section of that service. Guy Marienne, the initiator of this branch of the service, was the deputy of Captain Trautmann, head of the SR collection section that co-ordinated intelligence reports, and he was a close colleague of Colonel Gustave Bertrand, head of the cryptography section. The first director of Service 7 was Marcel Le Roy (also known by the code-name of Colonel Finville), who set up offices well away from the Piscine to make his operations even more secretive. French Intelligence has been much criticized in these early years after World War II, but in fact Service 7 was way ahead of many clandestine sections of other secret services of the world at this period. Not only were diplomatic pouches examined and bugging carried out, but hotels, residences and even, in some cases, embassies were entered to search for documents or to install bugging devices and arrange telephone tapping. Much of this surveillance was devoted to American offices.

The work of Service 7 became concentrated on North Africa, as, in the 1950s, increasingly French Intelligence had to pay closer attention to the whole of its North African territories, the protectorates of Morocco and Tunisia and especially Algeria, which was regarded as part of Metropolitan France and in many respects was the jewel in France's imperial crown. The rise of nationalism in those areas forced the French to concentrate a great deal of their overseas espionage in North Africa, while other European powers were chiefly tackling the problems caused by the Cold War with the Soviet Union and its satellites. Despite this the SDECE remained exceptionally well informed on other parts of the world, especially the Middle East and to a lesser extent the Eastern bloc.

Naturally some French ministers and politicians soon became aware of Service 7 and during those years sought to use it, sometimes against the Americans, sometimes against the Algerian rebels and other Arab nationalists, and in some cases the Soviet bloc. Thus SDECE gradually became liable to being manipulated in its covert operations by each new French government which took office, thus curtailing its own requirements as a neutral advisory body.

There was, however, some co-operation with the American

intelligence and security services, thanks partly to the efforts of Henri Fourcaud and Colonel Verneuil, who succeeded him in 1950. In 1951 Ribière was succeeded by Pierre Boursicot as head of the SDECE. Boursicot had a useful record in the Resistance as well as having been a director at the *Sûreté* before coming to SDECE. But he made himself unpopular with the military personnel in the service when he decided that civilian members of SDECE should be given the same rights and status as the military. It was, nevertheless, a rational move and one which gave greater stability to his agents' lives and a greater sense both of security and responsibility.

By this time the service was developing its counter-espionage section to build up substantial files on Communists and trade unions. This may have been very helpful to the SDECE in its relations with foreign countries such as the USA, but it created tensions and conflict with the counter-espionage service, the DST (*Direction de la Surveillance du Territoire*), which can be described as in some ways a French equivalent of Britain's MI5, which is solely concerned with catching spies and security at home and answerable to the Home Secretary just as the DST is answerable to the Minister of the Interior. The DST is totally separate from the SDECE, and the right of sole control of such purely domestic espionage was jealously guarded by its head, Roger Wybot. Ironically enough the DST was provided with offices in the former Gestapo headquarters in Paris. Wybot was a man with a passion for scientific detail and quite one of the most brilliant of French investigators.

One example of French aid to the USA at this time was the researching of the true identities of a couple known as the Baltchs, who had passports forged by the Russians in the name of Jackson. The FBI had found in the Baltchs' apartment in Washington a box of pills from a Paris chemist, and an entry in Mrs Baltch's address book: 'Laurette, 98 Rue Jean [then followed some indecipherable writing] . . . Villejuif.'[1]

The FBI asked the DST to help, and the latter carried out a diligent search for 'Laurette' which was much more difficult than it may have seemed to the FBI. Eventually they found that a young French girl named Alice Laure Eikenberry had lived at 98 Rue Jean Jaurès in Villejuif from 1941 to 1951. The DST tracked her down to a new address at a village in the Seine-et-Oise department south of Paris. Her nickname was 'Laurette' and her new married name was Alice Laure Ventis. It was 'Lanrette' who was able to identify a photograph of Baltch as Alexander Sokolov whom she had met in Paris in 1946. From then on the DST had only to check their files to discover that Sokolov had a pro-Soviet record, though he became a French citizen after his family left Russia. They found that he had joined the youth section of the Union of Soviet Citizens and the French Communist Party. Then, in 1947, he renounced his French citizenship and obtained a Soviet passport, leaving France for East Germany.

This information proved useful not only to the Americans, who realized that Baltch was Sokolov, but to the British as well, as a younger brother, Michel Sokolov, had some years earlier moved to England, served in the Royal Navy and married an English girl. Michel had added her surname to his name, making himself Sokolov-Grant.

The situation inside the SDECE had noticeably improved after Paul Ramadier, the Socialist Prime Minister, got rid of Communist and fellow-travelling ministers in 1947, but there was still a small corps of Communist sympathizers in its ranks. Slowly, these were investigated and ultimately thrown out of SDECE by the chief of counter-intelligence, Colonel Verneuil. France had had a lesson, which other secret services might well heed, that it is much easier for an intelligence service to be infiltrated by dedicated Marxist-Leninists than most people believe. At this time there was one factor which, surprisingly, French logic had ignored: army officers in the service were exempted from vetting. For this reason Colonel Verneuil had to pay close attention to such members.

It should perhaps be mentioned that French Intelligence developed a system which is wholly commendable – that of the occasional informant, the '*correspondent particulier et honorable*'. While agents were paid, *correspondents* were not, though they were not only welcomed, but encouraged to come forward and sometimes rewarded in other ways. In other words, the SDECE valued the patriot who might be helpful, if not today, possibly tomorrow. One must remember that anyone can ring up the service, whose number is clearly stated in the telephone book, unlike in Britain where such numbers are ridiculously guarded as a total secret, and the unknown informant is treated with suspicion or contempt.

Yet it was conflicting loyalties inside the service that led to SDECE being publicly involved in what came to be known as '*L'Affaire des Généraux*'. In late 1949 the Chief of Staff of the French Army, General Revers, and Colonel Fourcaud went to Indo-China where trouble was already brewing. On returning to France General Revers produced a highly secret report which not only criticized French policy in Indochina, but urged the replacement of the French High Commissioner there by a man of his own choice, General Mast. This information was somehow leaked to certain sections of the press and even picked up by the Viet Minh radio station.

An inquiry into the leak launched by the *Sûreté Nationale* revealed that General Revers had used as an intermediary one Roger Peyré to give copies of his report to both Vietnamese leader Bao-Dai's representative in Paris, Houang Van Co, and an agent of the subversive Viet Minh, Vinh Xa.

The scandal which developed did not help France's relations with other intelligence services, notably those within the NATO alliance. Clearly, SDECE, under the influence of Colonel Fourcaud, had done everything to protect General Revers to the extent of even failing to inform Ribière, then still head of the service, that SDECE had established contacts with Peyré. Peyré eventually fled to Brazil, and for a while there was a cover-up, with the government suggesting that the Revers report was not 'top secret' (indeed, not secret at all, according to some ministers), but in the end Revers and Mast retired from the Army and Fourcaud was retired from the SDECE. But Ribière did not escape criticism, though in his case dismissal took a politer form: he was given notice to quit SDECE, but not until the end of 1950.

In retrospect the delayed retirement of Ribière may well have been a major mistake. It aggravated relations between France and the NATO countries, and it was no easy matter to put these right again as long as Ribière was still in the saddle. This was not altogether the fault of the French: there was tactlessness, to put it mildly, on both sides of the Atlantic. The

Americans were almost equally divided between those on the ultra-right who saw the hand of Moscow in almost all other nations' activities and those who had known and understood what French Resistance had done to help achieve victory in World War II. But prejudice against the French continued among American right-wingers, despite useful cooperation between the FBI and DST. Then someone high up in the British SIS made the quite ridiculous suggestion that they should act as an intermediary between the USA and the European partners of NATO. For once Ribière was right: he ruled that the only realistic way out of this problem was for the USA to have an intelligence liaison officer in Paris and for the French to have a similar appointment in Washington. Thus one of his last acts was to appoint his own chief assistant, Philippe-Thyraud de Vosjoli, a former member of BCRA in Algiers, as France's liaison officer in Washington.

In the 1950s French governments came and went with remarkable rapidity and, though it is true that sometimes the SDECE was 'largely left to determine its own agenda', it is totally unfair to suggest as one critic has that, 'Poor in agents, denied any sophisticated electronic gear, and rich in traditions of political in-fighting, it not unnaturally concentrated its attentions on domestic French matters.'[2]

Scandals of a political nature there may have been and some undeniably concerned SDECE, but the service in the 1950s was neither poor in agents, nor denied electronic gear, and most certainly it did not concentrate on domestic French matters. There were a number of rumours concerning the service which found credence in certain parts of the world, but many of these were based on fiction. There is just one of these worth mentioning: it is part fact, part fiction and in many ways very amusing. In short, this story was that Mata Hari's daughter was working for the *Deuxième Bureau*!

The woman in question was given various names, or, if she existed, adopted aliases – Banda Macleod (Mata Hari's married name), Wilhelmina Van Deeren and Banda Gertrud. She was supposed to have been born in Batavia, then governed by the Dutch, and to have become involved in her late teens with a Dutchman many years her senior who was a government official. It is not clear whether they were married, or merely lived together. The Dutchman is said to have died in 1935 and to have left her a beautiful home where she carried on as a society hostess.

After that the story of Banda becomes more confused. One version was that she went to the USA to raise funds for Indonesia's struggle for freedom and that she was recruited by the OSS (the American secret service organization) who sent her to China. Then she is said to have gone to North Korea where she was shot as a spy. Yet another report stated that she was involved with a Russian general who was behind Soviet strategy in Indo-China. But the news which amused some and angered others in Paris was that she was actively spying all over South-East Asia on behalf of the French and in league with a Greek archaeologist.

General Sir Philip Christison, who was in command of the 13th and 15th Indian Corps from 1942 to 1945 and Allied Commander, Netherlands East Indies, from 1945 to 1946, stated that he knew the woman alleged to be Mata Hari's daughter under the name of Banda Gertrud in 1943 and that General Wavell, the Viceroy of India, knew her, too. Indeed, General Christison said that in September 1945 Wavell urged him to get in touch with her. Later General Christison was warned that Banda had been a collaborator with the enemy during World War II and probably the mistress of a Japanese general.

Certainly Mata Hari appears to have had at least two children, one of whom became a schoolmistress and is said to have died at The Hague in 1919. The truth of the story may never emerge.

Between 1946 and 1954 a number of French Union forces (particularly Foreign Legionnaires) defected to the Viet Minh and then fought for the Communists against the French. The Viet Minh had a massive propaganda programme devoted to recruiting French defectors, some of who are still in North Vietnam today, residing in a commune at Ba Vi. For many years the French had relied on intelligence from French Catholic priests in both China and Indo-China, especially during the Boxer rebellion. This intelligence had been first class, but suddenly it was realized that there were many left-wing priests whose help could not be counted on.

Indeed some of these priests informed against the French. Bazin, head of the French shock force against the Viet Minh's shock force in Saigon, was assassinated in April 1950. Only days before this Radio Viet Minh had broadcast, 'Bazin, you are going to die.' For it was Bazin who had discovered that the Viet Minh had created a unit called Battalion 905 to assassinate all French agents. But Bazin's work and that of many other French agents in Indo-China was ruined to some extent by information passed on to the Viet Minh by French defectors. The death of Bazin was a fatal blow to French Intelligence. Shortly before he was killed he had told a friend, 'I'm on the top of the blacklist, the people who are going to be wiped out. My killers have already arrived in Saigon. I've only a few days to get them. . . otherwise. . .' This was the beginning of the end for the French in Vietnam, and in many ways their Intelligence Services had been demoralized by French defectors to the Viet Minh and the changed attitudes of priests.

In 1954 Pierre Mendès-France became Prime Minister as much to rescue the nation from the impasse of Indo-China as anything else. The French had failed to put down the Viet Minh and there remained a situation in which South and North Vietnam were irrevocably at war. Successive governments had failed to find a resolution to the problems of French involvement in Vietnam. However, despite his tireless and brilliant attempts not only to find a solution to this question, but to introduce vital reforms at home and in North Africa, Mendès-France was frequently the victim of political mischief-makers and unscrupulous powermongers. Yet he brought about a settlement in Indo-China and if in the long term his objectives failed, he could hardly be blamed. The malicious plots of the powermongers were denounced at the Radical Party Congress in Gironde in 1945 as 'the abominable manoeuvres of cliques who are as much responsible for the misfortunes of our country as for the deterioration of the international situation'. However it was one particular such plot that was being attacked in this statement, and that was the extraordinary case of M. le Commissaire Dides.

L'Affaire Dides reduced France's National Assembly to an hysterical, abusive mob for some weeks. The Commissaire, in charge of the River Police, had been entrusted by the Paris Prefect of Police with keeping watch on Communist activities. As Dides left the Ministry for Tunisia and Morocco one day in 1953 he was surrounded by six detectives. A tough and natural fighter, he knocked two of the detectives down before he was finally overcome.

'We have orders to take you to the *Sûreté Nationale*,' he was told.

He was shown into the office of Roger Wybot, chief of the counter-espionage service. In his briefcase was found a summary of secret discussions held by the National Defence Council on 10 September 1954. It was learned that Dides had obtained this summary and other documents from a journalist named André Barranes. In the meantime Barranes had disappeared.

Worse followed. Two senior officials in the National Defence Council, René Turpin and Roger Labrusse, confessed to 'leaking secret information from the Council sessions'. It was learned that on at least five occasions in recent months information about the Defence Council had been passed on to the Communist Party.[3]

Only sixteen people were authorized to attend these Council meetings, President Coty and the Prime Minister among them. Similar leakages had also occurred during the previous Laniel government. The Mendès-France government was accused not only of hushing things up, but of having destroyed the work of an intelligence service which had operated successfully inside the Communist Party for three years by putting Dides in charge of investigating Communist activities. Dides' friends said that he had acted from patriotic motives by carrying on with his investigation of Communists, unknown to the authorities. Against them, though, Roger Wybot claimed that Barranes was really a Communist undercover man working with Dides. But the questions which baffled most people were, first, whether Dides was checking on the leakage of information when the documents were found in his possession, and, second, whether

Barranes secured the documents from the Communist Party or some unknown source.

All this happened on the eve of an important conference of political leaders in London in 1953 when Mendès-France himself was considered suspect in some Western circles, and once again doubts were raised in Washington about the reliability of France as an ally if top secret information of this sort could so easily reach the Communists. Mendès-France's supporters replied that if the document had ever reached the Communists, it had been planted on them to discredit the new government. They suggested that nobody had told the government about the previous stolen secrets. In any case, they argued, there was no proof that Dides' documents were genuine.

Dides himself launched a tirade of his own against both the detectives who had arrested him and the Government. Supporting him were Baylot, ex-chief of the Paris police, and Martinaud-Deplat, former Minister of the Interior and opponent of Mendès-France. The situation was also complicated by the feud between Martinaud-Deplat and the new Minister of the Interior, who was none other than François Mitterand, who later became President of France. To add to the farcical elements of the case Dides accused Roger Wybot of being a Communist. Wybot's response was promptly to sue Dides for £5,000 damages.[4]

Later Barranes was detained and a batch of other arrests were made. Captain Jean Cazalet, of the military administration in Paris, was charged with betraying military secrets. These were said to include plans for the evacuation of Paris and sabotage of key points in the event of an enemy occupation. Jean Mons, Defence Secretary-General, was dismissed from his post by the Prime Minister and charged with 'treason through negligence'. As a result of these arrests the Government enjoyed renewed prestige because all the wanted persons were located. Usually in such cases in France they tended to disappear abroad, leaving an uneasy feeling that the government of the day had deliberately let them escape.

A full-scale attack on the Government was nevertheless launched concerning the Dides case in December 1954, when Legendre, a dissident Gaullist, made a venomous personal onslaught on the Prime Minister and Mitterand. He accused the Prime Minister of trying to hush up inquiries and playing the Communists' game. He alleged that a secret report on Indo-China had come into the hands of d'Astier de la Vigerie, a deputy who edited a pro-Communist weekly, *Libération*, on which Barranes had worked. This report, claimed Legendre, was passed on to Mendès-France before he became Prime Minister. This the latter firmly denied. But Legendre did nothing to enhance his reputation by his speech. He tried to make out that Dien Bien Phu in Indo-China fell because of leakages of French secrets. In fact its fall was due to failure by French Intelligence to learn the secrets of the Viet Minh. In suggesting that no effort had been made to probe leakages which occurred during the term of office of the previous government, Legendre was treading on dangerous ground. There was indeed reason to believe that the new Government was not fully briefed by those Ministers from whom they had taken over.

L'Affaire Dides was never adequately cleared up. But in sieving fact from malicious rumour in this case, the possibility remains: perhaps the secret reports never reached the hands of the Communists, but were merely sold back to the Government by some enterprising person who wished them harm. Such action would be entirely characteristic of the time. The French Intelligence Services and the police had been infiltrated by Communists during the Liberation, so providing them with many possible means of access to official secrets. However, the allegation that Wybot was a Communist does not stand up and casts more doubt on Dides than on Wybot, for the latter had an excellent record over many years. He was an intensely patriotic Frenchman with no more association with Communists than any counter-espionage officer might have.

One last note on *L'Affaire Dides*: following his dismissal a classified advertisement appeared in a French morning newspaper. It read: 'Ex-chief Commissaire, sacked for denouncing treason, seeks honourable post. For further inquiries avoid Ministry of the Interior and telephone Jean Dides.'

18
The Red Hand

Those Frenchmen who are now denouncing The Red Hand, mainly the left wing, claim that it is a counter-terrorist organization which works in association with the French security service.
Sunday Times report from Paris, 12 July 1959

A fascination for the macabre and the horrific developed in the Paris of the middle and late 1950s. *Grand Guignol* was back again in a small, old-fashioned theatre. When in one of these ultra-realistic horror plays two old ladies pressed a girl's face on to a red-hot stove, stage effects provided the hissing sound and sickening stench of burning flesh. And if the cabaret artiste Mistinguette found it hard to preserve her legend of indestructibility, there was Patachou in Montmartre Village who obligingly cut off one's necktie with a pair of scissors as part of the evening's fun. If *existentialisme* wasn't depressing enough, there were joys such as these. Or one could indulge in the latest attraction – a conducted tour by boat of the Parisian sewers for a mere twenty francs.

The fascination with violence, horror and murder found its way into the political scene, too, both on the right and the left. Out of such obsessions was born the legend of The Red Hand, and a legend it still remains because all the reports about it are a weird mixture of fact and fiction. The origins of this ultra-secret society date back to the beginning of France's troubles in North Africa in coping with the threats from Arab nationalists. Rumours of the organization were heard in 1956, but it was not until three years later that the world's press started to pay attention to The Red Hand.

In July 1959 came the report of a bomb attempt in Rome against an Algerian, Tayb Mohammed Boulhouf, which killed

Cardinal Richelieu,
statesman and chief of
intelligence
(Mary Evans Picture Library)

Cardinal Jules Mazarin, Louis XIV's
intelligence chief
(Mary Evans Picture Library)

Left: The Chevalier d'Eon de Beaumont in female attire, from a portrait by G. Dance in 1793

(Mary Evans Picture Library)

Below left: Cardinal Guillaume Dubois, who adopted the 'cover' of a dancing-teacher while living in England

(Mary Evans Picture Library)

A	B	C	D	E	F
105.	102.	99.	96.	93.	
106.	103.	100.	97.	94.	
107.	104.	101.	98.	95.	
29	28.	27.	26.	25.	

ambr ou ambe . 108 camp . . . . . 157 Da
argent . . . 109 conjecture 158 la
afaire . . . 110 ces . . . . . 159 m
ali . . . 111 cette ou cet . 160 m
ance . . . 112 conclu . . . 161 les
ainsy . . . 113 commande . 162 m
armee . . . 114 comme . . . 163 m
affez . . . 115 condition . 164
au . . . 116 conseil . . . 165
ant . . . 117 consequence 166 cr
avec . . . 118 conjointement 167 ell
avis . . . 119 courrier . . . 168 cr
aussy . . . 120 cour . . . . 169 ce
autre . . . 121 croy . . . 170 ce
ay . . . 122 Comte . . . 171 cr
ayant . . . 123 castelan de . 172 cr
afseur . . . 124 Religion Cath. 173 cr
Allemagne . 125 le g. Cambellan 174 cr
archevesque de 126 le Czar . . . 175 cr
le Pce Alexand 127 m de Chamilly 176 cr
m. d'Autriche 128 Cosaques . . . 177 ef
Angleterre . 129 Chancellier . 178 c
les Anglois . 130 les Cercles . 179 c
Cujavie . . . 180 cr
Ba . . . 131 Kiovie . . . 181 cx
be. 132 . . . . . 133 Kaminick . 182 cx
bi . . . . . 134 Cracovie . . 183 E
bo . . . . . 135 Mr de Castag. 184 E
bu . . . . . 136 le Pce Constant 185 E
beaucoup . . . 137 E
besoin . . . 138 **Du** . . . 186 le
bien . . . . 139 de 187. 188. 189 les
bon . . . . 140 ci . . . . . 190 Eu
m le E de Brancas 141 co . . . . . 191 Es
Berlin . . . 142 eu . . . . . 192 m
m de Bethune 143 dans . . . 193 m
Breme . . . 144 demande . 194
Buczak . . . 145 des . . . 195
Boheme . . . 146 desir . . . 196 fc
Bataille . . . 147 depesche . 197 fi
Fredda . . . 148 devant . . . 198 fo
les Saxons 149 disposé . 199 fu
m l'abbé Bical 150 donne . . . 200 fa
cessim . . . 201 fu
Ca . . . 151 sont . . . 202 fu
ce . 152 . . . 153 Directeur . 203 fe
ci . . . . 154 Duc . . . 204 fi
co . . . . 155 Danezik . 205 fu

Right: Carl Schulmeister, Napoleon I's 'ace' spy inside the Austrian establishment

Below: A French secret service cipher of the eighteenth century

H	I	K	L	M	N	O	P	Q	R	S	T	U	X	Y	Z	Et	ns	es
84.	81.	78.	75.	72.	69.	66.	63.	60.	57.	54.	51.	48.	45.	42.	39.	36.	33.	30.
85.	82.	79.	76.	73.	70.	67.	64.	61.	58.	55.	52.	49.	46.	43.	40.	37.	34.	31.
86.	83.	80.	77.	74.	71.	68.	65.	62.	59.	56.	53.	50.	47.	44.	41.	38.	35.	32.
									24.	23.	22.	21.						

07 M de Teriel — 254
08 Cercles & Francon — 255
09 — *Ga*
10 *Ga* — le. 300
11 ge — 256 — lo
12 go — 257 — lu — 299 Madame de
13 gu — 258 — laisse — 301 moldavie
14 gard — 259 — les — 302 milan
15 general — 260 — leurs — 303
16 gouverne — 261 — leur — 304 *Na*
17 grand — 262 — luy — 305 ne . 353
18 guerre — 263 — tieu — 306 ni
19 Gnezne — 264 — lorsque — 307 no
20 gentilhomme — 265 — ligue — 308 nu
21 — 266 Lithuanie — 309 necessaire
22 *Ha* — 267 Leopol — 310 non
23 he — Livonie — 311 nos
24 hi — 268 liberte — 312 nostre
25 ho — 269 Lubimirsky — 313 nous
26 hu — 270 Lublin — 314 nouvelle
27 homme — 271 leswitz — 315 negociation
28 honneur — 272 Lipsick — 316 non obstant
29 hollande — 273 — 317 nt
30 hongrie — 274 *Ma* — 318 neantmoins
31 hambourg — 275 me . 322 — 319 nonce
32 hongrois — 276 mi — 320 naples
33 sans Pechine canal — 277 mo — nice
34 le D'Holstein — 278 mu — 321
35 les Hollanois — 279 mais — 322 me
36 — 280 maistre — 323 *Oit*
37 *Ja* — 281 mande — 324 oient
38 je . 283 — manque — 325 ois
39 ji — 282 marque — 326 on
40 jo — 284 ment — 327 occasion
41 ju — 285 mesme — 328 ordre
incessament — 286 mettre — 329 ordinaire
42 — 287 mon — 330 l'Ocean
43 intention — 288 mon — 331 Oginski
44 interets — 289 moy — 332
45 jour — 290 maison — 333 *Pa*
46 juge — 291 moyen — 334 pe . 381
47 jusques — 292 ministre — 335 pi
48 imperiaux — 293 M'ou M' — 336 po
49 imperatrice — 294 Monseigneur — 337 pu
50 les Pn. Iaques — 295 mediat ou med — 338 paix
51 il — 296 mecontens — 339 par
52 les Moscovites — 297 — 340 particulier
298 la Masovie — 341 pas
342 personne
343 persuade
344 plus
345 plusieurs
346 port
347 pour

349 pouvoir — 397 la Reyne de — 446 schonen — 495 Ukraine . 544
350 prenere — 398 le R. de Rom — 447 — 496
351 present — 399 Russie — 448 *Ta* — 497 te .
propozition — 399 Ruswick — 449 te . 497 — 498
352 M. le Prince de — 400 Ry Wick — 450 ti — *Zamoisky* 545
353 — 401 Resident — 451 to — 499
354 les Paysbas — 402 Riga — 452 tu — 500
355 M. le Enchart — 403 tres arc — 453 tant — 501
356 m. le Primat de Pr — 404 Reis — 454 temps — 502
357 le Palatin de — 405 Rois — tenir — 503
358 Prusse — 406 — 455 temoin — 504
359 Picinent — 407 *Sa* — 456 — 505
360 le Roy de Pologne — 408 sc. 456 — 457 terre — 506
361 Pomeranie — 409 Si — 458 tion — 507
362 la Poyolie — 410 so — 459 tost — 508
363 Pcolachie — 411 su — 460 tout — 509
364 Posnanie — 412 Sa Majesté — 461 toujours — 510
365 m. l'Abbé de Polignac — 413 sans — 462 traitte — 511
366 — scavoir — 463 troupes — 512
367 *Qua* — 414 secours — 464 trouvé — 513
368 que 415 — 416 service — 465 Tecué — 514
369 qui — 417 Sicur — 466 Toscane — 515
370 quo — 418 soin — 467 tiers party — 516
371 quand — 419 soit — 468 M de Torcy — 517
372 quartiers — 420 somme — 469 le q Tresoriet — 518
373 quelle — 421 son — 470 d'Iunchande — 519
374 quelque — 422 sous — 471 Transiluanie — 520
375 quil — 423 siege — 472 Turquie — 521
376 quoy — 424 sur — 473 Turc — 522
377 — 425 sur — 474 Tartares
378 *Ra* — secret — 475 Torne — 524
379 re. 427 — 426 subsides — 476
ri — 427 — 428 sujet — 477 *Va*
380 ro — 429 le Roy de Svede — 478 ve . 526 — 525
381 pe. 381 — 430 m't Elect de Saxe — 479 vi — 527
382 ru — 431 Silesie — 480 vo — 528
383 raison — 432 le Starosta de — 481 vu — 529
384 le Roy de — 433 Savoye — 482 vaisseaux — 530
385 ratiffi — 434 succession — 483 verit — 531
386 reeu — 435 Cercles de Svabe — 484 ville — 532
387 reeumons — 436 Saxe — 485 vos — 533
388 regiment — 437 Strasbourg — 486 vestre — 534
389 rend — 438 Stetin — 487 vous — 535
390 resolu — 439 Stokolm — 488 voir — 536
391 rien — 440 Svede — 489 vray — 537
392 rt — 441 Sapicha — 490 us — 538
393 Republique — 442 Sicile — 491 Varsovie — 539
394 Royaume — 443 Samogitie — 492 Vienne — 540
395 le Rhin — 444 Scandinavie — 493 Vilna

On prendra pour nul tous les caractères qui ne seront pas dans ce chiffre aussy bien que ceux qui auront une marque semblable a ce qui suit 50. 671. tis.

Tout ce qui est marqué ... chiffres ci dessus 600. 656. 700.

Tous les chiffres depuis 1 jusques 220 inclus sont nuls.

General Savary, Duc de Rovigo, the man who succeeded Fouché

Colonel Alfred Dreyfus at the time of the treason trial at Rennes

(Popperfoto)

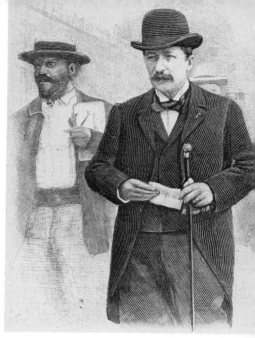

Lt.-Col. Georges Picquart, the man
who suffered in defending Dreyfus
(Mary Evans Picture Library)

Lt.-Col. Henry – a sketch made
during the Dreyfus trial
(Popperfoto)

Marthe Richer, an outstanding French secret agent in World War I, also known as *'L'allouette'* (The Lark) because she was a pioneer female aviator *(Popperfoto)*

'Colonel Passy', cover name for A. Dewavrin, head of the Gaullist intelligence bureau in World War II *(AFP)*

Jacques Soustelle, who
became intelligence chief in
Algiers after the invasion of
North Africa
(AFP)

Comte Alexandre de
Marenches, one of the
ablest of post-war French
intelligence chiefs
(AFP)

Admiral Lacoste, who was removed from his post as head of the DGSE after the *Rainbow Warrior* catastrophe
(AFP)

General Imbot, who served in the Maquis in World War II, succeeded Lacoste as head of the DGSE
(AFP)

an Italian child and injured six other people. The official line in Paris on this bomb attempt was that it was an act of vengeance by the Algerian rebels (the FLN), as Boulhouf was said to have betrayed FLN agents to the Italian police just before General de Gaulle visited Rome. Yet Boulhouf had been put under preventive arrest during de Gaulle's visit and had made no secret of his support for the FLN. Consequently, this version was much disputed, and an article was published claiming that this incident had 'started renewed reports about the mysterious body known as The Red Hand . . . They allege it is engaged in eliminating – by murder if necessary – dealers in Europe who are secretly supplying arms to the Algerian rebels. Successive French governments have been mute on the subject.'[1]

In an earlier incident in April 1959 Herr Heinz Wolf, the Public Prosecutor at Frankfurt, accused The Red Hand of having been responsible for ten murder attempts in Germany since 1956, and it was hinted that the French Ambassador in Bonn had been told to ask for an 'explanation'. Simultaneously it was reported that the Federal German Government intended to approach the French on the subject. In August 1959, a statement was made in Britain's Communist daily newspaper, *The Daily Worker*: 'On 14 April 1959, Heinz Wolf, Frankfurt Public Prosecutor, said: "Inquiries have established that they [the murders] were committed by a secret organization called The Red Hand, which works in co-operation with the French *Deuxième Bureau*, or is given a free hand by it." '[2]

Also in August 1959, Scotland Yard was asked to help Interpol in an attempt to hunt down The Red Hand. This time the allegation was made that The Red Hand had been sabotaging ships in Tangier, Hamburg, the Port of London and Belgian ports. One Brussels newspaper stated, 'The organization was French – *La Main Rouge* – and the ships were carrying arms for the Algerian National Liberation Front . . . Frogmen of The Red Hand had attached mines to the vessels.'[3]

From then onwards the world's press was full of news of alleged Red Hand atrocities. There was a court case in Paris in which six Algerian Muslims and seventeen French men and women were accused of helping and sheltering FLN agents in France. One of the defence lawyers stated that his colleague, a

M. Ousseidik, had been threatened by The Red Hand. 'He produced a letter signed with a red hand which read, "Your hour has struck, you will pay for this," and handed it to the tribunal.'[4]

At this time it was assumed that The Red Hand had vowed to keep Algeria as part of Metropolitan France. The Red Hand may have felt it needed to adopt ruthless methods after independence was given to Morocco and Tunisia in 1954, and the tactics of the more forthright and militant of the Algerian rebels may well have contributed to this. Yet The Red Hand was not so much concerned with killing off Arab rebels as with stamping out the supply of arms to the rebels from various European groups and firms. Much of this drive against arms suppliers was directed against West Germany, thus putting considerable strain on the Paris–Bonn axis. The main targets of The Red Hand were all collaborators with the Algerian rebels in Europe and elsewhere. Intelligence reports in both London and Paris revealed that several West German dealers were deeply involved with clandestine arms supplies to the Algerian rebels and that many of the secret meetings between FLN emissaries and their European contacts took place in Hamburg, Frankfurt, Bonn and Cologne. More than half a dozen of the murders alleged to have been committed by The Red Hand in West Germany were later confirmed as their work. In 1960 the West German authorities became worried about a wave of threatening letters. 'The burden of the threats is "Desist or Die". They have recently dropped through the letter-boxes of several prominent Germans, among them a German MP, Hans-Jurgen Wischnewski, and Herr Kempski, the reporter whose interview with General Massu [leader of French opposition to independence in Algeria] precipitated the last revolt in Algiers,' wrote the distinguished commentator Willi Frischauer.[5]

To try to understand the relationship between The Red Hand and the French Intelligence Services one must consider two important events. The first was General de Gaulle's return to power in 1958 and his turn-around of French policy from wishing to keep Algeria part of Metropolitan France to granting independence to that country. This at once made The Red Hand the opponent of the Gaullists. The second was the replacement of Boursicot by General Paul Grossin in 1957 as head of the SDECE. General Grossin had been born in Algeria, had had an excellent record in the Resistance and had at one time been a military aide of the Socialist Vincent Auriol, when he was President of the Fourth Republic. Grossin also had the admirable policy of wanting to recruit people of higher education into the service, and provide them with additional education of a specialized nature after they had joined. This policy was not particularly welcomed by those who preferred privileged sponsorship as the method of entry.

Grossin was fortunate in that his appointment was fully approved of by General de Gaulle when he became President. As a result he remained in charge of the SDECE until he retired in 1961. One can be sure he closely followed the de Gaulle line on Algeria, for he was regarded by the General as being the ideal intelligence chief to cope with all the problems resulting from the establishment of the Fifth Republic created by de Gaulle. Grossin was both a totally conscientious military officer of the old school and a man of the world with friends among the Socialists and other parties. He had to tread a very difficult path, fraught with obstacles at every turn, not least because de Gaulle, whom many had seen as the probable saviour of Algeria as part of Metropolitan France, swiftly became regarded as an enemy by many of the original settlers (*colons*) and especially by the OAS (*Organisation de l'Armée Secrète*), a group devoted to retaining French rule in Algeria.

Service 7 had already become involved in monitoring the Algerian rebels, concentrating on finding out their sources of arms and, whenever possible, preventing these from reaching the FLN. This service could be compared in some ways to the British SAS and it had operated since the late 1940s, being concerned principally with the task of parachuting agents behind enemy lines – either for instruction purposes or for the real thing. Colonel Fourcaud had developed *Service Action* (roughly equivalent to the British SAS) for operations in Indo-China and established a training school in which recruits were taught not only the arts of parachuting, but of demolition, sabotage and hand-to-hand fighting. Out of Fourcaud's development scheme evolved *Action*'s own forces, the aviation squadron (ELA/56) and the 11th CHOC (parachute regiment). In 1957, if not earlier, *Service Action* had links with The Red Hand and their operations against arms traffickers. One such example was the sinking of the ship *Atlas* in Hamburg harbour in September 1958 by *Action*'s frogmen. It should be stressed that the relations of *Action* with SDECE or even the Army were, for very good reasons, never too clearly defined.

But to what extent there was a close link between *Action* and The Red Hand will probably never be known. Other European governments sympathized with France in this problem of arms supplies to the rebels. One Belgian police chief told the author: 'One could not blame the French for making use of such methods. As it is legal to sell arms, what other course could they adopt? They took the view, quite rightly as a question of morality, that more French soldiers would be killed if such arms were allowed to go through to the rebels, so, logically, they took unofficial and unorthodox methods to stop this.'

Meanwhile the French officially denied that The Red Hand existed, suggesting it was invented by the media. Even Interpol declined to have anything to do with investigating the activities of The Red Hand. 'They are political crimes and we are not allowed to touch anything political,' was one statement made by Interpol's Paris HQ.[6]

In Paris the *Sûreté* claimed that The Red Hand did not exist and that, 'all crimes you mention were committed by individuals. There is nothing to link them together.'[7]

Yet there was one common factor linking three positive incidents in March 1959 – Algeria. Georges Puchert, an arms salesman, pressed the starter of his car in Frankfurt and it triggered off a bomb which blew him and his car into pieces. In Paris a barrister, Ould Aoudia, returned to his office one night and was shot dead as he put the key in the lock. In Ostend the Egyptian freighter, *Al Kahira*, loaded with arms, was blown up, and afterwards Belgian frogmen found it had been mined. In all cases the common factor was the dispatch of arms to Algeria. Puchert was selling arms to the Algerian Nationalists. Aoudia was defence counsel for Algerian terrorists who were standing trial in Paris, and the *Al Kahira* was delivering arms to the rebels.

In October 1959, Dr Felix Roland Moumie, the Communist-sympathizing rebel leader of the French Cameroons and self-styled 'liberator' of French Africa, arrived in London and was interviewed by Geoffrey Wakeford of the *Daily Mail*. He told the newspaper that his object was 'to kill Europeans and French soldiers as they kill us'.[8]

A few hours after this story appeared in print a man telephoned Wakeford and, speaking in good English and with a French accent, asked: 'Can you tell me where I can find this murderer? I am a member of The Red Hand, you understand? I have a job to kill him. You can be sure it will be done.'[9]

Certainly The Red Hand seemed determined to hunt down Dr Felix Moumie. In November 1960 Dr Moumie died of poisoning in a Geneva hospital, and it was reported that French security police believed The Red Hand to be behind it. The doctor had been poisoned during a meal he ate in company with some friends; a highly unusual poison, thalium, had been administered to him.

It was around the end of 1959 that it began to be bruited around that The Red Hand was not merely out to check Algerian Nationalists, but even to pave the way for a *coup d'état* against General de Gaulle, because this was the only way to preserve Algeria in the French Union. Obviously any such suggestion posed the question of how loyal the SDECE was to the new regime. In any other secret service in the world it would probably have been a fair question, did the service support its own government? But in France such matters are always subtly different. It is not so much a question of loyalty as of the overriding necessity of realism in a secret service. Put very briefly, this means that the secret service must always be ahead of governmental thinking. Looking back to the days of rapidly changing governments, there could be no question but that the SDECE had learned this one essential lesson. Thus the SDECE would need to retain links, however indeterminate, with The Red Hand, if only to be able ultimately to control it, or stamp it out, whichever policy became necessary.

In November 1959 the newspaper *Welt am Sonntag* reported that preliminary proceedings were to be taken against 'an alleged French terrorist organization known as The Red Hand,

and that evidence held by various authorities was to be handed over immediately to the federal public prosecutor's office at Karlsruhe'. These proceedings related to the murder of at least four people and the wounding of others, all connected with the sale of arms to Algeria. *Welt am Sonntag* also complained of the West German Federal Government's inactivity, its lack of support for the police and its failure to make representations to the French Government.[10]

The years 1958–66 were fraught with difficulty both for General de Gaulle in his efforts to provide France with a new and stabler constitution and for the SDECE in its response to the conflicting issues of these years. De Gaulle was to some extent distrustful of all 'special services' in the light of his wartime experiences and instinctively felt the need to reorganize the SDECE, some of whose operations he referred to with the unflattering phrase, *'ces affaires de basse police'*. One thing which tended to put the SDECE in an unfavourable light with the general was that the service had become so involved with preventing the sales of arms to Algerian rebels that they tended to opt out of operating against the diehard *Algérie Française* OAS and its leader, General Massu. Worse still, some SDECE agents had actually schemed against the Fifth Republic with the OAS. It was because of sympathies such as these that The Red Hand had been able not only to survive but to cover its tracks and extend its activities around the whole of Europe.

In 1957–8 when Algiers itself was threatened by the rebels, SDECE influence had been crucial in helping General Massu's paratroops to destroy the terrorist network inside the city. In the same way the SDECE had lent some of its own agents to The Red Hand to try to destroy the arms supplies. In all this the SDECE had played a vital part, and it is understandable that when de Gaulle surprisingly and suddenly revealed that he favoured granting independence to Algeria, it was felt that all this hard work had gone for naught.

Long before this in the previous decade the SDECE had been involved in two operations against both the Algerian rebels' FLN and the regime of President Nasser of Egypt. The Egyptian link with Algeria had in fact been a vital factor behind French military action against the Egyptians and the disastrous

Suez crisis. In what was a blatant breach of international law, French agents on 22 October 1956 had forced an Air Maroc plane flying from Morocco to Tunis to land in Algiers, hijacking such key men in the FLN as Ben Bella and Ait Ahmed and four others. This was one of many attempts to topple the Nasser regime in Egypt, but it was a totally misconceived policy because far from checking the Algerian rebels, it only made them fight with greater enthusiasm. The six Arab rebels spent more than five years in French jails, and were not released until de Gaulle granted Algeria independence in 1962.

The French and the Israeli intelligence services were far better informed on the secret policies of Gamal Abdul Nasser when he came to power in Egypt than either the Americans or the British. There was a good deal of co-operation and exchange of intelligence on these and other matters between France and Israel. Long before the disastrous Suez operation and the invasion of the Canal Zone there had been excellent Franco-Israeli relations in the sphere of naval intelligence, largely initiated by Admiral Pierre Barjot.

Much of the SDECE prejudice against the United States in the mid-1950s was caused by their knowledge that the CIA was secretly backing Nasser in the mistaken belief that he was a moderate leader who would support the USA against the Soviet Union. It was an SDECE agent who learned that the CIA had arranged for Nasser to be given three million dollars through a Swiss bank account. Again, it was the SDECE who learned that an Egyptian ship, *Athos,* officially supposed to be taking a consignment of arms from Milan to Pakistan, was in fact engaged in delivering these goods to the FLN rebels in Algeria. As a result the French intercepted the ship and discovered on board enough arms to equip a force of some thousands.

Incidents such as these and fear that Nasser would increasingly intervene on the side of the FLN paved the way to the secret Franco-British agreement on invading the Suez Canal Zone. In all this the SDECE played a vital role. Indeed, it was Pierre Boursicot, then the SDECE chief, who arranged the secret meeting outside Paris in October 1956 when Eden and Selwyn Lloyd planned the Suez operation with Guy Mollet and

Pineau. French Intelligence at the time of that operation took the view that both British Intelligence and the British Government were badly misled in believing that the Soviet Union might lead a counter-attack in the Middle East. As one SDECE officer said afterwards: 'Khrushchev was far too occupied with the revolt in Hungary to launch any rash campaign in the Middle East. It was typical of his effective bluff that such a threat should be taken seriously.'

In November 1961 the Egyptian authorities arrested André Mattei, head of the French diplomatic mission, along with three other members of the mission. Though diplomatic relations between France and Egypt had been broken off during the Suez crisis, this special mission had subsequently been stationed in Cairo and diplomatic immunity granted to all members in September 1959. Six Egyptians were also arrested and both they and the French were charged with espionage, conspiracy to murder President Nasser, planning riots in Egypt, plotting with Israel and the illegal transfer of currency.

At the trial which ensued, the prosecutor demanded a sentence of life imprisonment with hard labour for the defendants, but Jean-Paul Bellivier, one of the Frenchmen arrested, denied all the charges as 'nonsensical and monstrous and alleged that the statement he had written at the dictation of the investigators was quite untrue. He "had been threatened with death", he added, and "did not have the chance to tell the truth".'[11]

He further alleged that he had been systematically beaten on the back of the neck, thrown on the floor, stripped and put in a dark cell. He had also been threatened with 'brain-washing', and he said he wished to draw the court's attention to the fact that his interrogation after arrest took place at the intelligence department premises where, he claimed, he had been constantly intimidated by relays of intelligence officers.

It must be said that the French Government worked hard to see justice done for their agents. M. Couve de Murville, the French Foreign Minister, urged that independent arbitration was essential to settle this question of diplomatic immunity, and approached the Swiss Embassy in Cairo. Matters dragged on until April 1962, when the Egyptian newspaper, *Al-Ahram*, announced the release of 'the French spies' as a deal made in consequence of the Algerian ceasefire. But the charges were not dropped formally for another three and a half years.

At about this same time all news about The Red Hand ceased. With Algerian independence it seemed to die a sudden death: there was no underground counter-revolution masterminded by The Red Hand. It was quickly obvious that this had always been a destructive organization with no clear idea of how to do anything constructive. And, with Algeria independent at last, there was nothing to destroy, no more arms supplies to rebels.

19

The Problem of Jacques Soustelle and the Ben Barka Affair

They will use what France left there [in Algeria] to the last tractor, to the last bolt, to the last little teaspoon. After that, as in Tripolitania, they will let the goats graze where wheat formerly grew.

Jacques Soustelle

From the very beginning of the *Algérie Française* crusade Soustelle posed a problem for France's Secret Service. Not only was he a former Secret Service officer of high rank and distinction, but his crusade clashed violently with de Gaulle's approach to the problem of Algeria's future and the war which had been dragging on there for years. Soustelle was idolized by many of the French *colons* in Algeria. He was an anthropologist with a wide knowledge of non-European cultures. He had worked in Mexico before the war and had visited and studied the peoples of French Oceania in 1945, when he became de Gaulle's Minister for the Colonies. He was not what some would call a National Front extremist – very far from it: he approached the Algerian question from an academic and intellectual viewpoint. He was on record as having said that if the Aztecs had been left alone, they would have taken Mexico into the equivalent of the prehistoric Meiji era in Japan. It was with General de Gaulle's personal blessing that Soustelle was appointed Governor-General of Algeria in November 1954, even though at that time de Gaulle was not in power.

Soustelle said, in developing his theme of *Algérie Française*, 'True decolonization would have come from incorporation, with equal rights and an equal advance. But this was rejected: it was too difficult.'[1] It is important to note that Soustelle's own ideas for the future of Algeria were not nearly as reactionary as his enemies have made out. Far from it.

Soustelle had been invited to join the short-lived Mendès-France government of 1954, but he had refused largely because of his loyalty to de Gaulle. He was, however, always on the extreme left wing of the Gaullist Party, and it was Mendès-France who appointed him to the governor-generalship of Algeria later in 1954. Yet there was always a certain ambiguity in his political thinking, partly conditioned by his humble background, but equally by his obsession with anthropology, while his experience in the devious world of Gaullist intelligence services was yet another factor. Some discerning analysts of character have seen in him a kind of Jekyll and Hyde character. When he first came to Algeria the main fear of the French population was that he would extend the Mendès-France liberal policy into that country, paving the way for independence, but it gradually became evident that he had identified himself with the settlers and was committed to retaining Algeria as part of Metropolitan France. When he was withdrawn from the governorship in 1960 there was almost an open revolt in his favour by the settlers.

By 1958 he had taken over the leadership of the settlers' cause. He at first maintained a certain reserve about his ultimate intentions, and without doubt used his experience of intelligence to organize plots by both settlers and Army officers to prevent Algeria from becoming independent. He even claimed in an interview with *The Times* that he 'was convinced that the majority of the Muslim population of Algeria were in favour of integration . . . into France in an altered French Union'.[2]

At this stage de Gaulle and Soustelle remained close friends. Indeed in July 1958 de Gaulle appointed Soustelle as his Minister of Information. Two months later there was an attempt by Algerian terrorists to murder Soustelle only a few yards away from the Arc de Triomphe. He was sitting in the rear seat of his car when it was checked by traffic lights in the Avenue Friedland. He saw a Muslim with a revolver only a few yards away and dived to the floor just before the man fired and fled.

Then in 1959 Soustelle was given a new role: he had general responsibility for the overseas departments and territories, the

Sahara, and atomic energy. It was a year later that opposition
to Soustelle in Paris became most marked and there was little
doubt that this was partly Soviet and Communist-inspired
because of his role in the field of nuclear developments. In
January 1960 his own office denied reports in the French left-
wing press that he was using a villa near Chartres to make
wireless transmissions 'for disquieting purposes'. This villa,
known as La Chintraie, had been equipped with protective
barriers, searchlights and even dogs. This could obviously have
been a protection against further assassination attempts, but
the Communist newspaper, *L'Humanité*, concluded that it was
one of many headquarters of The Red Hand. Even *L'Express*
took up this story, claiming that the villa was used to maintain
clandestine wireless contact with military circles in Algeria.[3]

It was shortly after this that Soustelle was dropped from the
Government and later, in April 1960, he was expelled from the
Gaullist Party. By October of that year it was clear that
Soustelle was a vehement opponent of de Gaulle on the
Algerian question and at a press conference in Paris he inau-
gurated a new campaign for *Algérie Française*. The original
reforming liberal became what seemed to some a reactionary
leader of a settlers' revolt, though the truth was never quite
like that. Soustelle was soon forced into exile. In April 1961 it
was reported that he had vanished from his home in Paris and
police started searching for him. From then onwards he was
more or less permanently on the run, alleged to be plotting
against the de Gaulle regime in Italy, Portugal and Austria.
Often in this period he used the pseudonym of Jean Albert
Sénèque: it amused him to borrow the name of the Roman
philosopher who was accused of conspiring against the Emperor
Nero. But even in exile life was made difficult for him, partly
by the pressure put on him by French Intelligence, but also by
diplomatic influence. He was expelled from Italy, and banned
for a time by West Germany. On one occasion he was arrested
in a Lausanne hotel and expelled from Switzerland. He
declared, 'Two attempts were made to kill or kidnap me. The
first time I didn't know. The second time I knew. A clumsy
attempt had been made to bribe someone with a hundred

thousand dollars. We played hide-and-seek for a few days. Then I shook him off.'[4]

After an assassination attempt on de Gaulle in August 1962, threats to Soustelle increased, even though, despite his opposition to the general, he had always stressed his respect for him. The wildest allegations were made against him, including the suggestion that in September 1962 Soustelle had set up his headquarters for supporting the OAS in Lisbon and that he had secretly gone to Paris on the very day an attempt was made on de Gaulle's life. The right-wing weekly, *Minute*, reported that OAS commandos had assembled in Portugal, also alleging that Soustelle had been visited in Portugal by Colonel Argoud, one of the OAS leaders. One suggestion about why Soustelle might have been in Paris at this time was that OAS leaders summoned him to the French capital without giving any reasons so that he would be on the spot if the President were killed and a political opening was offered. There was never any confirmation of this, but there was a report from Brussels that he passed through Belgium at this very time and that secret crossings of the Franco-Belgian border were aided by an extreme right-wing group in Belgium.

In many respects Soustelle's cause had been helped rather than hindered in the minds of many French people when an arrest warrant had been issued against him on a charge of plotting against the state. Meanwhile his wife, also a distinguished ethnologist, continued to live in Paris at their apartment which had once been an unofficial Gaullist headquarters. She remained a staunch supporter of her husband. The Soustelles had always had friends willing to take risks on their behalf; Soustelle was once helped to escape from France hidden under luggage in a car, when he went to join the rebel generals in Algeria.

While Belgium granted Soustelle political asylum, the West German authorities made it plain that his safety in that country could not be guaranteed following the kidnapping of his friend, Colonel Argoud. Soustelle himself commented after French agents had left Argoud bound and gagged outside Notre Dame, 'They wanted me at the same time, but I was a long way from

Munich when they came for me. Several hundred kilometres away.'[5]

Later Soustelle claimed that he was warned of two attempts by *barbouzes* (special French undercover agents known as the 'bearded ones') to kidnap him. 'The second time I had a hair's-breadth escape. I knew for some days I was being followed. Then I found the flat where I was living surrounded by *barbouzes* who had taken apartments on either side. A friend called early in the morning with a car and we slipped away while they were off guard, leaving everything behind. Otherwise I am convinced I would have been delivered trussed up in Paris – or even quietly removed like Ben Barka.'

Late in 1966 there was a demand, signed by some nine hundred leading figures in French political and cultural life, for a pardon for Soustelle. But de Gaulle was a man whose resentments were long-lived and for a long time he stubbornly declined to agree to any such amnesty. Not until the general amnesty of 1969 was the way made clear for Soustelle to return to France. He was given a hero's welcome when he arrived from Geneva at Orly Airport, still insisting that he disapproved of 'the policy of so-called decolonization. . .which led to a disastrous failure in Black Africa and North Africa'. But there was no political comeback for this campaigner and he turned to authorship as some consolation.

It will be noticed that Soustelle said that he might have been 'quietly removed like Ben Barka'. It was the Ben Barka affair which resulted in a major reorganization and upheaval in the French Intelligence Services. For it showed up what de Gaulle and others around him had long suspected: that on the fringes of the French Intelligence Services there were men who frequently acted with complete contempt for the law. The Ben Barka affair was a major blow for the French Government, for de Gaulle himself (striving for an image which would show him as a friend of Africans) and especially for the SDECE. On 29 October 1965 the left-wing Moroccan politician, Mehdi Ben Barka, was seized by two police officers outside a place known as *Le Drugstore* on the Left Bank in Paris. He was taken away in a civilian car, seemingly kidnapped, without the police having a warrant. Ben Barka's friends pressed for information on what had happened to him and alerted various newspapers and periodicals, but the Ministry of Information managed to placate them until after the December elections. Then gradually a highly unsavoury story began to emerge, in both left-wing and right-wing journals.

It transpired that the two police officers, Souchon and Voitot, had not been working under orders from their superior officers, but from what was at first vaguely called 'another organization'. It swiftly became clear that the SDECE had been involved in the kidnapping. What happened to Ben Barka has never been cleared up: he just disappeared and was never seen or heard of again, and the inference was that he must have been murdered. The first name associated with the SDECE to be mentioned in the course of media inquiries was that of Antoine Lopez, employed at Orly Airport, who was the Orly contact for Service 7 of the SDECE. He was also associated with the *barbouzes* and had been promised a senior post at Air Maroc by General Mohammed Oufkir, the Minister of the Interior of Morocco, and an opponent of Ben Barka.

When Lopez's name was first mentioned his story was that he had tipped off his Service 7 chief, Marcel Le Roy, about a plan for kidnapping Ben Barka. Le Roy's reply was that the Paris police had been controlling Lopez's activities some months before the kidnapping, and that reports of plots against Ben Barka had been passed to SDECE headquarters where no action was taken.

Le Roy was kept in custody for some months and he later alleged that he had received no backing from SDECE. Eventually, when it came to a trial, Le Roy was acquitted, but soon afterwards dismissed from SDECE, while Lopez and Souchon were sentenced to seven years' imprisonment. De Gaulle was so infuriated that he even demanded that Morocco should bring a case against General Oufkir, and when there was no response to this, recalled his ambassador. When asked for his views on the Ben Barka kidnapping, de Gaulle's somewhat off-handed dismissing of the matter was to describe it as *'une affaire vulgaire et subalterne'*.

Nevertheless, however much he may have tried to play it down in public, in private his anger was ruthlessly directed against the SDECE. This was because the Ben Barka affair just would not go away. Despite action by the authorities and trials against individuals, the scandal simply kept emerging in new forms.

There was the case of the death of a Parisian gangster, Georges Figon. It was Figon who was supposed to have been used to lure Ben Barka into the trap which led to his kidnapping. A warrant for Figon's arrest was issued, but though police could not immediately find him, newspaper correspondents tracked him down and he talked to them freely. As a result two French magazines published Figon's account of the Ben Barka affair. Figon stated that he and Ben Barka met in a restaurant and that shortly afterwards two officers of the Paris vice squad 'arrested' Ben Barka and took him to a villa near Orly Airport owned by another gangster. Figon's story was that these two officers handed the Moroccan over to a senior person in the Moroccan Army. He claimed that Ben Barka was murdered by a Moroccan execution squad who slit his throat with a dagger and that the '*barbouzes*' disposed of the body.

These reports created a public outcry, although they were discounted by the police. General de Gaulle personally ordered the arrest of certain named Moroccans and asked Interpol to assist the French in finding them. Nothing further developed until January 1966, when sixteen policemen, armed with sub-machine guns, knocked at the door of Figon's apartment and shouted through the letter-box: 'Come out, Figon, and give yourself up!' There was total silence.

Eventually the door was broken open and police found Figon dead on the floor with a small blackened hole behind his right ear. The weapon that killed him, his own pistol, was beside his body. The police, of course, immediately said this was a case of suicide, but most people believed that Figon had been killed because he talked too much.

The mysterious death of Figon coupled with a sudden renewal of media interest in the Ben Barka case brought a speedy reaction from de Gaulle. He decided to attempt to reorganize the Secret Service. Here it is necessary to look back to a few years earlier. In January 1962 General Grossin had been replaced by General Paul Jacquier as head of the SDECE. Grossin was due for retirement. Jacquier was a staunch Gaullist who had been an Air Force pilot for the Free French. His plane had been forced down in Cyprus in 1942 and he had then been imprisoned in a German prisoner-of-war camp. Unfortunately he had had no previous experience of intelligence work. From the very beginning he had a hard task, not merely in eliminating those agents who tended to support the OAS but also in accommodating de Gaulle's mistrust of the CIA and understanding exactly what kind of intelligence de Gaulle wanted. De Gaulle's blunt indication to the SDECE had been that he merely wanted information, not suggestions on policy, but he also wanted the SDECE to look out for potential enemies who could be turned into friends and recognized friends who could become potential enemies. There were echoes here of the pleadings of Richelieu, Mazarin, Dubois and Fouché.

There was also a further problem for General Jacquier: the SDECE was still a relatively small intelligence service for a major power: the budget for 1960, presented to the Prime Minister's office, revealed some 1,300 employed at headquarters and only 300 at overseas posts.[6] It is very likely, though, that the smaller French service was in many ways more efficient than the far larger KGB and CIA services, but its resources were being overstretched. Initially de Gaulle's regime had certainly clamped down on the SDECE and not merely dissolved some of its undercover shock troops, but drastically limited its budget. The President's *chef de cabinet*, Georges Pompidou, made sure that the SDECE received no extra funds from other sources and at the same time actually ordered it to extend its operations, especially in scientific and industrial espionage.

Therefore, short of funds, Jacquier and the SDECE could do two things: either they could tamely acquiesce in the policy of the government of the day, as did the head of Britain's MI6 in the late 1930s, or they could find means of providing themselves with additional sources of income. The latter is a dangerous policy, sometimes justified, sometimes not: it all depends on that well-tried Machiavellian dictum of whether the end justifies the means.

In the case of the SDECE the service's decision to try and raise extra funds ended in disaster. Some of their senior officers thought the answer lay in a lesson they had learned during the war in Indo-China. This was, quite simply, that funds could easily and secretly be raised through the sale of drugs. Early on in the Indo-China war the SDECE had obtained the backing of Montagnard tribesmen by purchasing their opium and selling it elsewhere. However, some of these drug purchases found their way to the United States via traffickers in Marseille and this seriously marred Franco-American relations when the link between the traffickers and the French Secret Service was revealed by CIA operators.

Such unsavoury, not to say downright immoral, manoeuvres may have provided extra revenue for intelligence-gathering, but in the long run they brought only trouble with very little on the credit side. One former French Intelligence officer told me: 'Out of all these extra funds, considerably reduced through commissions and bribes by the time they reached the SDECE, all we really got was some cash to maintain the operations of the *Service d'Action Civique* [a civilian equivalent of *Service Action*] at the time they were fighting the menace of the OAS after the Algerian war. There, perhaps, extra funds were vital, but over the years drug-running nearly ruined the service.'

On 19 January 1966, de Gaulle dismissed General Jacquier, the head of the SDECE. The excuse for this was that the general had reached retirement age on his fifty-fifth birthday the previous June. This was a palpably fatuous attempt at justification as the new Director-General of the Service was General Eugène Guibaud, who was a year older than Jacquier. At the same time the SDECE was removed from the office of the Prime Minister and put under the Ministry of Defence, thus minimizing police influence.

M. Bourges, the Minister of Information, nevertheless insisted, 'The transfer was not the immediate result of the Ben Barka scandal,' but added that 'The Government had renewed its instructions made to previous administrations for the police to place before the courts and the examining magistrates everything useful towards establishing the truth.'[7]

Undoubtedly all the Intelligence Services had become

infected with the philosophy of 'anything goes', which might be all right on a night out on the town, but which is totally inappropriate when applied to either the SDECE or the DST. The biggest offenders were undoubtedly the *barbouzes*, who had become the shock troops of the service and made their own rules as they went along. Part of their job had been to protect de Gaulle against assassination and vengeance from the remnants of the OAS. They called him *L'Oncle*, a fact which led some wags among the American correspondents in Paris to refer to the *barbouzes* as 'the men from Uncle', a reference to that now old-fashioned TV series.

Unquestionably, the *barbouzes* had been erratically and none too carefully recruited, with vetting being a minimum consideration. Some were near-fascists and extremely right-wing, while others were from the underworld and not squeamish about the form their operations took. Jacques Foccart had been de Gaulle's chief intelligence co-ordinator (always highly regarded by the President) and, though others fell out of favour, he remained in office even after the Ben Barka affair, and despite the fact that the *barbouzes* had been partly under his guidance as well as that of the Interior Minister.

One must remember that in the early 1960s life had been made extremely difficult for the Intelligence Services by the outrageous operations of the OAS. In May 1964 the OAS were behind the sensational kidnapping of sixty-year-old Madeleine Dassault, wife of France's top plane designer, who was building up the nation's independent air striking force. The kidnapping had all the indications of a skilfully planned military operation. Mysterious phone calls followed, stating that Mme Dassault would be freed on receipt of £750,000, and if General Raoul Salan, former chief of the OAS then serving a life sentence, was released within seventy hours. Such incidents as these provoked ruthless responses from the *barbouzes*.

The appointment of General Guibaud as the new head of the SDECE seemed at the time to be no better than a stop-gap. This was the moment for an imaginative approach to the whole question of the SDECE and the choice of its controller, but at this time the President acted too cautiously. One reason, perhaps, was that after granting independence to Algeria he wanted to pay some tribute to his old idea of French Union overseas and build bridges to the old French colonies, especially in Africa. He wanted the SDECE to concentrate on Africa and the Middle East, now that the Algerian War was ended. Much of this bridge-building proved either futile or at best of temporary value, especially in the Middle East, though it must be admitted that French Intelligence in this area has always been of the highest. In the demand for paying close attention to Africa de Gaulle may have been expecting too much. Seen at its best, this was a French policy to win friends throughout the African continent while retaining close links with its former colonies. In very many respects this policy succeeded, if not perfectly, at least rather better than the British attempt to maintain the myth of Commonwealth in their own African territories. The French Intelligence Services went out of their way to encourage an increase in the number of independent states in Africa, but they clamped down on various African-sponsored coups, made various attempts to end the Gaddafi regime in Libya (sometimes, it is alleged, by assassination), and also sought a working relationship with South Africa's Bureau of State Security in Angola.

20
The Sapphire Ring

A colonel belonging to the Soviet special services goes over to the CIA and reveals there is in Paris an important Soviet network in which the two principal characters are a senior French official of NATO and a close colleague of de Gaulle. Anyone who is a little familiar with the corridors of power can name these worthy gentlemen at once.

Le Canard Enchaîné[1]

The scandal of the Sapphire Ring started with the publication of a book entitled *Topaz* written by the American author, Leon Uris. Uris was the son of a Polish immigrant to the USA and he had run away from school at the age of seventeen to join the US Marine Corps in World War II. His first book had been about his life in the Marines, *Battle Cry* (published in 1953), but it was with *Topaz*, published in 1962, a novel about a Soviet espionage network inside French governmental circles, that he made a sensational impact in more ways than one.

This book seemed to be an ultra-realistic spy story telling how the head of the KGB's anti-NATO bureau defected to the Americans and revealed the existence in Paris of a Soviet spy ring code-named *Topaz*, of which the two key members were a senior French official and a close adviser – code-name Columbine – of the French President.[2]

Le Canard Enchaîné, the satirical French weekly, suggested in its columns that Columbine was an accurate portrait of one of de Gaulle's most trusted Intelligence advisers. It added that another Soviet spy was probably a man convicted of espionage a few years earlier. *Le Canard* even guessed that the 'senior Soviet colonel' referred to in the book was Colonel Oleg Penkovsky, who was alleged to have been shot by the Russians in 1963. This last piece of speculation was, however, wide of the mark. Understandably, a spokesman at the Elysée Palace described such allegations as 'absurd', but this denial did not carry much weight when it was announced that *Life* magazine would shortly be publishing certain disclosures lending credence to Uris's story from Colonel Philippe Thyraud de Vosjoli, formerly head of French Intelligence in Washington. De Vosjoli had been a friend of Uris and there was further speculation that the central figure in *Topaz*, a French Intelligence agent named André Devereaux, was based on the real-life de Vosjoli. When questioned about this, Uris replied, 'If you are asking me to reveal my sources of information, I won't do it any more than you would.' At the same time he said he believed that there was a Soviet spy ring operating close to President de Gaulle in 1962.

Shrewd observers of the world-wide intelligence game probably paid more attention to *Le Canard*'s allegations than did the general public, for at this time it was relatively novel for spy fiction to be quite so 'factional'. Those engaged in the world of intelligence noted that the various spy rings organized by the Russians against NATO were known to use jewels for their code-names, although the ring that was supposedly organized against the French was known not as Topaz but as Sapphire. But though the book was a work of fiction, there were undoubtedly many elements of truth in it.

De Vosjoli had been an officer in French Intelligence for twenty-five years, and almost half this time had been spent as liaison officer with the Americans in Washington. He had worked closely with the Americans, got along with them extremely well and had helped them in many ways. Indeed, in Washington he was known as 'the Americans' favourite Frenchman'. He supplied the CIA with intelligence on Castro's Cuba. Information about all this got back to Paris at a time when de Gaulle was becoming increasingly critical of the USA in general and the CIA in particular. It was soon made clear to de Vosjoli that in Paris some at least in the SDECE disapproved of his close relations with the Americans.

When ordered back to Paris, he refused to go and resigned from the service, deciding to remain in the USA. From then on he was consulted frequently by the CIA, especially on revelations made by various Soviet defectors, notably Anatoliy Golitsyn. He gave as his reason for quitting the SDECE that they had been infiltrated by Soviet agents and that it was impossible to know who could be trusted. He continued to insist that there was a Soviet mole inside de Gaulle's own entourage.

Despite the official denial of the story propounded by Uris and seemingly backed by de Vosjoli, de Gaulle ordered an immediate inquiry into the allegations. He had reason to be worried, quite apart from the *Topaz* and *Le Canard* stories. For some time it had been clear that the USSR had made every attempt to learn NATO secrets through France and there had been some arrests as a result. Leonid Petrovich Kunavin, a colonel in the KGB, had commissioned a number of reports on prominent French officials known to be close to de Gaulle with the aim of finding out who among them could be recruited.

Kunavin's first target had been the new French Ambassador to Moscow, Maurice Dejean, who had served with de Gaulle in London during World War II and had been a diplomat in London, New York and the Far East before he arrived in Moscow in December 1955. In view of this, and knowing that he had been close to de Gaulle, the Russians kept watch on him from the moment he arrived, the aim being to win him over as an agent. The general idea of the plot seemed to be to make Dejean and his wife feel at home in Moscow, to flatter and charm them both so that they would return to Paris and influence de Gaulle and other Frenchmen in favour of the Soviet Union.

Early attempts to ensnare not merely Dejean but his wife as well failed somewhat farcically. Once a KGB agent had enticed Madame Dejean out on a picnic without her husband, but instead of carrying out his mission to flirt with her he drank too much and fell asleep! Needless to say, he got the sack. But ultimately Dejean was compromised by an actress, Larissa Kronberg-Sobolevskaya, in the pay of the KGB, who 'arranged' for her husband to find them both together. The husband threatened to expose the Ambassador and seek a public apology and compensation. Dejean immediately appealed for help to a high KGB official who promised to hush things up.

The mistake the KGB then made was to try similar tactics with a French attaché, Lieutenant-Colonel Louis Guibaud. The KGB confronted him with evidence of his illicit liaisons in the form of secretly taken photographs. They threatened instant revelation of the photographs to the French authorities, unless he promised to provide the KGB with information. Guibaud's unexpected response was to shoot himself. After that no further attempt was made to embroil Dejean, though the KGB may well have hoped to keep in touch with him when he was back in Paris.

But the Russians were stopped in their tracks when Yuri Krotkov, the agent used to trap Dejean and Guibaud, went to London with a group of Russian artists and writers and defected. He passed information to the British about the KGB's interest in Dejean and Guibaud, and they informed the French. Documentary evidence of Krotkov's disclosures was released early in 1971 by a US Senate Investigating Committee after his nine-day testimony on these matters.[3]

When de Gaulle heard these reports and confronted Dejean (who, it must be admitted, had never betrayed any French interests), he is said to have commented: 'Dejean, I understand that you like women.'

There had been other more disturbing incidents in previous years. In May 1965 the body of Jean-Marie Gastal was found in a wood at Gérardmer near the West German frontier. He was holding a revolver and first it was thought simply to be a case of suicide. But it was noted that though his passport described him as a student he had visas for the USA, Cuba, Burma and Tahiti (where the French were setting up their HQ for nuclear tests). Police also found permits authorizing him to enter all American and Canadian NATO installations. More sinisterly he carried a map on which an 'X' marked the very spot where his body was found.[4]

It was eventually deduced that he was a secret agent operating against NATO and that his apparent suicide might have been faked by hostile agents. Once again the question was, were these hostile agents Russian or French?

It did not take long for the French to discover one of the men hinted at in Uris's book. Georges Paques, a French press attaché with NATO, was arrested and eventually sentenced to imprisonment for spying. At the time of his arrest Paques was living in a luxurious Paris apartment while being deputy head of NATO's press and information section. The evidence against him was that he had passed on to the USSR quantities of top secret information since 1944 including a full report of the NATO Fallex combined manoeuvres exercise. Paques admitted having passed intelligence to the Russians, but insisted that he had done this because of his 'love for France', believing in a vision of a utopian Socialist society in both East and West Europe. He claimed he had even declined to be instructed in 'spy photography' on the grounds that this was 'vulgar' and 'ideologically unnecessary'. He was yet another agent Russia had secured when they extended their influence to Algiers after the liberation of French North Africa.

It was significant that after the Paques case French counter-intelligence began to achieve brilliant successes against the USSR in unmasking several Soviet agents and moles in their own ranks. Possibly de Gaulle was influenced by direct approaches by the US President, John F. Kennedy, who was reported to have been so disturbed about intelligence reports he received about a highly placed mole within de Gaulle's circle that he decided to warn the President with a personal letter. Naturally Leon Uris was questioned on all this, and his reply was: 'I feel that the basic thing – the infiltration of the French Government – is true and that it involves one or two people very close to de Gaulle. But I don't know who they are.'[5]

The charges against Paques did nothing to dispel the allegations about a mole inside the President's own circle. The role of Thyraud de Vosjoli remained questionable. From all he had said he was obviously a major influence. The French official view was that the de Vosjoli affair and *Topaz* were part of a CIA plot to embroil de Vosjoli and exploit anti-French feelings in Washington, possibly with the ultimate object of discrediting de Gaulle himself. Another view was that it was a deliberate ploy by the KGB to stir up anti-Americanism in Paris by involving de Vosjoli with the CIA and discrediting the French in American eyes.

Certainly, if one compared these two viewpoints, it was clear that the Soviet Union stood to gain more from such a contrived plot than did the CIA or the American Government. It was also suggested that behind these allegations was a KGB plot – probably planted on the CIA – to discredit one of the ablest Intelligence advisers in Paris, Jacques Foccart, officially the Secretary-General for Madagascar and African Affairs, but unofficially de Gaulle's chief adviser on all Intelligence matters and his watchdog on counter-espionage.

To complicate matters, inquiries by the intelligence services of France, Britain, the USA, Canada and Switzerland had revealed disquieting information on Jean-Marie Gastal's death. It was discovered that he had travelled widely in recent years, in Australia, Canada, Cuba and Vietnam, and that hidden inside one of his boots was a tiny black notebook which contained coded messages and figures referring to electronic and atomic research. The DST then became convinced that he was a secret agent for another power.

Obviously he had anticipated the possibility of being liquidated by one secret service or another for he also carried a note stating that in the event of his death his possessions were to go to his Moroccan-born wife, Zora, and his body should be used for medical research. Three years previously two Soviet spies had been arrested near Gérardmer, while a year before a German visitor had disappeared without trace in this same area.

Another incident which rebounded on SDECE was that of the discovery of a murder mystery by a farmer in Draguignand in 1963. Curious about a large barrel which had been stored in his garden shed by a man named Zoltan Ritter, he forced the lid off. Under a layer of wood shavings was cement. He took a pickaxe to break up the cement and discovered two hands stretched out. Shocked at what he had found, Guichard, the farmer, called the police, who investigated further, finding a dead body.

Zoltan Ritter was arrested, and he declared: 'It is true. I killed the man, but I am not a murderer. I killed a king rat. I am a member of the French Secret Service and I executed him by order of my superiors.'[6]

Ritter alleged that the dead man was a Russian master spy whose true identity was hidden under various aliases, but that his real name and title was Colonel Eli Betz, an officer of the Soviet Combat Intelligence Force.[7] He went on to say that Betz had learned vital secrets about French atomic experiments in the Sahara and that his mission was to kill him before he could pass on his secrets to Moscow.

I lured him into a trap by promising him more information. We met at midnight, in a secluded spot near Marseille. I ordered him to hand over his secret documents. He drew a knife and attacked me. I stunned him with a karate blow to the throat, stabbed him through the heart with a long steel needle, then crushed his face with a stone.

I took the body to my house, put him into the barrel and filled it with cement. I waited for my organization to dispose of the body, but there were delays. Later I left Marseille and took the barrel along. It travelled with me wherever I went.[8]

Ritter declined to say who his superior officers were and he was charged with first-degree murder. Police took almost three years to prepare the case, yet when he stood in the dock they still appeared to know little about either him or his victim. Ritter was found guilty and sentenced to fifteen years solitary confinement. What was most interesting about this verdict and sentence was the view taken both by French and other newspapers that a few years previously such a case would have been quietly settled between the police and the SDECE without any scandal or trial. But it was stressed in Paris that General de Gaulle had come down firmly on the side of the law and insisted that justice must be seen to be done. It seemed that Ritter was one of the first casualties of the clamp-down on the *barbouzes*.

Such incidents as these did not help relations between either the SDECE and the CIA, or the French and United States governments. On each side there developed a mistrust of one another, even though on both sides there were individuals who not only thoroughly understood the situation, but were prepared to ensure collaboration. Relations between the USA and France worsened considerably when de Gaulle's Government announced three new moves within the space of an hour, all of them calculated to upset the Americans. First of all France protested verbally that an American 'spy' plane had taken 175 unauthorized photographs of the secret nuclear plant at Pierre-latte in the Rhône valley. Secondly the French rejected an American proposal for a new international monetary confer-ence, and finally it was announced that André Malraux, a senior Cabinet Minister, was on his way to Peking. The secrecy surrounding the latter mission particularly angered the Ameri-cans, who had not been told about it in advance.

The French had some reason to be annoyed on this occasion: the US explanation that the reconnaissance plane was diverted by a thunderstorm was a little hard to accept. The Americans, then obsessed with the subject of China and regarding every move by any power in the direction of better relations with Peking as treachery, were intensely annoyed about not having been informed beforehand about the Malraux mission.

But it was the story of the Sapphire Ring which continued to create most tension between the United States and France. In 1968 a disturbing series of revelations were made by de Vosjoli. This man, who was for thirteen years head of French Intelli-gence in the USA, told how he had been ordered to begin spying on the United States. This allegation was fatuous, because any intelligence officer sent to another country has to report back on what goes on in that country. De Vosjoli accused one of de Gaulle's closest collaborators of being a Russian agent, but named nobody. De Vosjoli confirmed that President Kennedy had warned de Gaulle about a possible mole and that he had promised to help the French obtain confirmation of the report. The French President had then chosen General de Rougemont, who was attached to his own office, as the man to investigate the whole affair. After a visit to Washington and talks with the Soviet defector de Rouge-mont had flown back to Paris to make his reports to de Gaulle's trusted aide, Étienne Burin des Roziers. De Vosjoli had passed back what information he obtained to the SDECE in Paris, but he commented:

For some weeks I received daily cables pressing me to find out who the man [the Soviet defector] was, where the Americans were hiding him, and what he was telling them.

But I met a blank wall. Then, abruptly, there arrived a jarring order from Paris: I was to cease my efforts to track down the man and to stop asking questions about him. The reason for that peremptory, almost insulting directive was now made clear . . . It must have been that when Kennedy's letter reached de Gaulle, a decision had been taken to send de Rougemont secretly to Washington to assess the reliability of the source, and it was thought best to order me off the scent, lest I complicate matters.[9]

The mysterious Russian defector who is said to have made the allegations about a top-ranking spy in the President's entourage was given the code-name Martel by the French. It was apparent that while Martel was sufficiently knowledgeable about French Intelligence affairs that he could hint at traitors without actually naming them, he was in many respects distinctly vague in the evidence he provided. When interrogated he tended to hedge his answers and to say 'possibly' and 'perhaps' when he might have been more positive. My former French Intelligence mentor, *Le Bon et Vrai*, had this to say on the subject of Martel:

Who was he? Was he just one person, or was what we were told a hotch-potch of the evidence of two or three defectors? My distinct impression is that the Americans allowed themselves to be totally confused by questioning at least three defectors, and that Martel was constantly asked to confirm their testimony, which he couldn't. The truth is that the total evidence was extremely confusing and sometimes contradictory: it didn't add up. De Vosjoli claims we should have pursued Martel's leads more vigorously to a straightforward finding, for or against. But this just wasn't possible, however hard we tried.

The most important aspect of Martel's allegations concerned the Soviet network with the code-name Sapphire, which, according to him, consisted of more than half a dozen French Intelligence officers, all of whom had been recruited by the KGB while operating inside the SDECE. Certainly this was extremely hard to accept and few well-informed students of the intelligence world either then or since have accepted it. But, as will be seen later, there were several Soviet agents serving in important posts inside France as the Paques case had demonstrated. It became increasingly clear that this whole game, either deliberately or unwittingly, was amounting to little more than a ploy to destroy France's relations with the USA and to upset the Western Alliance. At the same time there was a suggestion – maybe no more than a smoke-screen thrown up by some of the critics – that de Gaulle had swung France behind the Soviet bloc, and it was pointed out that the President had visited the USSR and Poland and that he had recently supported the Kremlin view on Vietnam and the Israeli-Arab conflict. In fact de Gaulle had done no more than attempt single-handedly to maintain some kind of a European balance between the USA and the USSR. The spirit of this experimental policy had been felt inside the SDECE with some disturbing results.

In April 1968 *Le Canard Enchaîné* denounced the whole affair of a Soviet network in French Government quarters as being 'simply one move in a campaign of reprisals organized by the United States Intelligence Service' and that the man hinted at as a top mole in French Government circles was none other than Jacques Foccart, de Gaulle's Intelligence adviser. Not that *Le Canard* believed this to be true: there was, stated the newspaper, nothing to reveal. 'Far from being a Soviet plot, the affair was a most competent American operation which looked like succeeding in its purpose of leaving de Gaulle the loser, if only by slight damage to his self-esteem or his public image.'[10]

By any standards Jacques Foccart was a most unlikely candidate for a Soviet agent, but subtle propaganda and disinformation can achieve remarkable results even in this supposedly open society of the late twentieth century. A Jew who was also on the left of centre in politics, Foccart was married with two children and ran an import and export business of rum and sugar from Martinique. He was typical of those men of unsuspected talents whom de Gaulle had a genius for spotting. His devotion to the Gaullist cause had resulted in his being involved with the first Gaullist secret service, the BCRA, and long before de Gaulle returned to power in 1958 he had been a faithful adviser to the General. Certainly he was involved with the SDECE in a highly discreet way which linked him directly to the President, but he had never sought to make a career out of politics. It was his intellect, his ability to analyse difficult problems swiftly and to remain objective which commended him to de Gaulle. He made enemies on both the right and the left in consequence. He angered the extreme right by co-ordinating the Intelligence Services and the police in a drive against those plotters trying to overthrow the Gaullist regime, while the left accused him of making use of the *barbouzes*, something which he vehemently denied.

The astonishing thing about Foccart was that, despite his high office, he continued to run his business from an office in the Boulevard des Capucilnes, which was only five minutes' walk from the Elysée Palace. In some ways he was perhaps a natural candidate for victimization: it was carefully noted that some Americans were anxious to find a scapegoat in the French ranks after de Gaulle decided in 1963 that the cosy relationship which had been built up between the CIA and the French Intelligence Services should end. De Gaulle took the view – with some justification – that the French told the Americans far more than the Americans told them. There had been some appallingly bad relations between the two nations with a distinct lack on the American side of an understanding of all the subtleties of de Gaulle's foreign policies. The first step in curbing such misunderstandings was a ruling that in future CIA men should not be accredited to the French Foreign Office as diplomats, but to the Ministry of the Interior.

A side issue of the allegations against Foccart was his support for Biafra during the Nigerian Civil War which the Russians, who were backing the Nigerian Federalists (like the British Government), wanted to check. De Gaulle loyally stood by Foccart, but when Poher became the interim President in 1969, he dismissed Foccart from office. There was an immediate outcry against this and when Pompidou became President Foccart was restored to his post. This was one of the most extraordinary examples in modern times of a novel having such far-reaching effects on trans-Atlantic politics, and it all arose out of a mischievous, if amusing, review in *Le Canard Enchaîné*.

No doubt there was much jealousy of Foccart's powers, his influence with de Gaulle and the fact that there was a controversial duality about his functions. Brian Crozier, an expert in the field of strategic studies, has raised the question of the

extent to which Foccart's secret functions overlapped with those
of the SDECE and the DST.

The answer, inevitably, was not very clear, and ill-intentioned rumour
attributed much undercover work to Foccart, often without founda-
tion. The other half of his secret attributions, however, was even more
controversial since it involved keeping an eye on, and if necessary
defending, the Gaullist movement which was not, in any constitutional
sense, an organ of the State.[11]

Philippe Thyraud de Vosjoli continued to assert that there
were Soviet agents inside French Intelligence in his book
Lamia, published in 1970, from which it became clear that he
had provided the background material for Uris's *Topaz* novel.[12]
Martel is now generally supposed to refer to Anatoliy Golitsyn.
But as *Le Bon et Vrai* logically put it:

How did we know whether Golitsyn was not what you call the 'fall-
guy', a useful cover for the real informant? That sort of thing does
happen in this espionage *mazarinade*. What got us really worried and
annoyed, too, if you like, was that Martel never came out with definite
names. In checking up with the Americans and Martel we had to
submit names of possible suspects within our own ranks. We were
giving away names without getting very much in return. If we had not
been extremely careful, we could have given away far too much
information. Martel did as much harm as good. True, we caught a few
villains such as Paques, but we never found any sign of a Sapphire
Ring.

One must remember that at this time de Gaulle had what
some would call a dream, others a brilliant thesis: he felt the
way towards ending the Cold War was for France to give a lead
by establishing improved relations with Russia's satellites. De
Gaulle may have hoped to bring back some of the nations of
Eastern Europe into closer touch with the West, but it is hard
to believe that he could ever have hoped for any such success
with the Soviet Union. It was an imaginative policy, based as
much on France's strength and influence in world affairs as
anything else, but certainly not on any weakness or attempt to
appease. Did this policy frighten some people within the CIA
so that they sought to check it by the Martel stories? There is
ample evidence that this was the case.

Some litigation was perhaps inevitable after the wild allegations made all around the world at this time about spies in high places in Paris. Foccart not only took legal action against certain right-wing newspapers which claimed he was a Russian spy, but he successfully sued both the Communist *L'Humanité* and *Le Canard Enchaîné*. Similarly, when de Vosjoli was attacked as having defected to the USA from France and being a double agent, he denied this and said he had only left the SDECE because he was so distressed by the unsatisfactory state of affairs in the service. In 1972 he was awarded damages of $138,000 by a Los Angeles court against Leon Uris in a dispute over a contract they had signed sharing profits from the *Topaz* novel. This time de Vosjoli claimed that the novel was based on a manuscript he had written.

21

France's Drive Against Soviet Agents

At least fifty undercover Russian agents are operating inside France. About thirty have been identified, but no action can be taken because there is no evidence against them . . . Information is still being sent to Moscow by high-speed transmission. We can't trace the transmitters. It is all over in a fraction of a second.

> Désire Parent, deputy head of French counter-intelligence

The above statement was made by Parent somewhat ruefully during a trial in Paris in 1969 of four Frenchmen accused of spying for Moscow. Technologically, the Russians had made great advances in their espionage techniques by the late 1960s and one of the most important of these was the improvement in high-speed communications with agents. By this time Soviet agents all over Europe were regularly sending information to Moscow by high-speed burst transmissions. The high-speed burst was the aural equivalent of a microdot.

Nonetheless, it cannot be stressed too much that, despite this extremely honest statement and all the allegations made in the previous chapter about Soviet infiltration of high French circles, French counter-intelligence at all levels launched a most impressive drive against Soviet agents inside France with repeated results and with brilliant and inspired operations. Many of these were being initiated long before the *Topaz* story created such a furore. Results were, in fact, beginning to come through just when the *Topaz* accusations began.

In March 1968 Maurice Picard, former head of the French Civil Defence organization and a former member of the wartime Resistance, was called to the headquarters of the DST and questioned for eight days. Eventually he was charged with having contacts with the agents of foreign powers 'of a kind to harm France's diplomatic situation or her essential economic interests'.

Picard was a civil servant who suddenly developed a passion for collecting secret documents almost as a form of investment. He had worked under the Vichy administration, but had been disappointed at not getting the promotion he felt he was entitled to. He had even denounced a local Resistance group, yet he claimed that eventually he had become a member of the Resistance. His devious tactics and easy adjustment to switches in political opinion resulted in his appointment as Prefect of various *départements* prior to becoming head of the French Civil Service organization. Not only did he make contact with the West German Intelligence Service under General Gehlen, but with the KGB through Sergei Kuznetchev, counsellor of the Soviet Embassy in Paris from 1959 to 1964.

Picard's mistake was to extend his activities to other powers: the swapping of intelligence became not only a way of life for him, but a means of investment. He started to make contacts with various secret services, the British, the American and the Spanish. No doubt it was this double-dealing, quickly noticed by the Russians, which led to his detection. He had warned the Spaniards about Russian Communists on their territory while passing information about the inefficiency of these agents to the Russians.

When he was brought to trial in October 1968, alleged to have passed official secrets to American, British and West German agents, he was accused of having played a double game with the Nazis during the occupation of France and since then of supplying information to a number of powers. The Russians had obviously become suspicious of him because of the contacts he had and it is even possible that they were partly reponsible for his arrest. Picard in 1968 was the perfect alibi for some of their own activities in France and his arrest detracted attention from the Sapphire Ring accusations.

Picard had been in the Fresnes Prison hospital since his arrest, suffering from respiratory troubles and a weak heart. He described his interrogation by French police as 'a real brain-washing. At the end of it I was ready to commit suicide.'[1]

His counsel, Maître Richard Dupuy, stated that Picard was

threatened by disclosures about his private life, obtained by telephone tapping, and that he 'was terrorized and told them everything they wanted. He was a victim of blackmail.'[2]

Eventually Picard was found guilty of having damaged the national interest by consorting with American, British, German and Soviet agents and diplomats and given a seven-year prison sentence. At the same time the prosecutor made it clear that Picard was tried neither for espionage nor treason. Shortly afterwards the French Supreme Court quashed the sentence owing to 'extenuating circumstances' and Picard was released a year later after friends had intervened on his behalf.

In one sense action against Picard, though not vital to French interests, was taken as a warning to all servants of the State and, of course, Intelligence agents, that communications with foreign countries, even if not treasonable, were liable to have a damaging effect. The French were by this time well aware that not only the Americans, but the British as well, were deeply concerned about allegations of leakages of NATO secrets from inside France.

France had left the military organization of NATO in 1966, while remaining a member of the Atlantic Alliance, and French civil servants continued to work in the civilian administration of NATO which had moved from Paris to Brussels. Much of the brouhaha about the arrest of Picard came from the fact that de Gaulle's plans and ideas about the EEC were regarded as top secret and it was believed that the British in particular were anxious to know exactly what they were. This was almost pathetic insularity and nationalism carried to extreme limits in what was entirely an economic sphere, but the fact was that French secrecy about this subject and de Gaulle's antagonism to British entry to the EEC caused the British Secret Service to put 'Common Market Intelligence' on the top of its shopping list.

This is an oblique approach to the question of France's drive against Soviet agents within its territory, but it must be made clear that year by year the French started getting results in the combined action of the DST and SDECE. Much of the drive was against French suspects in the civilian administration of NATO in Brussels. This work had been going on since 1962 when the combined Intelligence Services began to come to grips with the problem after reorganization. The need for constant vigilance had been learned after the Georges Paques case in 1964, and subsequently there were a number of French arrests of officials on defence secrets charges. Jean Pickus, a 28-year-old engineer, was sentenced to fifteen years' hard labour for spying for Poland by passing on information about French secret weapons while serving in the French Navy, and Joseph Adam Bitonski, a journalist, was sentenced for four years for espionage on behalf of Poland. Bitonski's wife was acquitted. Later Georges de Kobor, a Hungarian-born engineer, was sentenced to ten years' hard labour for giving information to the Polish Embassy in Paris on pipeline projects in France and Algeria. It was claimed on his behalf that all the information he had provided had been published in technical journals. A Polish woman whom he had met brought pressure on him to hand over the information, hinting that his mother in Hungary might come to harm if he refused.

The French also learned something from the British in this period. Though in MI5 there was an obsession for spying on the French, in MI6 there was still a considerable degree of the old-time camaraderie which resulted in a number of useful tips to the French on villains inside their own ranks. It is still said in Paris that it was a tip-off from the British which led to the arrest of Georges Paques. The great embarrassment for the French was that they had officially sponsored him for his NATO post.

During the 1960s the French Intelligence Service compiled a handbook called *Espionage – A Reality*, which was distributed to 9,000 heads of industrial firms and others in key positions, putting them on their guard against methods likely to be used by foreign agents to procure industrial secrets. This was in many ways a sensational departure from normal secrecy on such matters, but it was based on evidence which showed that many agents from East European countries had entered France years ago as emigrants or specialist workers after training at a centre in the Ukraine and that they were working for a vast industrial espionage network. The book stated that such people, engaged as ordinary workmen, were well able to read and copy the most complex blueprints, or, as foundry hands, identify strategic materials. The book counselled industrialists to be more circumspect in recruiting staff.

Though France had withdrawn from NATO's structure militarily, under French law French citizens who spied on NATO countries were liable to the same penalties as those who spied on France. In 1966 French Intelligence was able to smash a spy ring which used dolls to smuggle secret NATO information into East Germany. This intelligence was revealed when four West Germans who worked in the press office of what was then NATO's Paris headquarters were arrested. They were two married couples, Kyranick and Bammler. They had used French-made 'Douchka' dolls to channel the information they collected for East Germany via Prague. One doll in each of several regular export consignments sent to Czechoslovakia could be unscrewed and inside it was packed a despatch from the spies. This espionage operation was said to have begun in 1960 when Kyranick had been discharged from the French Foreign Legion and obtained a post in the archives of the French military headquarters in Berlin. While there he met Bammler, an East German secret agent, to whom he gave details of troop movements. In 1963 Kyranick was transferred to Paris where he married a secretary in the West German Embassy and then arranged to get a job in NATO. The Bammlers had been living in Paris since 1964, using false identity papers. Bammler was the son of a *Wehrmacht* general and had once been head of the Entertainment Department of the West Berlin Municipality. Nevertheless he was a professional agent of the East German Intelligence Service and since 1964 he had been sending out information by a powerful radio transmitter.

There was some delay in actually exposing this spy ring because two French security men who had discovered what was happening took over the network by channelling false information into it. This was fed to the agents in an effort to uncover other links in the Communist espionage chain.

This was the second espionage affair to have been uncovered by the French in the NATO press service. As a result Peter Kyranick was jailed for twenty years and his wife for fourteen years, while the Bammlers received sentences of eighteen and twelve years respectively. At the same time a Prague barman was arrested for attempting to recruit an Air France official into espionage for Czechoslovakia by blackmail tactics while he was on a visit to France.

Suddenly it became abundantly clear to the DST that a major drive for all manner of NATO secrets and intelligence on nuclear and other scientific developments was being mounted by Moscow against France and that the Russians were using not only their own nationals as agents but also Czechs, East Germans, Romanians, Poles and Bulgarians. Between 1965 and 1975 there was case after case in France involving nationals of these Soviet satellite countries. Astonishingly enough sometimes these people wormed their way into the French security services, though on occasions, one suspects, they were lured in with a view to entrapment. One such affair was that of Czech-born Pierre Cardot, who had served with the French Army in Germany and on demobilization was attached to the French counter-intelligence service. When he was arrested in November 1967, charged with spying for a foreign power, the police were said to have found in his one-room Left Bank apartment a secret radio transmitter, a developer for invisible ink and secret codes.[3]

One of the problems which faced the DST was that inside France in this period there were no fewer than 1,310 representatives of Eastern bloc countries, including 780 from the Soviet Union. Over and above this there was also the problem of the *rabcors*. This, in Communist jargon, was an abbreviation of the *rabotchi correspondent*, who belonged to a network of Communist factory workers who sometimes supplied intelligence to the USSR from various parts of the world.

Many of the leads which the DST obtained in tracking down the spies in their midst pointed in the direction of Romania. There was the classic case in 1969 of Francis Roussilhe, a French translator at the Brussels HQ of NATO, who was charged with treason. Roussilhe was arrested by the Belgian police as he was leaving his office in the NATO building in Brussels and handed over to the French authorities.

Roussilhe had joined the NATO staff in 1952 and was

reported to have been given a security clearance twice. Married, with three children, he was alleged to have been recruited several years previously by Romania. The judge at his trial stated that he had access in his work to documents ranging in classification from 'confidential' to 'top secret' and 'cosmic'. Altogether, between 1963 and 1969 he had passed 12,000 pages of documents to Romanian agents for which he had been paid some 100,000 francs in gold. He told the court that the Romanians had 'persuaded me that the information I transmitted could avoid a conflict between the NATO and Warsaw Pact nations and that I was also helping Romania to free itself from Soviet domination'. He was sentenced to twenty years' imprisonment.

Another incident involving Romanians occurred when a French National Service private, working in NATO Central Europe Command headquarters at Fontainebleau (prior to France leaving NATO) was arrested and charged with having knowledge of espionage and failing to report it to his superiors. He was alleged to have become friendly with a military attaché at the Romanian Embassy in Paris in May 1961, when articled as a lawyer's clerk. The attaché was Lieutenant-Colonel Mandachem, whom, it was claimed, he knew to be indulging in espionage. Meanwhile the Romanian colonel had returned to Bucharest.

The Romanian Connection gave the DST and, to a lesser extent, the SDECE, a great deal of hard work and many headaches over a long period. In November 1969 seven people were arrested by the Paris security police, including six French citizens (two of them officials in the French Foreign Ministry) and a member of the Romanian colony in the French capital. These arrests arose out of detailed and laborious inquiries by the DST following the Roussilhe case, and as a result three members of the Romanian Embassy in Paris were asked to leave the country. The other seven who had been arrested were charged with 'spying on behalf of Romania', and at the same time the files on all Romanian residents in France were transferred to the office of the prosecutor of the Court for State Security.

Among the Frenchmen charged were Robert van le Wilhe

Français, a former employee at NATO; Pierre Richeron, a former secretary of the French Embassy in Washington; a man named only as 'M. Pierre P', said to be a cipher officer at the Foreign Ministry in Paris; and Eugène Rousseau, a French counter-espionage officer.

Coincidentally only a week before these arrests Lieutenant-Colonel Bernard-Marie du Cheyron de Beaumont d'Abazac de la Duze was driving his car near Budapest International Airport and was killed instantly when a lorry was driven at high speed out of a side road and crushed his car. Although the colonel was understood to have been head of the East European section of French counter-intelligence, it was officially denied that his death had any link with the spy arrests. That denial was not altogether convincing, especially as this was a time when the Quai d'Orsay (the French Foreign Office), under much prompting from de Gaulle, had been trying hard to strengthen friendly relations between France and Romania. Indeed, there was undoubtedly considerable pressure to hamper the DST and police inquiries into these matters, the theory of the French Foreign Ministry being that the less the public knew about espionage matters conducted by foreigners the better.

De Gaulle had for long set his sights on Romania as being the ideal satellite to be wooed to France's side, largely because the Romanian President, Ceaucescu, had always tended to resist any moves from the Russians to dictate policy to him. On the other hand, as wiser counsellors might have pointed out, this by no means meant that he did not fully support Soviet international policies: that he did so was indicated by the tough measures he took to protect Romania from all outside pressures. What the Romanians had done was to take full advantage of France's friendly advances towards their country by stepping up their own espionage. This extension of espionage by Romania was actually going on at the very time that de Gaulle, on 18 May 1968, paid an official visit to Romania, a visit which had to be cut short because of violent clashes between students and security police in Paris and the occupation of factories by French workers.

It was a confusing picture which Romania then presented to

Western intelligence chiefs and the problem was that few seemed to take a balanced view of it. In the 1950s the Romanians made several arrests following reports of agents being landed in their territory by parachute for what were termed as 'subversive activities for the United States'. In October 1953 thirteen people were condemned to death on this account. In June 1955 the Romanian Ministry of Internal Affairs broadcast a statement which said that two 'American spies' who had surrendered had been granted a pardon and were being permitted to choose freely their future occupation. Their names were given as people of Romanian origin, though they were said to have been trained by the Americans in West Germany and parachuted into Romania via Athens. But, the statement added, they had refused to become 'traitors' to their fatherland and after surrender had confessed their crimes.[4]

At the same time it had been made absolutely clear not merely to Russia but also, by devious methods, to Western diplomats, that President Ceaucescu was totally opposed to any kind of occupation of his country by Soviet troops. Twice the President had felt that Romania's borders were threatened by the Soviet Union – in 1968 at the time of the Russian invasion of Czechoslovakia, and shortly afterwards when Ceaucescu was heavily criticized by other members of the Warsaw Pact for visiting Peking. He was not invited to a special Warsaw Pact meeting on one occasion and there had been reports that the Soviet Union wanted to make a demonstrative march across Romania to hold manoeuvres in Bulgaria. After this a number of Moscow-trained officers were removed from top jobs in the Romanian forces and replaced by men trained primarily in Romania. All this intelligence suggested to de Gaulle that here was a chance to hold out a hand, and gradually to win back at least some of the Eastern bloc into accord with the West.

Yet for many years to come the Romanian Connection was to continue to provide the DST with enormous problems. But everything that the French managed to uncover in the 1960s was nothing compared with what they were to learn in the next two decades, culminating in the mysterious case of Colonel Z which erupted in 1982. Romania had espionage problems, too, and in September 1972 a Romanian general, Ion Serbe, was in fact executed by a firing squad 'for passing information on defence to the Soviet Union'.[5]

In the meantime arrests of other nationals for espionage continued in France; two Algerians and a woman secretary at the French Foreign Office were jailed for espionage in connection with the Franco-Algerian oil negotiations. The Frenchwoman was Beatrice Halegua, who had worked for the director of economic affairs at the Quai d'Orsay. As a reprisal for the French arrests the Algerians disclosed the embarrassing fact that the SDECE's counter-espionage organization had been caught running a telephone-tapping system in Algiers which had enabled them to listen in to talks of Algerian Ministers.

Two Frenchmen, one a Communist mayor, and six Poles were charged with being members of an espionage network. The mayor was Gregoire Leleux from the village of Fenain, who was detained at Lille after police searched his home. Workers at the brickworks where he was employed came out on a 24-hour strike in protest against his arrest. Various Czechoslovaks were also arrested in Toulouse and Grenoble where the French had a nuclear studies centre. One of these was Dr Rudolf Lenk, a scientist who had been working at the centre.

There was also the case of the secretary who worked for a company which operated a Government atomic pile at Canderache in Central France, and who was suspected of leaking secrets to the Communists. When she went on holiday, security men shadowed her every move until they suddenly caught her taking a plane to Prague. It was then they discovered that she had been the secretary of a Communist Party cell all along and she, too, was arrested for passing on secrets.

Then on the eve of a visit to France by the Soviet leader, Leonid Brezhnev, Dimitri Volokhov, a 39-year-old French physicist, was arrested and charged with espionage activities for the Russians dating back eleven years. It was alleged that he had betrayed to Moscow most of France's nuclear secrets, including the innermost workings of the top-secret Pierrelatte nuclear centre responsible for the ground work on France's *force de frappe* (nuclear strike force).

Volokhov had worked for French firms engaged in classified

activity on behalf of France's civil and military nuclear programme and he had access to all of France's atomic centres.
Security officials said he first started passing secrets to the
Russians after a visit to the Soviet Press and Information Office
in the Rue de Prony in Paris in 1960, when the Russians offered
to 'exchange scientific data' with him. Afterwards Volokhov
was controlled by a series of Soviet diplomatic spymasters first
from the Press and Information Centre and then from the
Soviet Embassy.

The son of a White Russian emigré and certainly with no
Communist background, Volokhov was slowly and extremely
cleverly recruited. Probably he was drawn into the net by
friendly and casual talks which led to indiscretions without his
being at first aware of what was happening. He found that his
Soviet contacts changed every two or three years. Then for
some reason which puzzled French security officials Volokhov
suddenly decided to retire from nuclear work and he joined a
French building and construction firm. It could well be that he
had had a change of mind, or equally that he realized the
longer he went on serving the Russians the more likely he was
to be found out. Soon after this his controller, Lieutenant-
Colonel Yuri Rylev, gave Volokhov his last assignment. He
was told to make a complete list of all friends and business
contacts whom he had met during the past eleven years,
together with a list of their weaknesses in the following order:
women, drugs, homosexuality and money problems.

One of the names on the list provided by Volokhov was that
of a senior French diplomat in the Quai d'Orsay whom he had
described as being 'a man with large debts and serious financial
worries'. French Intelligence officers believed that Rylev
approached the diplomat soon after this and disclosed the fact
that he had confidential information about his financial problems. Possibly Rylev was under orders to get quick results in
connection with the Brezhnev visit. Otherwise it is hard to
account for such untypical 'crash tactics' used by the Soviet
attaché, as this is not normal routine by KGB controllers.

The French diplomat not only refused to be blackmailed into
providing information to the KGB, but he immediately
informed the French counter-intelligence service with the result

that Volokhov was arrested. It could be that as soon as Volokhov indicated he wanted to quit the espionage game the Russians decided to get rid of him in this manner, that is to say by allowing him to approach a French diplomat who would unhesitatingly report on him.

Over the years the KGB have made persistent attempts to penetrate a number of United Nations agencies, but nowhere was this more effective than in the Paris headquarters of UNESCO (United Nations Educational, Scientific and Cultural Organization). They were, of course, helped by the number of senior members of UNESCO who were openly pro-Soviet. In December 1971 it was stated that there were seventy-two Soviet officials in the organization, fifteen belonging to the USSR's permanent delegation and the other fifty-seven on temporary posting.

Russia had long regarded UNESCO as an ideal sphere for its operations not least in the scope it gives for propagating theories and themes helpful to the Soviet cause. So much importance did Russia attach to this organization that both the KGB and the GRU (military intelligence) used 'agents of influence' within its ranks. One of the most important of these, and still underestimated by many, was Charles Pathé, the son of one of the earliest and best known of French film producers. It was during the 1950s that Pathé had been suggested to the Russians as a likely recruit for their cause when he was working in the UNESCO offices in Paris. He moved in top governmental circles and was regarded as an eccentric but staunch Gaullist with liberal leanings. Before World War II he married a former beauty queen, Miss White Russia 1927, Ariane Guedonoff, but on the insistence of his family they were later divorced. He spoke fluent Russian and visited the USSR on a number of occasions.

It was not until 1980, twenty years after his acceptance as a Soviet agent, that he was charged with what amounted to the 'continuous process of disseminating Russian "disinformation"'. It was an unusual charge and a trial quite out of the ordinary run of such cases, for Pathé had made no secret of his pro-Soviet leanings. He was sentenced to five years' imprisonment, while Alexandrovich Kuznetsov, his controller and a permanent delegate to UNESCO, was expelled after claiming diplomatic immunity.

During the period Pathé was operating it was reckoned that nearly one-third of the Soviet officials working permanently in UNESCO were full-time members of the KGB or GRU. For all this time Pathé had been cunningly inserting Soviet-produced material into articles he wrote for the French press, making special use of the newsletter, *Synthèsis*, which he personally directed. Though *Synthèsis* was only in existence for three years – 1976–9 – it was reponsible for massive disinformation during that brief period. It deliberately set out to create mistrust between Europe and the United States: Pathé's scheme was to defend Soviet interests and actions largely under cover of attacking the USA and appearing to boost French national interests. In many respects this skilful campaign of disinformation (Pathé always avoided downright untruths which could easily have been spotted) probably did more good for the Soviet cause than much straightforward espionage. When Mitterand became President in 1981, Pathé, then aged seventy-one, was released from prison on humanitarian grounds.

From 1967 to 1972 the director of the DST was Jean Rochet, who proved outstanding in his efforts to keep the Soviet espionage campaign in France under control. Prefect Rochet has recalled his initial surprise on his appointment as head of the service at the manner in which it was hindered not only by dissensions and rival groups within its own ranks, but also by the light penalties which some of the judiciary imposed on spies, once convicted. Gradually Rochet sought to remedy this state of affairs by constantly pressing on people that Soviet spies existed everywhere in France.

Yet within a year he was facing a new and dangerous problem in the exploitation of student unrest and riots in Paris in May 1968. This was at that time a world-wide phenomenon, most marked in the USA, but to a lesser extent in Britain, often inspired by students' own left-wing beliefs rather than Soviet influence, though doubtless the USSR helped it along in some cases. Rochet himself, however, declared unequivocally that these incidents were provoked by and 'taken in hand by outside ringleaders with the purpose of overthrowing the regime'.[6]

In Paris, if not in other centres in France, this may well have been true, though there has never been any positive linking of those 'outside ringleaders' with Soviet Russia. Rochet was very conscious of the part played by disinformation in not merely winning over people to the Soviet cause, but also in fomenting demonstrations. He had obtained first-hand evidence of how such organizations as the *Tricontinentale*, which met in Havana in 1966, had promoted strife against capitalist regimes, linking them with anti-Vietnam and pro-Peace demonstrations. To tackle this problem the DST chief arranged for students to be given briefings on this subject so that they would be fully alerted to the Soviet campaign. Indeed, he went further than this by making a personal appearance on French television in a special programme on espionage. Some two hundred and sixty questions had been put forward by the public and three journalists took part in the discussion. The French Foreign Ministry were not at all happy about this most unusual action by a counter-espionage chief, but it was well received by a listening public estimated at some fifteen million.[7]

It was many weeks before senior officials in the French Foreign Ministry quite recovered from their shock at Jean Rochet's 'Hunt the Spies' programme: not that they could do much about it, for the DST still came quite firmly under the Ministry of the Interior. Not only did the DST chief show the tools of his trade in the television programme (such items as mini-microphones and cameras), but he gave a solemn warning about the traps likely to be laid for unsuspecting French citizens when they visited countries of Eastern Europe. What irked the men at the Quai d'Orsay most was his reference to French diplomats who 'became the dupes of agents of Iron Curtain countries' and condemned 'the cast-iron *ésprit de corps* among them which hindered the work of the DST'.[8]

Just to rub in this lesson Rochet specifically described as 'imprudent' the evidence given by Jean-Pierre Brunet, director of economic affairs at the Quai d'Orsay, on behalf of his secretary who had recently been convicted of passing to Algerian agents documents dealing with petrol supplies. The secretary had received a suspended sentence of five years'

imprisonment, while the two Algerians involved were each sent
to prison for eight years. Rochet asserted that the papers were
important and that they included records of meetings in the
Elysée Palace. The inference was that possession of them had
strengthened Algeria's hand in recent oil negotiations.

Certainly Rochet made no attempt to appease the Quai
d'Orsay, and he astonished many of his viewers with some of
his revelations. One of his stories was about the daughter of a
foreign-based French Government employee who, he said, 'was
filmed in bed with an enemy agent. Then she was told that the
film would be published if she did not hand over the keys to
her father's safe.' He also pointed the finger at one of the rival
organizations in French Intelligence, telling of a male warrant
officer who gave the Poles the secret of a French military code
after having been trapped into an illicit affair with a woman
acting for the Poles. 'Fifty per cent of the diplomats in the
Eastern bloc countries in Paris are Secret Service men,' he
alleged. Giving statistics to back up his assertions, he added
that the East German Government had been involved in
thirteen spy trials held in France during the past ten years;
Czechoslovakia had a hand in twelve cases; Russia was involved
in ten; Poland in seven; while in a recent case no fewer than
fourteen Romanian diplomats were implicated.[9]

Many cases investigated by the DST and others remained
unsolved, but on the whole the vigilance of its agents was highly
commendable in this era. In November 1970 a murder and an
attempted murder resulted in intensive DST inquiries. The first
involved an unknown assassin who called at a block of flats
near the Eiffel Tower and inquired about the number of an
apartment held by Pierre Aimedieu, owner of a factory which
produced various electronic bugging devices and transmitters
for the Security Services. The mystery man made no attempt to
hide his face and even chatted to the *concierge*. Aimedieu was
shaving when he heard the sound of a pistol shot, and ran from
the bathroom to find his wife slumped dead on the floor of the
corridor. He swiftly tackled the intruder and, though slightly
wounded by another shot, managed to knock off the man's
glasses and his hat. At that moment his young daughter ran

from her room into the corridor and was shot dead. The assassin then fled.

The second incident that month was more sinister. Commandant Jacques Lamercier, a senior Security officer, was found dead in his home. Beside his body was a box of some lethal pills and the burnt remains of a mystery package he had just received. Lamercier had been head of counter-espionage activities in Eastern France and had recently been engaged in some highly secret investigations. For this reason it was the military police who took charge. The magistrate who headed the inquiry into Lamercier's death commented, 'There must have been something very momentous in the letter to make the man kill himself.' One rumour circulating at the time was that the package contained a letter ordering Lamercier to kill himself, but few believed this.

Another mysterious affair occurred when a seventeen-year-old boy, Serge le Petit, the son of a French nuclear technician, was found dead on a cliff near Cherbourg, overlooking the English Channel. He had been shot at point-blank range with a single bullet and detectives believed he might have been shot because he was mistaken for a spy. On the day of his death Serge le Petit left a note at his home saying he had decided to go abroad for two years. Yet he had only taken with him a sandwich, a torch and his cameras. Later that day he asked two fishermen at Cherbourg to take him to Alderney in the Channel Islands, but they refused.

There was absolutely no suggestion of suicide and no weapon was found nearby. The youth was well known for his secretive behaviour and police took the view that this may have led to the suspicion that he was trying to pass information to a foreign power. They discovered that the day before he was murdered Serge was visited by a blonde woman. Blonde hairs were found in his bed and there were traces of lipstick on his pillow. Cherbourg's investigating magistrate expressed the view that the youth was 'coldly and professionally executed. It is an unusual crime and we have ruled out nothing.'

One theory was that a foreign agent had secured information

from him and killed him so that nobody should discover this leakage. Out of such incidents are novels born. On the other hand, as is gradually being realized, true-life espionage is very often much stranger than fiction.

Reforming the Intelligence Services

The SDECE no longer fits in with republican order . . . I feel with all
conviction that the SDECE should be abolished.

General Pierre Billotte

This statement was made by General Billotte, a former Minister
of Defence, in 1968 when he launched an attack on the current
Defence Minister, Michel Debré. He claimed that a long time
ago he had urged that, if the specific measures he had suggested
for reform of the SDECE were not taken, a major scandal
would eventually erupt. It was scandalous, he said, 'that a
foreign prosecutor can accuse high officials of the SDECE of
engaging in the drugs traffic and no stinging denial, formulated
in detail and completely convincing, could be opposed to his
allegations'.[1]

That such a statement as this above should be made by a
senior officer of the armed forces in any other part of the world
about his nation's secret service is almost inconceivable.
Equally, few if any politicians around the world would make
such a sweeping condemnation: all they would wish would be
that the intelligence services of their nation should be serving
their true purposes.

General Billotte, a Gaullist deputy, made this forthright
comment because he honestly believed that the SDECE no
longer fulfilled the duties it had been charged to undertake. A
year before he made this statement he had also produced a
report recommending reorganization of the SDECE in an effort
to prevent fresh scandals.

The background to all this was the allegation of drug-running
in the Secret Service. This emerged once again when one Roger
Delouette was arrested in America as he went to the dockside

to collect his Volkswagen which had been shipped over from France. A US customs officer then discovered heroin hidden under the floor of the car. Delouette, anxious to avoid the severe sentence which a drug smuggler could be given in the USA, decided to help the American authorities to track down the other miscreants. The suspicion was that the CIA were already on his track and in a position to put pressure on him to tell all.

Delouette's story was that he had worked for the SDECE and that his superior officer, Colonel Claude Ferrer, chief of SDECE's North American section (cover name Colonel Paul Fournier), had organized the whole operation. This allegation was vigorously denied by Ferrer and the official French response to this was that Delouette had invented a drug ring in order to minimize his own guilt. Immediately there was a dispute between France and the USA, the former wanting Delouette to be returned to their jurisdiction, while the latter wanted to prosecute Colonel Ferrer.

The Americans maintained they had a list of other French officials, including some other SDECE members, customs officers, politicians and civil servants who had shielded drug traffickers. Meanwhile it was claimed that SDECE had carried out its own investigation into the drugs trade which revealed that some members of the CIA had been working for the Mafia by arranging the transportation of gold to pay for drugs procured in Europe and the Middle East and that a number of CIA agents were involved in the supply of narcotics to North America from Asia.

Then came a new revelation on Radio Luxembourg from Colonel Barberot, who was chief of the BDPA (*Bureau pour le Développement de la Production Agricole*), which was ostensibly an organization for helping underdeveloped countries, especially those which had links with France. Colonel Barberot, for whom Delouette had worked for a number of years, confirmed that Delouette was a member of the SDECE and even suggested that 'there was probably something in the story'.[2]

This was a particularly damaging statement at a time when American security services, both CIA and FBI, were alleging that they had compiled detailed evidence of complicity by individual French intelligence officers in world-wide drug trafficking, which, it was added, cost the US economy around $1,000 million a year.

General Billotte's denunciation of the service came when Debré, speaking as Defence Minister, described the drugs scandal surrounding the SDECE as 'a fairy tale worthy of a *concierge* and of page fifteen of a third-class newspaper'.[3] This was a statement with which such highly reputable Parisian newspapers as *Le Monde* and *Figaro* disagreed.

However, this over-the-top statement by General Billotte was a little unnecessary, because at this time Michel Debré was already planning to reform the Intelligence Services, albeit in an unostentatious manner. Despite the departure of de Gaulle in 1969 following a referendum and a brief period with Poher as President before the arrival of Georges Pompidou as head of the nation in 1970, France was still not only remarkably stable, but economically far ahead of many of her neighbours. It was at this time – 6 November 1970, to be precise – that the SDECE acquired a new director-general, the Comte Alexandre de Marenches, who remained in office for eleven years and was able to reform and modernize the service in a remarkably efficient manner. He was in fact the longest-serving head of the Secret Service of modern times.

De Marenches proved to be one of the most outstanding spymasters of the century. He not only managed to curb the SDECE of its often illegal excesses, but also eliminated dissension within its ranks and brought it into the computer age. His work was certainly not helped by the diatribes of General Billotte, or, for that matter, of Jacques Soustelle who alleged that the SDECE was 'infected by gangrene and it suffers from its political connections and from the integration into its ranks of shady characters'.[4] Some of these allegations were true and without doubt the whole service needed reforming, but open criticism could be counter-productive. In any event, for all its shortcomings, the SDECE was still a relatively efficient organization which obtained results. French Intelligence had never been less than good; it was only a question of making it better.

What de Marenches did was first of all to curtail the espion-age fantasies which had been attempted by the *grands caimans* (big operators) in earlier years. At times what these agents had attempted was almost to copy the wildest escapades of spy fiction. De Marenches knew that he had inherited what was basically a devoted and patriotic team of professionals and that the main object was to bring them under a tighter and more cohesive organization. What he eventually achieved was to make France possessor of one of the most effective secret services in the world, not in any ostentatious way, but in terms of results and influence.

Huge is perhaps the most apt word one can apply to de Marenches both in intellect and in physical size. At any gathering or party his figure dominates the whole room, stand-ing head and shoulders above anyone else, and this applies as much to his personality as his dimensions. He is an aristocrat and an internationalist (at least in his thinking), an army colonel, a member of the Jockey Club and a Knight of Malta. In many ways his background was more of an Allied one than that of a French nationalist; de Marenches would have no doubt whatsoever that the one fitted into the other. Born in 1921, he was brought up by an Irish nanny and English and German governesses and was later educated in Switzerland. He joined the army in the cavalry at the age of eighteen and, after the fall of France, he had several adventures in the Resistance campaign before escaping on foot over the Pyrenees in mid-winter. Then he re-enlisted in the Algerian Spahis and volun-teered to fight under General Juin in Italy. He was seriously wounded at the battle of Cassino, after which he became Juin's ADC.

His father, Henri de Marenches, after gallant service in World War I, had served as an aide to the American General Pershing and met such future generals as MacArthur, Marshall and Patton. He married an American, Marguerite Monahan. Alexandre himself, while serving Juin, acted as a liaison officer with the British and Americans between 1942 and 1944. Of this work he later said: 'The Anglo-Saxon world and we French were then, and thank God we still are, in the camp of liberty.

My objective has always been to first of all promote the French view and then the Allied.'[5]

This statement was made long afterwards when de Marenches, who had avoided any kind of publicity during the eleven years he was head of the SDECE, broke silence in a series of interviews with the French journalist and television personality, Christine Ockrent, in 1986.

At the end of World War II de Marenches left public life, mainly occupying himself with his estate in Normandy and a few business interests. Despite the fact that he could have been an influential figure, he had no desire whatsoever to become involved in politics, though he was still prepared to maintain various international contacts on behalf of his country, including some delicate and highly confidential missions.

De Marenches entitled his memoirs *Dans le Secret des Princes*, a peculiar choice in many ways. However, this referred not merely to such figures as General de Gaulle and General Juin and friends in British and American circles, but also to his personal friendships with the Shah of Iran and King Hassan of Morocco. Yet, if he disliked the idea of a political career, he felt it a duty to accept the challenge which President Georges Pompidou gave him in 1970 of taking over and reforming the SDECE. Maybe this was because, as an old friend of Pompidou, he was given a free hand to do what he thought best.

De Marenches' mission had been made abundantly clear to him; he was quite ruthlessly to purge the service of its unruly and undesirable elements, to reorganize it on much more professional lines and to curb the tendency for it to be divided into various rival sections. In brief, he was to end the Gaullist scheme of things which, whether the General had intended this or not, meant that the SDECE had been run according to the dubious policy of divide and rule. De Gaulle had refused to allow the concentration of power in a single security service. Maybe experience had told him that he needed to listen to many diverse voices and opinions before he made a decision, but this policy had seriously interfered with the development of the SDECE in many respects. But in the 1970s first under Pompidou, then under Giscard d'Estaing, the SDECE underwent considerable changes for the better. The main improvements were, of course, the stamping out of any links between the service and drug trafficking such as had been shown up in the Delouette affair, and in recruitment. De Marenches was sufficiently disciplinarian to cope with this formidable task which was made more difficult when he was attacked by two prominent army officers – Colonel Roger Barberot, who complained that the purge of the SDECE was incomplete, and General Billotte, who was said to have developed a dislike of both Pompidou and de Marenches.

Some extremely wild allegations about the misdoings of the SDECE were being bandied around at that time, one of them about its involvement in what the French media called the Markevitch affair. This was yet another irritation for the new chief. Like many such scandals linked to the French Intelligence Services the Markevitch case was largely irrelevant. It concerned the murder of the bodyguard and chauffeur of the film actor, Alain Delon, and at this distance of time can be tersely dismissed as a squalid gangster episode. Pompidou, himself, when he became President, ordered an investigation into this whole affair, and the inquiry, while producing little in the way of hard evidence one way or another, is said to have encouraged him to ensure that the SDECE was thoroughly purged of any possible criminal elements.

Far more important to the reputation and future of the SDECE was the sudden escalation of the drugs scandal which threatened to have international repercussions. While this had originally been triggered off by Roger Delouette's claim that at the time of his arrest he was acting for one of France's Intelligence chiefs, it was made worse when in October 1971 a French businessman, allegedly an SDECE officer stationed in Haiti, was detained because police discovered 106 kilos of heroin in his car. Shortly before this another man with SDECE connections, Michel Mertz, who was known in the Intelligence world as 'Commandant Baptiste', was jailed for five years on drug charges. To make matters worse, John Cusack, then European chief of the US Narcotics Bureau, bluntly stated that, 'People in high places in France were shielding drug smugglers.'[6]

Le Bon et Vrai states:

It may be an extremely cynical assertion to make, but it has surely long been known that many of the world's intelligence services, both eastern and western, have been involved in drug trafficking if only to raise the extra money they need and which their governments won't give them. Maybe that sounds like an apologia for the SDECE, but from my own knowledge this is certainly true. Much of the funds raised in this way are deposited in Swiss bank accounts and later invested in a variety of ways. This illicit traffic doesn't only concern drugs but also counterfeit currency, various forms of forgery and sometimes commodities such as silver or works of art. At one time Tangier, when it was an international zone, used to be a centre for this kind of thing.

De Marenches sacked no fewer than twenty of his top executives in the SDECE within a month of taking over. Meanwhile his temper must have been sorely tried by having to spend up to two hours at a time being interrogated by an examining magistrate at the law courts. Other intelligence officers were also questioned.

For a while some French commentators bore out something of what *Le Bon* has suggested, alleging that some members of the CIA were also involved with drug trafficking and had been working with the Italian Mafia for the transport of gold to pay for drugs procured in Europe and the Middle East. Nevertheless, it is only fair to say that neither the SDECE nor the CIA in any way suspected that either organization was 'officially' involved in any aspect of trafficking. It is usually the lone agent, of whom not too many questions are asked, who becomes involved in this kind of traffic for one reason or another. The reasons may vary from the need to obtain information, to blackmail, the trapping of an enemy agent, or personal greed. But by his summary dismissal of so many SDECE top executives, de Marenches effectively both silenced critics outside the service and squashed clandestine influences within it.

De Marenches soon discovered that in the latter years of de Gaulle's presidency the SDECE had paid insufficient attention to intelligence-gathering inside the Iron Curtain countries. That he must very quickly have reversed this trend seems obvious from the opinion of one British SIS agent in this period: 'The change in this respect was remarkable within a year or two of de Marenches taking over. Our own relations with the SDECE were also enormously improved.'

Improved relations with other Western Intelligence Services was also one of the new chief's prime aims. He regarded this as of paramount importance and, as a cosmopolitan with friends in many other countries, he felt he was in an excellent position to bring this about. When asked about SDECE's relations with other Western Intelligence Services, he commented: 'It was not the SDECE which brought me relations, but, if you will pardon my saying so, I brought my own relations to the service of France.'[7]

What helped enormously, of course, was the fact that de Marenches had established so many close and warm friendships with both British and Americans in the war years – far more so than many of the Gaullists. He was able to smooth over past differences more easily, some of which were due to faults on both sides. One problem for Anglo-French relations had been the fact that under de Gaulle's presidency the French Intelligence Service had actually instigated a campaign, backed also by some other Western countries, to support Ian Smith's UDI rebellion in Zimbabwe (then Rhodesia) against Britain from 1965 to 1980. This was in a sense part of a continuous French policy to maintain the friendliest relations with all African powers while being realistic in selecting those who best served French foreign policy. It was a purely opportunist policy, and could just as easily mean lending support to a right-wing white government on one occasion as to a Marxist independent state, providing it was efficient and did business, on another. It was a realistic approach and one which the Secret Services of both Britain and France thoroughly understood.

De Marenches as a young man had farmed in Rhodesia and had been delighted with the country and its steady progress towards self-supporting statehood. There have been suggestions that long before de Marenches became head of the SDECE he had been approached for help and guidance by Rhodesians. On this subject the Comte remains silent. But Ken Flower, the former head of Rhodesian Intelligence, referred to the remarkable co-operation he received from Paris, though he never made clear whether this was official or unofficial. He said in 1987 that he had asked de Marenches for help in 'flying our beef and other high-value exports to Europe and the Frenchman pointed to a map of Africa and said: "Pick any Francophile country – we will get you landings rights." '[8]

Indeed Ken Flower, who has since died, claimed that the 'French Connection' was a godsend for the Rhodesian regime of Ian Smith, who also had some support from the Italian Secret Service, headed by General Michelli. It must be admitted that in the 1960s the British Secret Service was desperately short of worthwhile intelligence on Rhodesia to such an extent that Harold Wilson, through his intelligence liaison ministerial colleague George Wigg, had to rely on information about Rhodesia from acknowledged right-wingers and even some White Russians who had contacts inside that country. This has been attributed partly to the fact that Ken Flower bamboozled MI6. However, he would almost certainly not have managed to bamboozle the Comte de Marenches. And although he may have misrepresented himself as an honest broker to MI6 on Rhodesia (one prime reason why they desperately needed to obtain new intelligence on that country), it is more than likely that he gave a false impression to the French. Equally, the main channel of communication between Rhodesia's intelligence service and both France and Britain in this period was through Rhodesia's intelligence officer in Paris, a Mauritian who was on almost equal terms with MI6 and the SDECE.

It is also interesting to note that Ken Flower eventually became intelligence chief to Robert Mugabe when the African majority achieved independence. Nor is it without significance that Flower went on record as saying that he and Ian Smith had never liked each other and that, 'Never in seventeen years did he call me by my Christian name.' As Flower is now dead he cannot be questioned on some of the statements which were later contained in his book, *Serving Secretly*.[9] But despite the fact that the Wilson government mishandled the whole situation and that other Western governments took their own views of the UDI situation, my own impression is that what Flower said about de Marenches sounds unlike the way the SDECE chief would speak, is totally exaggerated and should be regarded with some suspicion. In any case de Marenches did not become head of the SDECE until some years after Ian Smith declared UDI. When de Marenches did take over, however, he had to deal with allegations like this in rebuilding happier relations with Britain.

The new French Secret Service chief was also on excellent terms with George Bush, later to become President of the United States, but then a senior officer in the CIA. While de Marenches had never been directly linked to any branch of French Intelligence in the earlier years of his career, herein lay his great strength once he took over, and it was particularly helpful when it came to restoring relations with United States Intelligence after the Sapphire Ring affair and other matters.

Franco-American relations had also further been upset by an incident in 1964 which created an acute scandal behind the scenes. A particularly attractive French countess had crept into the bedroom of President Kennedy's Under Secretary of State, George Ball, when he was staying at a hotel in Cannes, and stolen secret papers from his jacket pocket while he was asleep. In his memoirs the former SDECE Colonel Marcel Leroy stated that this mission was conducted at the request of Valéry Giscard d'Estaing, who was then French Prime Minister. According to Colonel Leroy, he personally photographed the papers in a room he had booked on the floor above that of the countess and then returned them to Ball's jacket. The hinges of the door to Ball's room had been well oiled so that they would not squeak when the door was opened.[10]

One story circulating about this incident was that the countess hoped to continue this kind of work and even offered to use her wiles to seduce one or two European politicians for whom she had developed an attraction. However, it would seem that she was advised that 'enough was enough' and that to attempt more would be disastrous.

Despite de Marenches' personality, his *bonhomie*, which won him the nickname of 'Porthos' of *The Three Musketeers* fame, and his popularity as a figure at parties, he maintained a very low profile prior to becoming head of the SDECE. Even afterwards he tended to copy the British technique of keeping their heads of the SIS out of the headlines as much as possible, and this was marked by the fact that he was not listed in the

French *Who's Who*. Indeed at the time of his appointment not a single photograph of him was to be found in any French newspaper library. There was hardly any publicity given to the fact that in 1972 Queen Elizabeth II of Britain gave him the KBE (Knight of the British Empire).

De Marenches had two advantages: that he was close to Pompidou, and that the SDECE now came firmly under the control of the Elysée Palace. As a result he was given a largely free hand and this enabled him to extend his relationships in many fields, some old, some new. He was one of the architects of France's improved intelligence-gathering in the Middle East and Africa. On African affairs he had a less narrow view than most of the Gaullists: in other words he was interested in areas outside those which had formerly been French colonies. This did not always please some of his subordinates.

De Marenches also paid close attention to the Far East, believing that in China and Japan were two nations whose drive into building a better future would be ignored only at the peril of the Western world. He paid particular attention to China, which had escaped from the farce of the Cultural Revolution. It has been said that he flew to Peking for talks with the chiefs of China's own Intelligence Services, but this is untrue. This is an item of disinformation, but what quarter it came from is still unclear.

Le Bon et Vrai comments:

What de Marenches achieved in intelligence on Far Eastern affairs was something of a major coup. But the truth is that much of this information came from other people who had visited China and talked to its leaders. As to French agents' links with the Chinese, perhaps they are helped by the fact that in some ways we regard them as an oriental version of the French, while they – as their philosopher, Lin Yutang, has said – look upon us as a Western version of themselves. One or two of us were able to keep the KPCC [Kuomintang Party Central Committee] informed on Soviet matters, especially on defence, whereas very often the Chinese could help us enormously on other nations of the Soviet bloc where we had business interests.

One can draw a parallel between *Le Bon*'s comments and those of de Marenches: 'The Chinese are interested in Africa,' he observed, 'especially when there is an opportunity to thwart the Russians.'[11]

At this time the SDECE was said to have possessed 2,500 full-time agents and at least as many 'honorary correspondents'. I asked *Le Bon* for his opinion on the latter. 'This may sound better than it really is,' he replied.

It might suggest that we have 2,500 or more patriots who will supply intelligence for no payment. There are two things to bear in mind. First, unlike you rather pig-headed British, who seem to suspect any patriot of being some kind of an imbecile, especially in your intelligence and security services, we tend to pay attention to anyone who, without wanting payment, thinks he, or she, has something worthwhile to tell us. This, surely, is logical: what have they to gain from telling us things except possibly our respect? But of course much of this kind of information proves worthless, so, when you talk of 'honorary correspondents', the number of those who are truly useful or valuable is comparatively small. But the point is that we French probably get more bonuses that way than you British. Having at one time had a close liaison with the British, I do know that sometimes intelligence passed to them by some of their compatriots has been rejected and that later it has come our way and been accepted.

While previously far too much of the counter-intelligence work had been left to the DST alone, under de Marenches the SDECE shouldered much more of this burden and increased its involvement in domestic surveillance. This was largely responsible for France's steadily increasing success in catching spies within its own domain. But even within a short time of his taking over the SDECE, de Marenches faced opposition from many quarters. In December 1971, the Senate halved the budget of the service, at a late-night sitting, largely on account of the allegations of its past links with drug trafficking. In spite of a declaration by the Minister of Defence, Debré, that if this were done a number of officials would not be paid the following year, the Senate adopted by 176 votes to 110 an amendment recommending the reduction and also giving the Government six months in which to reorganize the service. At the end of that time a commission representing the National Assembly and the Senate would decide whether the money could be restored.

Debré was either naïve or practising disinformation when he

told the Senate that the SDECE's responsibilities were abroad and that no meddling with domestic affairs was permitted. He said that it was because this rule had been transgressed that there had been certain dismissals. This may have been true regarding certain illegal operations, but to a large extent the DST had suffered from lack of help from the SDECE. Debré went on to say, 'There are men risking their lives in this service. There are very serious affairs to settle, involving behaviour which is not necessarily that of the average Frenchman. On all this, as you will understand, I remain silent. No Parliament in the world has shown so keen a curiosity.'[12]

On one point on the subject of intelligence de Marenches was emphatic. He believed that in the Western world the leadership of the Intelligence Services changed too frequently: during his term of office there were at least three changes at the head of Britain's MI6 and as many as six changes in the directorship of the CIA. Not only was he a first-class administrator with what is known in the intelligence world as long-distance thinking, but he had the imagination to reorganize the service for the future. He believed that France should have a National Security Council which would in effect co-ordinate the ministries of Foreign Affairs, Defence and the Interior, with the SDECE coming under this new body. At the same time he thought that counter-intelligence work conducted by the SDECE should be totally transferred to the DST, which would also come under the National Security Council. This made sense in many ways, not least in clearing up the rivalry, jealousy and muddle which sometimes occurred when both the SDECE and the DST were involved in counter-intelligence. But de Marenches did not see such proposals adopted during his period of office.

In the early 1970s there were many reports in French newspapers, including such distinguished papers as *Le Monde* and *Figaro*, that the French General Staff was collecting intelligence on the 'anti-militarist' and subversive activities and opinions of political parties and trade unions. While much of this information was said to be little more than a summary of items culled from the local press, some of the reports were described as 'quarterly intelligence bulletins on the internal enemy', and were classified as 'confidential – defence'. This led to some wild speculation in the media. A British newspaper reported:

The French Security Services are well equipped for keeping a watch on people. They inherited from the Gestapo a listening-in apparatus that is probably unequalled outside Soviet Russia . . . Fifteen thousand telephone numbers in Paris alone are constantly tapped, and one can be sure that among them are the phones of politicians, diplomats and civil servants who go out looking for private fun [a reference to a 'call-girl' scandal which was current in France at the time].[13]

This was a period in which the French were seriously concerned more than at any other time in the previous decade about the involvement of so-called Soviet diplomats in espionage. In February 1972 three top Russian spies were expelled from France as a result of information given in London by the Russian defector, Oleg Lyalin. All three worked at the Russian Embassy in Paris. The most important of these was Alexei Krokhin, a counsellor, who turned out to be a general in the KGB. This was one of the early bonuses of improved co-operation between the French and British Secret Services. Britain's Secret Service had provided the French with a full account of the revelations made by Lyalin, whose defection had touched off the mass expulsions of Soviet diplomats in the United Kingdom.

Yet even after this the French Foreign Office were pretending that no Soviet diplomats had been expelled and that if any had left Paris in recent weeks, it was because they had been recalled by Moscow. Of the other men who were asked to leave the most interesting was Viktor Volodine, who had been accused of 'recuperating' (another ambivalent phrase) with the scientist Fedoseyev when he disappeared during the Paris air show only to turn up later in Britain. While the French Foreign Ministry had their own reasons for playing down or denying the expulsions, such as maintaining good relations with Moscow and not providing propaganda to the French Communist Party, Constantin Melnik, former adviser on intelligence to the previous Prime Minister, was much more forthright. He had described Britain's expulsion of Soviet officials under the Heath government as 'the most important affair of its kind since the war' because 'it strikes at not a single agent or network, but at the entire system of massive espionage under diplomatic and commercial cover'.[14]

Melnik went on to say that the various Soviet and East European missions in France then had about 1,000 members of whom sixty per cent were considered to be agents. Each spy could normally control ten agents, which could indicate that up to 3,000 French informants were under orders from East European and Soviet espionage services in Paris. 'This means that there are more spies than the entire staffs of the SDECE and the DST put together.'[15]

At various times during administrations of de Gaulle's era there had not merely been tension between the British and French Intelligence Services, but mistrust and in certain circles enmity on both sides. On the British side, according to *Le Bon et Vrai*:

[There had been] some rather clumsy attempts to obtain the ciphers we used during the early 1960s, but things were never as bad as some writers have suggested. After all, it is sensible intelligence work even for allies to be wary of one another in case there is a clash of interests. You can be sure we kept up to date on your own technological developments in electronic equipment. For example, we knew that the British still had some rather old-fashioned Typex equipment in their Embassy in Paris.

Gradually there was improved co-operation between the two nations on intelligence matters, first with contacts between MI5 and DST, later between MI6 and SDECE. There was co-operation on the problem of two Communist networks directed against Concorde and other Franco-British aerospace developments of recent years. One was run by Sergei Pavlov, head of the French office of Aeroflot, the Soviet airline, the other by Herbert Steinbrecher, an East German. The French had got on to the trail of these networks as early as 1965 when Steinbrecher was uncovered by a double-agent, Dr Jean-Claude Soupert, of Luxembourg, who specialized in industrial chemistry. Both MI5 and the DST were working together on this and getting some surprising information as a result of their co-operation.

First of all it turned out that Dr Soupert was organizing agents for East German Intelligence while also working for the Belgian Security Service. He informed the Belgians that two of his agents working for East Germany were British businessmen. This information eventually reached MI5, but though the two Britons were charged, they were acquitted. Then MI6 learned that Steinbrecher's agents had obtained details of the Anglo-French Concorde's electronic systems.

Soon after this another Concorde spying operation came to light when an East German agent was caught at Montpellier analysing textiles manufactured specially for the interior of the aircraft. Samples had apparently been sent from Bristol by a textile merchant claiming to be an Italian. A year later, in 1966, two Czech spies, disguised as priests, were arrested and charged with sending illicit information on Concorde to their home country.

However, while nothing can be proved, it would seem that once the networks against Concorde were detected, a great deal of false intelligence was fed through to the spies by French Intelligence, not only on Concorde, but regarding other aerospace matters as well. Indeed, it is believed that some of this disinformation caused some serious errors in Soviet aircraft construction work, resulting in one disastrous air accident.

In 1977 French Intelligence struck again, largely due to improved co-operation between the DST and the SDECE. Just as the Soviet leader, Brezhnev, was about to visit Paris, Vladimir Rybatchenko, attached to the scientific section of UNESCO, was caught red-handed by French agents with top secret documents about a new computer system for the French armed forces. He was expelled from France, though news of this was kept relatively quiet. Indeed, there was even an attempt to play down Rybatchenko's espionage, Government sources insisting that he was seeking industrial rather than military secrets.

A month later it became clear that the French had uncovered a spy network which had for the past fourteen years provided 'a foreign power' with intelligence about French and NATO defence installations and methods. The phrase 'a foreign power' was generally supposed to be either the USSR or another

Eastern European nation. Four Frenchmen and an Italian were arrested. According to the DST the leader of this network was a Yugoslav-born, naturalized Frenchman named Serge Fabiew, who was managing director of a small company specializing in fire protection systems. DST agents discovered a highly sophisticated transmission system at the headquarters of the company controlled by Fabiew southwest of Paris. It enabled him to pass his information directly to the foreign power concerned. 'I had a romantic desire to have a homeland,' Fabiew stated at his trial. 'For me it was not the Soviet Union, but the Russia of my parents.' He had been offered a free holiday in the USSR and there he spent ten days in a spy school learning how to use a radio transmitter, write coded messages and use invisible ink. Two of the men involved with him were said to have joined the network for ideological reasons, but had received payments of up to £30,000.

23
Yet Another Crisis in the Service

I wonder if in the whole of French history there is an episode as
ridiculous as the Abu Daoud affair. I don't think so.

Jean Dutour in *France-Soir*

Frenchmen both in the media and in literary circles are almost
permanently critical of their Intelligence Services. So much so
that they often stir up and even invent crises when none exist.
The sole reason for quoting Jean Dutour's comment in *France-
Soir* is that it is yet another example of a French writer seeing
a major problem when only a minor one existed. In the years
1977–8 even some of the leading French newspapers, such as
Le Monde, were talking about a new crisis in both the SDECE
and the DST. It was true that by February 1978 a series of
events had contributed to the voicing of such a theme, but
probably it was the Abu Daoud affair which really touched
this off.

Abu Daoud had long been a member of the PLO (Palestinian
Liberation Organization), though not a particularly important
one. Though he was alleged to have been the man who plotted
the Black September gang's massacre of Israeli sportsmen at
the Olympic Games in Munich on 5 September 1972, he had
always stubbornly denied being involved in any way in this
incident. He had applied for a French visa to attend the funeral
in Paris of another Palestinian extremist, Mahmoud Saleh, who
was shot as he was shutting up his Arab bookshop, allegedly by
the Israeli Secret Service. Though Abu Daoud was still wanted
on twelve charges of complicity in murder, eleven charges of
helping to take hostages for a Palestinian extremist group and
one of helping to cause an explosion, his visa and those of two
other Palestinians were granted with unusual speed at the

French Consulate in Beirut two days after Saleh's death. He was wanted on such charges by more than one power.

All three Palestinians boarded a plane for Orly the day they got the visas, Daoud travelling on an Iraqi passport under the name of Youssef Raji Hanna. On arrival in Paris they were given accommodation by the French Foreign Ministry in a small hotel, the Résidence St Honoré, where they spent the following day making arrangements for Saleh's funeral. Daoud was reported as claiming that he was 'in France with an official delegation to see the French authorities. We wanted to speak about the assassination of Palestinians and to sort things out.'[1] If this claim had in some way been supported by the Foreign Ministry, perhaps that is the likeliest reason for the party being given official accommodation. On 7 January 1977 Daoud with other Palestinians was received at the Quai d'Orsay by Pierre Cerles, director of the Middle East Department of the French Foreign Office.

Meanwhile the DST in co-operation with the SDECE had been watching these moves and carefully monitoring all that went on. Either before or after he got his visa they soon found out that the Iraqi, Hanna, was in fact the Palestinian Daoud. There was no problem in identifying him because of his height (six feet two inches) and his photograph which was easily obtainable. When Daoud returned to his hotel DST agents were waiting for him and took him to the police station at the Rue des Saussies where he was interrogated until two o'clock in the morning. Later he was brought before a magistrate's court where he was remanded in custody in connection with a West German request for extradition.

Raymond Barre, then French Prime Minister, claimed that he was only informed of the Palestinian's arrest three hours after it happened. Undoubtedly, the DST and the SDECE (whose relations with the West Germans had greatly improved) wanted to ensure that Daoud was extradited. The DST immediately telephoned the Munich police and the West German Ministry of the Interior and an arrest warrant was issued by the Munich police for Daoud's alleged complicity in the murder of the Israeli athletes. Delay by the West German Government in endorsing the Bavarian request for extradition prevented the

DST from succeeding in their plan. In a mere twenty minutes a French Appeals Court ruled that the Germans were out of order and Daoud was released from jail.

The background to all this was that Giscard d'Estaing, the new French President, had been seeking a role as arbitrator along with President Sadat of Egypt in solving Middle Eastern problems. Behind the scenes, too, was the much respected figure of Mendès-France who had acted as a mediator at various talks involving both Arabs and Israelis. This followed the setting-up in December 1975 of the Council for Israeli-Palestinian Peace with General Matityabou Peled, professor of modern Arab literature at Tel-Aviv University, as its chairman. In all these manoeuvres the French Foreign Office was playing a considerable part and one which, on some occasions like that of the Daoud visit, conflicted with the normal processes of law and order. Meanwhile the Minister of the Interior, Michel Poniatowski, to whom the DST was responsible, was well known as being an enthusiastic supporter of Israel, a trend which to some extent went against the government's policy. Certainly the whole affair suggested that one section of French government did not know what the other was doing and brought little credit to France. It was really a minor matter, but was blown up out of all proportion by the media and, as so often in the past, the Intelligence and Security Services were blamed. In reality this was a mild incident compared with several others which have concerned French Intelligence in post-war years such as the Delouette affair, the case of Ben Barka, or even the various problems linked to the name of Dewavrin. However, that did not stop the left-wing press, or rather the 'intellectual-left-of-centre' press of Britain and France, from making it sound like a major disaster. 'How the secret service put France on the spot' was the London *Observer*'s headline to its report of the affair, while *The Guardian* made the ponderous comment that, 'A year's successful contacts in France between the Palestinian Liberation Organization and leading Israeli opposition politicians, encouraged by the Israeli government, have been imperilled by the arrest of Abu Daoud, the alleged leader of the Munich Olympic massacre.'[2]

The SDECE took a keen interest in the gradual moves towards revolution in Portugal as well as the Breton and Corsican nationalist movements. When revolution came to Portugal in 1974 there were allegations from Lisbon that the SDECE had co-operated with PIDE, the secret police created by President Salazar, in providing information on Portuguese exiles living in France. It was even alleged that the service had organized the blowing-up of the Corsican nationalist radio station on the Italian island of Elba.

In 1976 *Le Nouvel Observateur* devoted four pages to an account of how relations between the French Intelligence Services and the CIA had improved first under Pompidou and then Giscard d'Estaing. It was announced that technicians of the SDECE had attended a course at CIA headquarters in Langley, Virginia. Even Victor Marchetti, a former CIA agent and one of its author-critics, stated in 1976 that, 'In spite of some snags, relations between the SDECE and the CIA seem to be more harmonious under Valéry Giscard d'Estaing than under de Gaulle.' He added that they were 'surprisingly good now'.[3]

Certainly such co-operation led to further successes in tracking down Soviet spies. In 1974 Giscard d'Estaing personally called on the Polish Ambassador to clear out the spy ring operating from the Embassy. This followed the expulsion of two Polish diplomats allegedly caught trying to bribe a French agent in the bar of a Mistral express train. Two years later after the extreme left-wing daily newspaper founded by Jean-Paul Sartre, *Libération*, published the names, addresses and telephone numbers of forty-four Americans alleged to be 'employees or agents of the CIA', *Le Nouvel Observateur* named two Russian diplomats in Paris as chief representatives in Paris of the KGB and the GRU (Soviet military intelligence). At the same time this paper attacked *Libération* for failing to distinguish between senior and junior CIA officers, clerks and analysts, also adding that it was somewhat naïve of *Libération* to offer to publish the names of the KGB men 'if the American Embassy cares to let us have them'.[4]

Was this an astute piece of public relations by the SDECE to engage the media on its side for a while? It may well have been the case as at the same time the right-wing newspaper, *L'Aurore*, alleged that 'one of the most eminent' Soviet agents in France was the military attaché at the Soviet Embassy, who was a member of the GRU. *L'Aurore* alleged that the attaché's father had played an important role of the same kind under Stalin and that the son began his career as an agent in 1951. Between 1951 and 1953 he had been an agent in France and much later he had emerged as a key agent of General Giap in Hanoi to prepare the takeover of South Vietnam.

A London reporter of the *Daily Express* tested some of *Libération*'s claims and found that nearly all of the telephone numbers of alleged CIA agents had either been changed or were unobtainable. There was one exception: a young girl answered on a number given for one of the ten women on *Libération*'s CIA list. 'Me a spy?' she giggled. 'How exciting. So that's why everyone has been phoning me. I thought they were people trying to date me for dinner.'[5]

In July 1975 the DST revealed that the world's most wanted terrorist, Carlos Illich Ramirez Sanchez (generally known as 'the Jackal'), had planned to assassinate up to one hundred of the leading Jewish public figures in Paris, London and elsewhere, mentioning that at the top of Carlos' list was the name of Asher Ben Nathan, the Israeli Ambassador to France. The DST claimed that so carefully had Carlos plotted this attack that he had found out every detail of the Ambassador's daily movements, the make and numbers of all the Embassy cars and the names and numbers of the security guards stationed in and outside the Embassy. This information, the DST claimed, was contained in 'minutely detailed plans' found by their agents. 'If we had not discovered the existence of Carlos, the consequences are too horrible to contemplate,' said an Intelligence Services spokesman.[6]

Carlos was, of course, the Venezuelan terrorist who had received backing from the Cuban Secret Service and the Soviet KGB as well as working as controller of a range of terrorist groups including Arab, West German and other guerrillas. The son of a Venezuelan doctor, Carlos was a hard-line Communist who had been educated at the Patrice Lumumba University in the Soviet Union. After graduating in 1971 he went to Paris and was assigned to the Palestinian terrorist organization known as *Parisienne Orientale*.

French counter-intelligence officers had an extremely hard and dangerous life in this period, mainly because they had terrorists as well as spies to contend with. There was one occasion in 1975 when two agents of the DST were shot dead in a gun battle with terrorists in an apartment on the Left Bank in Paris, while a third was wounded and died later in hospital. In the apartment were found sub-machine guns, pistols, grenades, dynamite, plastic explosive, detonators, and home-made bombs. It was Carlos who was reputed to have shot the DST officers, all of whom surprisingly were unarmed. This seemed particularly strange in view of the fact that they knew Carlos was an armed terrorist, a skilled and ruthless operator and ideologically committed to all kinds of fanatical organizations.

On this occasion the DST named one of the three victims as Michel Moukarbel, a Lebanese who had agreed to collaborate with the French authorities in tracking down Carlos, even though he had been personally named in a Beirut newspaper as the founder of the self-styled 'Arab Armed Struggle Organization'. In other words Moukarbel had actually co-operated with Carlos in the past and had collected money on his behalf.

Carlos escaped quite easily after shooting the three men as – even more surprising – no police were stationed around the building to keep watch. However, apart from the extensive arms haul which was made in the apartment, the police discovered documents which led to the dismantling of the terrorist network set up by Carlos and Moukarbel. These papers revealed links between Carlos' organization and German, Japanese and Palestinian terrorists with notebooks giving details of various raids and operations planned for the future. There were also accounts of previous operations including attacks on French embassies. That night raid on the apartment in the Rue Amélie in the Seventh Arrondissement of Paris may have been costly in lives lost, but it was also highly productive.

In October 1977 a war-time Resistance hero, Georges Beaufils, then aged sixty-eight, was arrested and charged with spying for the USSR. The following year the State Security Court in

Paris sentenced him to eight years' imprisonment, finding him guilty of passing French defence documents to the USSR through agents posing as correspondents of Tass, the Soviet news agency. His name was struck off the roll of the *Légion d'Honneur*

Success by the DST was not always rewarded by the government of the day, however. Not only was this obvious by the response to the arrest of Daoud, but in the treatment of Jean Rochet, who was without doubt a highly successful chief. It was true that Rochet took the view that, in assessing the future worth of any individual or potential agent, 'once a spy for Russia, always a spy for Russia'. This was the attitude which, perhaps somewhat unfortunately, he adopted in 1972 when he banned the ageing Leopold Trepper, the former head of the Red Orchestra anti-Nazi spy network in World War II, from entering France at a time when Trepper was seeking refuge from repression in Poland. Trepper, after his return to the USSR for whom his network had operated, was imprisoned in the Lubyanka for ten years. After Stalin's death he was returned to his native Poland.

In 1972 Trepper's wife requested a visa for France, apparently to support the campaign for her husband to enter that country. At the instigation of the DST this request was turned down. Immediately a hue and cry was raised in the media with accusations against Rochet, notably an attack on him personally in *Le Monde* for slanders on a hero of the Resistance. Rochet replied to this in a letter to *Le Monde*, giving as his reasons that Trepper was engaged in espionage activities in France for the USSR dating from 1930, and that his behaviour was suspect after his arrest by the *Abwehr* in 1942 and the subsequent arrest of most of his collaborators.

As a result of this letter the Committee for the Defence of Trepper arranged for Trepper to bring a case against Rochet for defamation of character. Rochet's reply was that, with the approval of the Minister of the Interior, he had defended the DST against unjust allegations. But Rochet was not helped when the day after the trial opened there was an official announcement that he was leaving his post as Director of the DST and being transferred to the post of Prefect at Nancy.

When the trial was resumed Rochet had already left for Nancy and, though the court agreed that no libel was involved, they found 'lack of objectivity' in Rochet's letter to *Le Monde* and awarded one franc in damages to Trepper and fined Rochet 1,000 francs. It was a most unsatisfactory ending to a case which had little substance.

Another mysterious incident magnified by the media into a crisis was the murder in 1978 of Prince Jean de Broglie, a former Cabinet Minister, who had arranged contracts to supply some of the latest weapons, including strategic missiles, to various Arab countries. The affair was never satisfactorily cleared up. De Broglie had been warned by the DST that his arms dealing was, in their own words, 'upsetting a foreign power'. He had been involved with a company called Brincom, which had an office in Paris and headquarters in Luxembourg as well as representatives in West Germany and Algeria. A French judge ordered an inquiry into his relationship with Brincom and demanded that DST officers should be questioned by lawyers. Prior to this the Minister of the Interior, Poniatowski, had declared on television that a £500,000 insurance pay-off was behind the Christmas Eve murder. The suggestion was that business associates of the Prince had arranged for him to be killed so that they could benefit from the insurance policy on his life, a theory which was vigorously denied. The judge's decision caused some of the media to cast doubts on the 'official' theory of the killers' motive as expounded by Poniatowski.

So many of these incidents had only the slightest connection with the Intelligence Services that to dwell upon them would be pointless. Matters were not helped by the revelations of Marcel le Roy, the former head of *Service 7*, in a book published in December 1980 about alleged French espionage operations in the United States. Le Roy claimed that the practice of spying on America had been initiated by General de Gaulle when he ordered American diplomatic bags to be intercepted in Africa and US activities in France to be monitored. This was most unhelpful at a time when Franco-American relations in the intelligence field had improved so much, even though it referred to events that were now a matter of history.

The Bokassa diamonds scandal in 1978 did much to spoil the presidential career of Giscard d'Estaing, though it was grossly exaggerated. The truth was that Bokassa, leader of the Central African Republic, often gave industrial diamonds on special mountings to his visitors; they were never of any great value. The real scandal, if any, was that French political leaders tended to overlook the atrocities the Emperor Bokassa perpetrated as well as his alcoholism because he provided them with big game hunting. Finally the SDECE decided it was time for action when they learned that Libyan commandos in civilian clothes were being infiltrated into the Central African Republic. They flew in some 150 paratroopers who performed the remarkable feat of ousting Bokassa and putting the overthrown President David Dacko back in power without a shot being fired.

Looking back on this operation a few years later in 1986 the Comte de Marenches said the incident reinforced his argument that not only should France have a professional Intelligence Service (and he put particular emphasis on the word professional), but that inside this service there should be an Action division with its own air, sea and land troops capable of being put into action at short notice. With what seems like a nicely ironic touch of humour, the Comte said, 'Action Service is midway between sending a diplomatic note and sending an expeditionary force.'[7]

What the Conte had in mind was undoubtedly a much more disciplined and professional Action Service than the cowboy outfits which had prevailed previously.

In February 1978 there were various reports of both a crisis and a witch-hunt in the French Secret Service. *Le Monde* stated that two agents had committed suicide and that the director-general was about to resign. At that time there was no question of de Marenches resigning. As an example of what it called the malaise in the service, *Le Monde* cited the case of a high-ranking officer at the organization's Paris headquarters who, it was alleged, had been locked up and manhandled during investigation on suspicion that he was a Russian agent. According to the newspaper, the agent had been cleared of suspicion, there had been an intervention from on high on the man's behalf and a prosecution in the courts had been narrowly averted.[8]

Later it was confirmed that no fewer than three agents working for the SDECE radio-monitoring centres which eavesdrop on foreign embassies had committed suicide, one of them in Berlin, and one in Turkey, while a 38-year-old colonel who had been seconded to the service inexplicably fell to his death from the Paris–Marseille express. The Defence Ministry made no comment on the report in *Le Monde*, nor on the subsequent report of the colonel's death.

In case it should be thought that sometimes the SDECE's counter-espionage section was competing with the DST, it should be explained that in combating terrorists it was important for the SDECE to be able to pinpoint the movements of such people overseas and to warn of their impending return to French soil. In this sense the two services complemented one another.

This was a period in which both the SDECE and the DST were involved in a ceaseless war against terrorists of all kinds, and it was because of this that on many occasions interrogations had to be ruthlessly conducted, bending the normal rules of procedure. Many suspected terrorists being questioned had already been well trained in how to deceive their interrogators. Both Britain and France have found to their cost that when tackling terrorism, whether Arab, Armenian, Irish or any other variety, they are in a hopeless situation whenever they overstep the mark, however slightly. 'Shoot to kill' is the catchphrase employed to criticize the security services on many occasions, but sometimes who shoots first wins.

Early in 1980 the appointment of a senior Gendarmerie officer to head the counter-espionage section of the SDECE was assessed as being a move to end what had been dubbed in the media as witch-hunt methods. Major Jean-Michel Vernière succeeded Guy Laugère, a veteran member of the SDECE, in this post. This followed allegations of extensive telephone-tapping and 'bugging' of offices and homes.

De Marenches was sometimes attacked because he was so very successful, not only in the sphere of intelligence, but in foreign policy successes arising out of his analysis and initiative. He tried to support a cautious but intelligent policy for settling Middle Eastern problems, even though this made him many enemies. True, on occasions he was authoritarian and terse, and this led to his delivering reprimands quite frequently. One of the troubles was that, intellectually, he was far superior to his predecessors. He was always looking ahead of events and he became impatient with what he regarded as the short-sighted, short-range views of many European governments. One of his great beliefs was that the benefits in education which France had given to her former colonies and protectorates in North Africa provided the basis for close links between France – and indeed Europe as a whole – and Algeria, Morocco and Tunisia, connecting European capital and equipment with African manpower and resources.

There was, of course, during the whole period of his director-generalship the seemingly eternal problem of Colonel Gaddafi's Libya. The resignation of his deputy Colonel Alain de Gaigne-ron de Marolles in 1980 over this issue probably troubled de Marenches more than anything. A graduate of the French military academy of St Cyr and a paratroop officer, de Marolles had always been something of an expert on North African affairs even before he was appointed to head the Action Service of the SDECE. Then in 1977 he was appointed head of the most important section of the SDECE, one which in effect formulated policy from information-gathering. He was always particularly interested in maintaining French links with all of North Africa, and was anxious to take all possible steps to counter the Libyans' efforts to destabilize the situation in the Middle East. Increasingly and logically, he made it his task to pave the way for the overthrow of Gaddafi. France was not the only Western Intelligence Service to attempt to do this: the British had planned a similar operation a few years earlier, not directly using the SIS, but mercenaries who linked up with the deposed Senoussi regime and sought to return him to power through a military coup. The British plan was to land a team of volunteers on a Libyan beach from which they would proceed to a prison where some hundred or more political prisoners were held, rescue them and pave the way for a restoration of the monarchy. Unfortunately this plan misfired for a variety of reasons, one being the illness of the chosen leader at the time. The French were well aware of the British plan and some of them co-operated unofficially, not least in arrangements for the transport of arms via Douala to the Cameroons and Chad.

One French view was that the failure of the British plan put Gaddafi on the alert and so militated against any success for de Marolles' own plans. These were similar in many ways to the British plan, but involved the setting-up of a Libyan government in exile to get things moving. Undoubtedly French Intelligence had had some close co-operation with some Egyptians in these plans, for this was a time when the late President Sadat's relations with Libya were deteriorating, something which ultimately led to his assassination, indirectly if not directly. At the root of all this was the fact that Libya had been intervening secretly in various African and Middle Eastern states, usually by funding movements which followed Libya's foreign policies.

Leakages of secret information had not helped de Marolles as over the years they had resulted in unhelpful publicity in newspapers around the world. Surprisingly, some of these leakages came through agents of Israel's Secret Service which certainly had more reason to dislike Gaddafi than de Marolles. *Le Monde* stated that there had been 'disagreement in the SDECE over policy in North and Black Africa, leading to technical mistakes', and added that in 1977 the Israeli Secret Service had attacked de Marolles for allegedly helping Egypt's military co-ordination in its border skirmishes with Libya.[9]

Ultimately there was a hasty attempt to bring things in Libya to what was hoped would be a swift victory. SDECE agents attempted to worsen relations between Paris and Tripoli by spreading stories through French media contacts that a Libyan armoured column was advancing on the Chadian capital of N'Djamena, and that the President of Chad, Goukuni Oueddei, had either fled or been killed. For a while these reports were believed, even, it is thought, at the Elysée Palace, until envoys and journalists arrived in Chad and reported otherwise. There had also been an incident in August 1980 when Libyan troops rebelled in Tobruk, but this revolt was promptly put down.

It was partly as a result of disagreements within the SDECE, unwanted publicity and the failure of the Libyan coup to take place that Colonel de Marolles resigned from the service in September 1980. He was the fifth person to head his department while de Marenches was director-general of the SDECE. It was a bitter disappointment to him that his plans for a Libyan government in exile linked to a popular rising in Benghazi and Tobruk had failed.

Nevertheless 1980 provided some considerable successes for the Intelligence Services, notably the luring into a trap of a former head of the East German air force, General Heinz Bernhardt Zorn, who in World War II had been a Luftwaffe pilot. The general, who had retired three years earlier, visited France as a tourist and he was shadowed from the moment he arrived. When he was arrested and charged with spying in September 1980, he was apparently carrying secret material on French tanks and anti-tank weapons.

Earlier in the year DST officers caught a Soviet consular official in Marseille, Gennadi Travkov, as he was taking delivery of defence secrets concerning the Mirage 2000 combat aircraft. This was the plane scheduled to replace the Mirage 3 fighter of the French Air Force. Four prototypes of this plane were undergoing trials at Istres, near Marseille. It was reported that he had attempted to infiltrate Snias, the aircraft construction firm. Shortly afterwards Travkov was recalled to Moscow. A month later yet another Soviet consular official in Marseille, Viatcheslav Frolov, suddenly left France for Russia after being questioned by the DST. Once again the DST claimed to have found secret documents in the possession of a consular official.[10]

If there had been several alleged mishaps in French Intelligence in this period, there had certainly been many successes. When analysed, as has been seen, the alleged mishaps, crises and scandals amount to very little, while the positive gains are considerable. Sometimes the mention of the word crisis has been cleverly used by French Intelligence for making changes in their own way, while often it has been merely an attempt by politicians, generals and others to gain publicity.

24
A Change of Name

What's in a name? That which we call a rose by any other name would smell as sweet.

William Shakespeare

When François Mitterand became President of France in 1981, the SDECE was suffering badly from the various publicized incidents mentioned in the previous chapter. The new President was besieged by demands not only from the extreme left wing, but also from those in the centre, who wanted the SDECE to be totally disbanded. One factor behind these demands was the accusation of extensive telephone-tapping at a centre near Les Invalides. This was particularly condemned by the new Minister of the Interior, Gaston Deferre, who brought in a new government edict banning such activities unless national security was involved. Deferre declared that any violation of this edict would be severely punished.

There was some panic within the SDECE when the Socialists came to power and the Action Division of the service was said to have burned many, if not all, of its papers. The reports about this which subsequently circulated were probably grossly exaggerated. Although it is true the Action Service took such steps, one treats with some suspicion the story (probably circulated as a cover) that the outgoing Minister of the Interior, Christian Bonnet, ordered the destruction of thousands of files on left-wingers and that the SDECE also emptied their archives. Nonetheless, undoubtedly in this period some files were 'lost'.

De Marenches resigned within twenty-four hours of Mitterand's election triumph and some others resigned in sympathy with him. There was no doubt that within the service he was highly regarded. There was an oblique tribute to him published in the *Sunday Times* from its Paris correspondent: ' "Porthos" has left the Swimming Pool. This cryptic message sent *frissons* of alarm around the world's spy centres when the news broke. To those in the know it could only mean one thing: the mastermind of some of France's most extraordinary intelligence coups, Count Alexandre de Marenches, had left the French Secret Service.'[1]

Certainly his departure was regretted by many among both the American and British Intelligence Services, but he was also highly regarded elsewhere. But from the viewpoint of the new presidency there was the fact, indisputable to those in the know, that under the presidency of Giscard d'Estaing keeping a watch on the President's opponents had been to some extent a feature of SDECE surveillance. The word opponents covered in the main the extreme left wing, the Communists and some trade unions. It was even suggested that Mitterand himself had been spied upon by the Intelligence Services over a period of many years. His telephone had been tapped and his apartment bugged and there was supposed to be a dossier numbered 403 which contained a file on him.

However, fortunately for the SDECE, the new President was a realist and, though he appreciated that some of the criticisms may have been justified, he showed no signs of giving way to the more extreme demands for disbanding the SDECE, which were totally unrealistic in view of the vastly improved record of the service. Instead he compromised by giving it a change of name, and in April 1982 the SDECE became the DGSE (*Direction Générale de la Sécurité Extérieure*). In this new name was one subtle change: the reference to *Contre-Espionage* was dropped in deference to the DST. There had, of course, been clashes between the SDECE and the DST over internal counter-espionage and there was a strongly held view, especially among Socialists, that only the DST should handle this. However, the change of name could never alter the fact that the DGSE must still pay some attention to counter-espionage internally, if only on the strength of information it obtained from overseas. The sensible point that was made was that the service should harmonize much more closely with the DST.

The new head of the service was Pierre Marion, an Air France executive, the idea being that he should introduce management techniques into the service. Any such idea was almost bound to be a failure in an intelligence organization. No doubt Mitterand thought this idea would work and that it would harmonize with his own theories of how a modern, disciplined intelligence service should operate. Marion was an absolute outsider as far as the hierarchy of intelligence was concerned, but he was a friend of the new Defence Minister, Charles Hernu, and had also served in the Aerospace Consortium under the President's brother, General Jacques Mitterand. Prior to that he had spent nearly thirty years with Air France. At one time he had been head of Paris airports. Latterly he had been controlling operations in the Pacific and at Tokyo, where he had been a part-time agent.

Marion's brief was to carry out a thorough reorganization. This, and the renaming of the SDECE, was Mitterand's answer to those of his supporters who wanted to see the service suppressed. Some fifty agents were prematurely retired and orders were that the Action Division was to be one of the first casualties. This Action Division, or Military Security Unit (it was given so many names that one suspects it was always being reborn in some new guise), had been accused in the past of unauthorized surveillance of left-wingers and suspected subversives. When set up in 1961 its chief aim was to prevent the theft of French military secrets and to check attempts by foreign powers to recruit French servicemen as spies. From 1982 onwards orders from the President and the new Minister of Defence were that surveillance should be left to the DST and that in place of the former Action Division there should be a pool of air support commandos and some naval personnel. At the same time Gaston Deferre, the new Minister of the Interior, let it be known that he would appreciate counter-espionage officers paying rather more attention to right-wing extremists than to left-wingers. Here he was undoubtedly pointing towards not merely former members of the OAS ('Algeria for the French') but those of the SAC (*Service d'Action Commune*) founded by Pierre Debizet when de Gaulle returned to power and which had, on occasions, linked up with the old SDECE.

Its original role had been to combat the OAS underground, but very soon it had become a recruiting organization for gangsters. Latterly the SAC had been desperately trying to eliminate its criminal members.

Gaston Deferre had for many years been Mayor of Marseille: that city was his power base. One of his first acts upon becoming Minister of the Interior was to send a team of police officers from Paris to Marseille to investigate suspected links between the SAC and the Marseille police. Nobody knew better than Deferre that there had always been a clandestine relationship between politicians and the underworld in this Mediterranean port. Within a few days of the dispatch of the Parisian police team to Marseille six members of the family of a local police inspector named Massie, including the inspector himself, were murdered in the village of Auriol just outside the port.

When, shortly afterwards, six men were arrested for the murder, it transpired that they were all SAC members, and that Massie had also been a former regional head of SAC. It looked very much as though, to please the new Minister of the Interior, Inspector Massie had provided some information against his old SAC colleagues. They suspected him and the massacre was the outcome.

While Marion may have introduced some improvements into the service, he did not succeed in taming the Action Division or allied sections. Generally, his term of office was not very successful. A dour man, almost the opposite of de Marenches, he was not popular with his subordinates and latterly his relations with the new President also became strained. Their relationship may have foundered because Marion decided the DGSE should have an important role to play in counter-espionage and that all should not be left to the DST. This was a lesson he learned fairly quickly and, despite the embargo on the DGSE mounting such operations, he pleaded that his service should at least play a role in catching terrorists. He also claimed that he did not get the co-operation he desired from the DST. In 1986, four years after he resigned from the DGSE, he told the weekly news magazine *Le Nouvel Observateur* that his men in the DGSE had discovered that bombs and guns were being brought into the country in diplomatic bags while the terrorists who were going to use them would arrive by plane and train. 'During that period,' he declared, 'we identified six [terrorist] contacts in Paris. I proposed to M. Mitterand that my service should eliminate them physically. The President refused.' Other terrorist contacts were identified outside France and again the 'elimination' process was refused.

While in office, Marion used his managerial skills to improve the gathering of scientific and economic intelligence and he made some useful new appointments. He also resisted attempts to close down the organization known as GEPAN (*Groupe d'Études des Phénomènes Aerospatiaux Non-Identifiées*). This was the organization which, with government backing, systematically compiled reports on unidentified flying objects. GEPAN was established in 1977 by the CNES (*Centre Nationale d'Étude Spatiale*), which is the French equivalent of the USA's National Aeronautics and Space Administration (NASA). It was reported at the time that President Giscard d'Estaing took a personal interest in it. At that time GEPAN had a committee of seven scientists and was closely associated with the Gendarmerie and, to a limited extent, with the Intelligence Services.

GEPAN confined itself to the study solely of French UFO reports, most of them passed to it through the Gendarmerie who naturally first of all sifted out the ridiculous and totally improbable and only presented those which seemed worthy of further examination. By 1979 it was reported that GEPAN 'has received 800 sighting reports so far, and the Gendarmerie (which does a very efficient job of investigating reports) passes twenty a month on average to GEPAN for further study'.[2]

At this time France was apparently the only country apart from America's Center for UFO Studies which received UFO reports, though this, of course, did not mean that other nations were not making their own investigations, even if these were conducted covertly. Nevertheless GEPAN had its opponents and more than once it was on the verge of being disbanded, presumably because some saw it as a waste of time. Doubtless because of his lengthy association with airlines and personal knowledge of air pilots who claimed to have seen and even

chased unidentified flying objects, Marion fought hard for the
retention of this service, fully backing the appointment of a
new director in Alain Esterle, an aeronautical engineer with a
doctorate in applied mathematics. He won the support of the
new Defence Minister, Charles Hernu, for the continuation of
GEPAN, and since then all findings of this organization have
been passed on to what is euphemistically called 'the military'.
There is obviously a certain amount of hush-hush policy concerning GEPAN, probably as much to avoid the criticism of
those who denounce all UFO investigation as the work of
cranks as on the grounds of national security. It is interesting
to note that Jean-Jacques Velasco, head of GEPAN, stated in
1985 that GEPAN had collaborated with the Gendarmerie 'to
log about 1,600 UFO reports and that while the majority have
been explained as natural phenomena or aircraft . . . as many
as 38 per cent do not fall into this category'.[3]

In the early stages of GEPAN one reason put forward for its
creation was that 'it was necessary to tranquillize public opinion
concerning the UFO phenomenon, and it was in this spirit that
GEPAN was created'.[4] Possibly, but somehow this sounds an
improbable excuse for so highly intelligent a race as the French.
In any event this viewpoint seems to have been contradicted by
the fact that there is far more secrecy today on GEPAN findings
than there was in the past.

GEPAN distributed 15,000 of its manuals to police stations
all over France for guidance on ufology, and this did result in
the Gendarmerie exposing two hoaxes. On the other hand
there was a case in 1983 when even GEPAN scientists were
totally baffled. A farm worker in the Gard region of Southern
France reported that he had heard a slight whistling sound and,
looking up, saw 'a strange machine coming down very fast. It
was not spinning and there were no flames or smoke . . . After
hitting the ground it took off almost immediately at a tremendous speed.'[5]

GEPAN scientists investigating this report found that plant
life had mysteriously changed in character in the vicinity of this
incident. Analyses in four separate laboratories produced surprising results. Chlorophyll and other substances in the plants
had been reduced by between 30 and 50 per cent, while an

analysis of soil samples indicated that an object of heavy weight had scraped along the ground, having both thermal and mechanical effect, and leaving a residue of what appeared to be combustion. Alain Esterle declared that: 'For the first time we found a combination of factors which leads us to accept that something similar to what the eyewitness described actually did happen.'[6]

Le Bon et Vrai has his own views on the need to keep watch on ufology:

It isn't so much whether or not UFOs exist, as what other powers think about the subject and whether they exploit the phenomenon. What was brought home to us in French Intelligence was the keen interest in both the USA and the USSR on the subject. Not only on the subject of UFOs, but all manner of experiments which come under the heading of the paranormal. Maybe some other powers, notably the Russians, use disinformation on this subject and hope thereby either to frighten us or waste our time in chasing lunatic reports. I have an open mind on the subject myself, but one must take some notice of Professor Felix Zigel of the Moscow Aviation Institute when he says that 'of all the offered hypotheses the most probable is that the UFO is an extra-terrestrial probe'. He also added that it was a very hard nut to crack.

The last days of Marion's regime at the DGSE were marked by confusion and delay in getting vital reports from the Middle East, especially the Lebanon. In addition the service was suffering from the failure of coups aimed indirectly at Libya, though launched in Chad and the Central African Republic. On one occasion the DGSE was unable to provide information about reported coups because its agents were away for the weekend and out of touch. Confusion also occurred because information held by SDECE agents, some of whom had been sacked, was kept back from the DGSE. For example, under Marion, the DGSE supported Goukuni Oueddei, the Chad President, while not having been informed that his rival Hissène Habré had recently been resupplied in an operation involving the old SDECE, the CIA and the Egyptian Intelligence Service.

Marion was succeeded in 1982 by Vice-Admiral Pierre Lacoste, an unusual choice, as never before in France had a naval officer been in charge of the Intelligence Service. Lacoste had graduated from the *École Navale* of Casablanca in 1943, after having been interned for some months in Spain while trying to join the Free French Forces. He had served for a long while in the Far East and later at Brest and Toulon. In 1955 he was promoted to a senior staff officer's post in Paris, returning to sea two years later to the command of the *Jean Bart*. In 1959 he attended a course at the naval war school in Paris, usually a signal that an officer is expected to rise to one of the highest offices in the French Navy. Various promotions followed until in 1975 he was attached to the office of the then Defence Minister, Yvon Bourges, having previously taken command at the *École Supérieure de Guerre Navale*. Three years later the admiral became chief of the military cabinet of the Prime Minister, Raymond Barre. His appointment as head of the DGSE was, of course, welcomed by those members of the service who had served in the armed forces.

It was bruited around at the time, not only in Paris, but in some overseas capitals as well, that the real reason for the appointment of Vice-Admiral Lacoste was that his contacts with foreign service officers could help in obtaining contracts for the sale of French military and naval equipment. No doubt he could have helped in this direction, but it is highly improbable that this was a major reason for his appointment. Others said it was simply an attempt to placate the armed forces, but the real answer was that there was so much internal friction within the service that a change was almost unavoidable. Probably it was felt that this was the right moment to make changes at the head of both services, the DST as well as the DGSE, as on one November day in 1982 *France-Soir* announced '*c'est une double bombe*', giving the names of the new heads of the DGSE and the DST. The DST's new head was Yves-Louis Bonnet, Prefect of Mayotte, a tiny French island in the Indian Ocean.[7] However, although the appointment of Bonnet was to prove a great success, the DGSE was to remain a major problem. The appointment of Vice-Admiral Lacoste may have pleased the military officers in the service, but it has now become increasingly clear that control of an intelligence service (especially in modern times) by a senior officer of the armed forces is not the answer. Britain learned this lesson after the disastrous regime of Major-General Sinclair in the early post-war years, but France was rather slower in coming to terms with it. The Comte de Marenches was, of course, an exception: he was not only a soldier, but a thinker and a cosmopolitan with a feeling for the intricacies of international politics. But, generally speaking, the truth is that in the DGSE the bright civilians, unhampered by any traditional disciplinary rules, usually got the right answers, though their methods were not always orthodox. The military officers never managed to control these people, while they also failed to keep a tight grasp on their own 'action services'.

While the DST seemed to have improved its methods of recruitment, the DGSE had come up against difficulties. Attempts to attract civilians with scientific, linguistic and economic skills to the DGSE through scholarships and advertisements in *Figaro* did not succeed. The obstacle all along was not so much that the pay was not particularly encouraging, but the feeling that the service was dominated by the military and that they were the people who got promotion. The word went round Paris when there was an attempt to recruit members of the prestigious *École Nationale d'Administration* that 'the graduate of the ENA does not want to be a spook [spy]'. Another problem was that most of the military officers of the DGSE were uninterested in economic and more modern forms of espionage. De Marenches and even Marion had done their best to combat this trend, but there was still a long way to go.

While there may be blunders, mishandling of situations, and fairly frequent scandals in French Intelligence, there is the indisputable fact that quietly, often unnoticed, the service is all the time improving in a variety of directions. And, as will be seen in the next chapter, whatever shortcomings the DGSE might have been suffering from at this time, these were more than made up for by the successes of the DST.

Yves Bonnet and His DST Triumphs

The tiny island of Mayotte hardly seemed to provide a good training ground for the head of one of the world's most efficient counter-espionage services.
French media comment on Bonnet's appointment as head of the DST

At first impression the appointment of Yves Louis Bonnet as the new head of the DST service seemed an extraordinary decision, taking into account that his previous post had been that of Prefect of such a faraway island. The first explanation put forward was that this marked a return to a tradition that the DST should always be headed by a Prefect: there had only been two chiefs of the service who had not come into this category previously, Roger Wybot in the 1950s and Marcel Chalet in the late 1970s. In fact Bonnet's experience covered far more than his post as chief commissioner of police in Mayotte. He had graduated from the Institute of Political Studies in Paris and had served in the police since 1958. He had previously been commissioner in Manche in 1963, and French Guiana in 1966. In 1971 he was detached from his usual duties to become a counsellor at the Ministry of the Interior, where he undoubtedly made a name for himself as an efficient administrator. Then in 1974 he was appointed Prefect in Arles for a brief period.

By 1982 Marcel Chalet, the head of the DST, had reached the age limit of sixty, so his departure was not a great surprise. He was an astute counter-espionage chief who understood remarkably well the workings of other counter-espionage services. Chalet probably knew more about the workings of Britain's MI5 than did some senior members of that service. One excuse given for why no senior member of the DST could have been appointed in Chalet's place was that out of three possible choices one was too old, another too ill, and the third too young! The probability was that the government felt on safer ground with a Prefect.

Fortunately for Bonnet he took over a first-class service that had improved enormously over the previous decade under two such outstanding chiefs as Wybot and Chalet. Not only had the DST relentlessly and efficiently tracked down one Soviet spy after another, but it had also made a point of recruiting particularly talented men to the service. There was at last a demand for people of higher education. The computerized dossiers and filing system of the DST were already the envy of many other security services. When Bonnet arrived he had at his disposal computer files on some 30,000 terrorist suspects readily available for instant action at frontier posts, ports and airports. The DST not only fulfilled a role equal to that of Britain's MI5 and the Special Branch of the Metropolitan Police combined, but also received copious information from the French police service, the *Renseignements Généraux*, which keeps millions of files on private citizens.

The DST's speedy mastery of the use of computers had given it a considerable advantage over most other counter-espionage services in the world. French logic and a natural demand for quick results, combined with the importance attached to computer science by DST executives, had allowed the French to master this subject better than most nations, the Japanese excepted. The DST has used the new techniques to extend its knowledge in a variety of ways, especially in spotting the smuggling of savings out of France and any illegal deals which might be linked to espionage from overseas. The Customs Investigation Unit linked up with the Defence Ministry's computer to probe into the secrets of various Swiss banks. Thus in 1984 the computer revealed the names of several thousand Swiss bank account holders, who may have been using these accounts to hide illicit funds, and a round-up of such people was made. This struck a devastating blow at Swiss banking's highly valued anonymity. In other words, by skilful use of computers the DST claimed to have cracked the secret codes of the *Union de Banque Suisse* and other Swiss banks. As well as this, in an attempt to check any illegal flow of capital from France to Switzerland, agents posing as tourists were used to look for currency smugglers.

A special operation entitled BUS (allegedly an anagram of UBS – *Union de Banque Suisse*) was launched late in 1982 after agents who raided an apartment in Nice discovered a print-out listing the names of a number of French businessmen with numbered Swiss bank accounts and the sums in these accounts. This information was all in code, but the authorities were helped when yet another list came into their hands. There was co-operation between customs, DST and the Army in trying to crack the code. But eventually, with the help of the Defence Ministry's own computer, the lists were fed into Eureka, as the computer was named, and some three hundred names were obtained. It resulted in an instant crackdown on holders of Swiss bank accounts in all parts of France.

Despite these successes, however, there was some criticism on the grounds that French governmental computers could also be infiltrated by outsiders and even exploited. *Le Canard Enchaîné* claimed that it learned some of the secrets of France's nuclear testing area in the Pacific and details of a laser project when it broke into the Government computer information bank with a home computer terminal. The newspaper asserted that this operation was 'as easy as entering a public park'. Responsibly, however, the newspaper itself censored most of the information it had gleaned in this way.[1]

Two years later three young students admitted that they were the pirates who broke into one of France's top secret data banks. The break-in came over an Easter weekend at the *École Polytechnique* where a huge Cray-One computer was based.

It was under Yves Bonnet that the DST achieved some of its greatest triumphs in tracking down and exposing enemy agents inside France. From the very start of his term of office Bonnet had acquired a reputation for tracking down Lebanese, Iranian and Armenian extremists. Then he revealed that the chief KGB 'resident' director in France was one Vladislav Vlasovitch Nitchkov, and it was his dossier on Soviet industrial espionage which forced President Mitterand to take action.

Bonnet was largely responsible for the expulsion of forty-seven Russian diplomats in April 1983. Shortly before this five Frenchmen suspected of having passed secrets to Russia were arrested by intelligence officers, though this was kept secret until after 5 April, when it was officially announced that forty-seven Soviet officials, forty of them diplomats, had been expelled from the country – an almost unprecedented step for France to take. The Ministry of the Interior issued a statement saying:

Counter-espionage operations conducted for some time by the DST uncovered the systematic pursuit on the national territory by a number of agents of the secret services of the USSR of scientific, technical and technological intelligence, particularly in the military sphere. The multiplicity and gravity of the acts undertaken on behalf of this foreign power by agents mostly benefiting from diplomatic status justifies the departure of the persons concerned.

Neither de Gaulle, Pompidou, nor Giscard d'Estaing had ever made such a drastic move against the Soviet Union, and it is some considerable tribute to the promptness of Mitterand's decision that he unhesitatingly made it despite the fact that there were four Communists in his government. The expelled Russians were almost immediately taken to the airport in two buses and six mini-buses. They included Nikolai Chetverikov, the First Secretary at the Soviet Embassy, three diplomats working at UNESCO and the head of the Russian Tass news agency in Paris, Oleg Chirikov.

Of the five Frenchmen who had been arrested, three were released after questioning, but two were kept in custody and charged with working for a foreign power. One of the two held prisoner was an engineer and inventor who had been caught red-handed as he was passing important secrets in the Bois d'Arcy on the outskirts of Paris to a Soviet contact man. These arrests did not lead directly to the expulsion of the Russians, but they were linked to the whole affair.

President Mitterand, on the eve of a visit to Switzerland in 1983, when interviewed by Swiss television, said: 'It is normal that when a country discovers illegal activities being carried out on its territory, it reacts. That should surprise no one. It is not a special act of hostility towards the country in question . . . My relations with the Soviet Union will be excellent the day that both of us understand that mutual respect is the best of international law.'[2]

The Soviet leader, Yuri Andropov, replied in a mildly conciliatory tone, 'I do not wish to blame the French Socialists, let alone the Communists, for this provocation against the Soviet people,' he declared, but added that in his view, 'Behind the decision of the French government, there were forces interested in damaging the good relations between France and the Soviet Union.'

Though it was the DST who took most of the credit for the unmasking of the Soviet spies who were expelled, it is almost certain that the DGSE played an important role in providing information which led up to this. Indeed, it was probably the combined weight of DST and DGSE intelligence which forced Mitterand's hand. Thierry Wolton, a journalist on *Le Point*, spent more than two years researching the story behind the expulsion of the Russians, believing that Mitterand's action was so unprecedented for a French goverment that there must be something unusual behind it. In 1986 he claimed to have discovered the existence of a French mole at the heart of the KGB code-named Farewell – an unusual code-name, surely, for anyone with links to French Intelligence, though the word itself is a nicely ironic touch for a disillusioned KGB operator. Farewell, it was alleged, was the person most responsible for the expulsion of Soviet spies in 1983, and, according to Wolton (backed by confirmation from one other source), he passed about 4,000 top secret documents to the DST between early 1981 and November 1982, when he 'disappeared'.[3]

Farewell was allegedly introduced to the DST when a Frenchman (possibly an 'honourable correspondent') walked into the DST offices in the early part of 1981, carrying two letters which he said 'a Soviet friend high up in the Russian civil service' had given him. In the letters the Russian claimed to have served in the Soviet Embassy in Paris in the 1960s and that he would like to be of service to France. He was said to be a top officer serving in Department T of the KGB's First

Directorate. This department covers scientific and technical intelligence collection as well as indulging in some clandestine operations.

Farewell had apparently made contact with this French friend while the latter had been temporarily resident in Moscow in 1981 and he had offered to provide intelligence. This proved to be a highly successful operation efficiently directed by Raymond Nort, chief of DST's Soviet section. It was later reported that Farewell had been tried for murder and executed. In 1981, according to DGSE sources, a senior KGB officer was convicted of the murder of a policeman, and it was later confirmed that this man was Farewell.

Thierry Wolton has certainly alerted not only his own country, but others as well to the dangers of the Soviet quest for advanced technology which their own systems lack. For example, the French are now much more aware of the importance and implications of the US Strategic Defense Initiative, not only because of its implications for a revolutionary defensive system, but for other technological advances which they think it may bring. But behind all this one suspects there is rather more than just the story of Farewell. *Le Bon et Vrai*'s comment is that:

There is never one, but very many passages to the truth. Never in any worthwhile intelligence service would one lone informer's story be accepted today, least of all on the basis of an 'honourable correspondent' who made such an introduction. Not that in any way I am playing this down: it shows the value of such informants. But you can be assured that the vital part of this story lay in the checks made on Farewell's information. French Intelligence has more contacts in the Soviet Union than you would think. Much work was done on Farewell's material and checks were made with both the Americans and the British on all this. The picture we got was an inside view of how the Russian Industrial Commission in co-operation with the GRU and the KGB acquired industrial and high technology secrets. If you want evidence pointing in this direction, in October 1985 there was a report from Washington that a French double-agent in the KGB had handed over details of Operation Fagin, a brilliantly successful Soviet spy school which trains agents to steal Western defence secrets. This news came from the Pentagon and you can take it that this double-agent was the same man as Farewell. France did the whole Western world a good turn in this case and it resulted in demands by the USA and

Britain for stricter enforcement and monitoring of the COCOM [Co-ordinating Committee for Export Control] controls, as Farewell was able to reveal how Russia had been getting away with all manner of illegal acquisitions of high-tech and other vital goods. Similarly, you British have been able to make a very detailed analysis of Farewell's reports.

The Comte de Marenches' personal comments on Farewell are interesting in view of the allegations from time to time that the SDECE and the DST did not always co-operate fully. While praising Rochet, he commented in 1986 that, 'As head of the SDECE, I knew nothing whatever about him [Farewell]. In fact, I had never heard of him until people started talking about the book. Some commentators found it very curious that the head of the SDECE was not aware that other French services had a mole at their disposal, but such compartmentalization was accepted practice among the Secret Services of France that serve the state.'[4]

Another interesting case for Bonnet and the DST was that of Colonel Z. This was a sequel arising out of the Romanian Connection which the DST had first unearthed back in the late 1960s during their drive against Soviet agents. Of all the countries in the Eastern bloc it had been Romania which again and again over the previous twenty years had been caught spying inside France. But it was in 1982 that the Franco-Romanian connection really hit the headlines with one of the most puzzling espionage stories of recent times. Both the DGSE and the DST were already fully alert to the problem of Romanian espionage. But it was the DST with their recently developed talent for getting information from other territories which can rightly claim credit for the series of coups which followed, the most important of which was this case concerning the mysterious Colonel Z.

Colonel Z's real name was Matei Haiducu. He held the rank of Lieutenant-Colonel in the Romanian *Securitate*: in other words he was an investigative agent of the Intelligence Service. For some eight years prior to 1982 he had worked as an undercover agent for AMRI, *Applications Mécaniques et Robineterie Industrielle*, a French company specializing in the manufacture of valves and turbine blades for nuclear power plants.

Without doubt he had passed back to Bucharest many of France's vital secrets, and, of course, all this intelligence was passed on to Moscow. Maybe he was so efficient in passing on the right kind of information that the Romanians began to regard him as a super-spy. Yet he was not all that clever. Though he had graduated from the Bucharest Academy of Economic Sciences, he was not highly regarded by AMRI, who were planning to sack him. He was a fast spender and even boasted about this. He loved to be seen around with celebrities such as the Romanian tennis player, Ilie Nastase.

Up to 1982 he had had the best of all worlds, with steady promotion and increases in salary. Then in February 1982 he was ordered back to Bucharest. There he was suddenly faced with the kind of tasks which took him away from straightforward espionage to much more unpleasant missions. It would seem that this change was sprung upon him without any warning or any real understanding of the psychological make-up of the man. He was told that his next mission was authorized by no less a person than the Romanian President himself, Ceaucescu. He was to return to Paris to kill two well-known Romanian dissidents who had been given political asylum by the French.

Unquestionably the Romanians had picked the wrong man for this kind of job, probably because they thought he loved the money he was getting so much. He did, but they had failed to discover that he also had a conscience and that this told him he should not kill his own countrymen. One man he was told to kill was the dissident writer, Virgil Tanase, who had enraged President Ceaucescu by writing an article for a French magazine which attacked the President as 'King Nicolae the First of the Communists' for his 'court of two hundred relations appointed to high State posts, and his wife, "Queen Helene", for her luxurious tastes and vulgarity'. The other man selected for assassination by Matei Haiducu was another Romanian writer, Paul Goma, who had exposed the political repression and torture used by the Romanian state in his book, *The Dogs of War*.

Haiducu was appalled by such instructions and, though he had accepted espionage as a job he was prepared to do, he was totally opposed to turning himself into a killer as well. As a result, when he returned to Paris in April 1982 he called in at the DST offices and handed in to the guard at the door a piece of paper upon which was written the single word *Securitate*. This was enough to get him admitted at once to a senior officer.

Haiducu lost no time in making the point that, though a spy, he was not a killer and that his masters had given him two months in which to kill Tanase and Goma. He then took out of his pocket a fountain pen which was filled with what was supposed to be an untraceable poison. The DST were immediately impressed because they knew that there had been various other attempts against dissident Romanians in France, including not merely threats to kill, but also the actual stabbing of a Romanian journalist the previous year.

The DST's usual reaction to an approach such as Haiducu's would have been to arrange for his immediate defection and safety. But in Haiducu's case this was not easy because his wife and children were still in Bucharest, and he knew full well that this was a prime reason for the Romanians giving him this appalling mission: his family would be held as hostages.

However, the DST handled this case with superb efficiency and imagination. They worked out a plan which was calculated not only to safeguard the colonel and his family, but the two men under sentence of death from assassination as well. Haiducu was told to return to Bucharest on the pretext that he wanted to clarify certain details in his assignment for the assassinations, and arrange for his family to take a holiday in the West. At the same time he was enrolled as an agent of the DST, then controlled by Marcel Chalet who, to ensure his own position in this very tricky affair, obtained the personal permission for it from the Minister of the Interior, then Gaston Deferre. The latter referred the proposal back to President Mitterand, who also approved it. It was then that Haiducu was given the code-name Colonel Z.

When Haiducu returned to Paris he immediately came back under the control of the DST. The French were certain that the Romanians would keep close watch on Haiducu and ensure that he carried out his mission to kill the two dissidents. The

French were under no illusions on this score and quite certain that Haiducu would be shadowed at all vital moments.

In May 1982 Haiducu, posing as an autograph hunter, was invited to a dinner in Paris at which Goma was the guest of honour. Haiducu, having taken with him his fountain pen, furtively pumped its deadly contents into the glass from which Goma had been drinking. This was all done just in case another Romanian agent was there to see that Haiducu carried out his assignment. But, to make sure that no harm came to Goma, a DST agent cunningly knocked the glass to the floor, giving the impression of an accident.

A report went back to Bucharest that Haiducu had carried out his assignment efficiently and without being detected, but that an accident had saved Goma's life. Colonel Z's reputation was maintained. Indeed, it was enhanced even more when on 20 May 1982 Virgil Tanase, his other target, was seized in a Paris park, and forced into a car which swiftly sped away before anyone had taken its number. The story of this incident was swiftly leaked to the press and it was immediately assumed that Tanase had been kidnapped. Indeed, there was a tone of outrage in the press reports that a man who had recently been made a French citizen could be kidnapped and whisked away, presumably by Romanian agents. Even President Mitterand expressed his concern about the affair and not only promised to investigate, but to cancel a forthcoming visit to Romania.

By this time, the Romanians had assumed that, having failed to kill Goma with the poison-filled fountain pen, their man had decided on other tactics to eliminate Tanase. He was rewarded with one of his country's highest orders and at the same time his family were given permission to join him for a holiday in the West.

The mastermind behind this cunning plot was the gregarious but highly efficient head of the DST, Marcel Chalet, who had set up a team of five Eastern European specialists to advise on the whole project so that Bucharest could be convinced that Haiducu had really tried to carry out his mission. But behind all this was an attempt at an even more spectacular coup, the luring over to France of Romania's Intelligence chief, General Nicolae Plesita.

This plan was ruined as far as can be seen by leakages to the media from inside the DST, which resulted in Bucharest slowly realizing from reports in the French press that all was not as it seemed to be. Tanase's kidnapping had, of course, been carefully conducted by the French Secret Service and he had been hidden away in a farmhouse in Brittany. His wife was told the truth about what was going on and she gallantly played her part by reporting Tanase as missing and giving details of the brutality of the Romanian Secret Service and their tactics. The timing of these tactics could hardly have been better from the French viewpoint. Almost immediately there was a purge of some two hundred and fifty officials of the Romanian Communist Party and an explanation from the President, Ceaucescu, that a transcendental meditation sect had infiltrated the party with the goal of 'overthrowing his regime, taking Romania out of the Warsaw Pact and achieving world domination'.[5] An unlikely possibility, but that is how it was presented to the people.

Then in September 1982 news of the phoney kidnapping was leaked to at least two French papers. Jean-François Bizot, director of the monthly magazine, *Actuel*, and Bernard Poulet, of *Le Matin*, said in separate television interviews that Tanase was alive and well under police protection somewhere in France. 'An extremely complex operation by the French counter-espionage services resulted in the failure of the assassination of Virgil Tanase,' said Bizot.[6]

Almost immediately a press conference was arranged and Tanase emerged after being in hiding for three months. Alongside him was the bearded figure of Haiducu who was referred to only as Colonel Z. He admitted that he had been sent to France by the Romanian *Securitate* to kill Tanase.

Armed guards attached to the DST kept watch while the press conference took place. To see the nominated killer and his nominated victim sitting together and answering questions was a rare enough spectacle in itself. Tanase described how his 'kidnapping' had been organized by the DST. On 20 May he had gone to a rendezvous in the Luxembourg Gardens and it had been arranged that witnesses should see him being bundled into a car, while his wife complained to the police that he had been kidnapped. Both Tanase and Colonel Z revealed that President Mitterand had been personally involved in this fake kidnapping and that he had been aware of what was going on since April.[7]

One of the main reasons why the DST welcomed Haiducu's approach so readily was that they had long been concerned about the presence of Romanian hit-men in France. There had been reports of a mysterious Romanian carrying a suitcase said to contain radioactive material which could be beamed at exiled Romanians who were opponents of the regime. When a Radio Free Europe broadcaster died mysteriously after the visit of a man said to be carrying such a suitcase, this caused the DST to step up their watch on visitors from Romania. There had been other attempts against the lives of outspoken Romanian exiles. In February 1981 Goma had received a parcel at his Paris apartment containing two volumes of Khrushchev's memoirs: the books were wired to explosives and a police bomb disposal officer had been hurt when the package exploded. On the very same day Nicolae Penescu, a former Romanian Minister of the Interior living in France, had been slightly injured when he opened a similar package.

Their failure to lure the Romanian spy chief, General Plesita, to defect to France was a blow to the DST. In September 1982 two newspapers stated that he might well have defected to France if the French press had not revealed how French agents had foiled the Romanian murder plot. *Le Quotidien de Paris* and *France-Soir* quoted intelligence sources as saying that the premature disclosure of this affair had wrecked a plan by General Plesita of the Romanian external intelligence service, CSEI, to leave for France. 'If only a high official had not revealed the affair a few hours too soon to a journalist friend and fellow Socialist, General Plesita would without doubt today be seeking asylum from the Minister of the Interior,' stated *France-Soir*.[8]

On the other hand it could equally be argued that the lack of information concerning General Plesita could have been a deliberate plot, possibly to create confusion and panic inside the Romanian Secret Service. This was not the end of the matter, as the Romanian Connection continues to plague

France to this day. As late as January 1986, there was yet another incident involving Romanian espionage inside France. It began when the European Parliament decided to investigate a report which alleged that a French MEP was in fact a Communist agent who had paid a bribe to obtain his seat. This report claimed that Gustav Pordea, a member of Le Pen's National Front, had paid $500,000, which had been supplied by the Romanian Secret Service.

Pordea, a Romanian-born French naturalized citizen, had been elected to the European Parliament in 1984. He angrily denied the allegations made against him and threatened legal action, claiming that he was an 'anti-Communist' and that the smear campaign against him had been set up by the Soviet Union. Le Pen took the same view, saying that 'one can imagine that Moscow is trying to harm us'. Certainly Pordea sat in the European Parliament as a member of the European Right, whose chairman was Le Pen. The whole truth of this affair was never satisfactorily resolved. Somebody deep down in the intelligence underworld of one country or another might still be making play with the Romanian Connection, or even attempting to level the score over Colonel Z.

26

An Astonishing Chinese Adventure

> Six in the third place means
> Forward and backward, abyss on abyss.
> In danger like this, pause at first
> and wait,
> Otherwise you will fall into a pit in
> the abyss.
> Do not act in this way.
>
> from the *I Ching*, or *Book of Changes*

The principal story of this chapter is so unusual, enthralling and puzzling that it calls for the pen of a master of fiction to put it into perspective. As has been noticed in earlier chapters many incidents in the history of the French Secret Service seem more improbable than anything produced in fiction. But the tale of Bernard Boursicot and Shi Pei-pu is easily the most remarkable of all. It is a narrative which at first sight seems almost impossible to accept as the truth, yet it has been fully documented and may be taken as absolute fact. The material is perhaps too bizarre for Flaubert, but Guy de Maupassant would have revelled in it. So, too, in a totally different manner might Jean-Paul Sartre.

This strange and in some ways endearing story crept into the headlines in July 1983, when it was announced that Bernard Boursicot, a diplomat, had been arrested and charged with passing secrets to Peking. Bernard Boursicot was the son of an accountant who had joined the French Foreign Ministry in 1964. He had been quickly selected as an adaptable, intelligent and pleasant personality with a certain talent for languages and, despite the fact that he had had little experience and was only twenty years of age, was posted to Peking in August 1964.

This was probably due to the fact that at long last France and China had agreed to exchange ambassadors.

Peking then was, however, a somewhat bleak place for any diplomat, let alone a young man outside his own country for the first time. Even senior diplomats were writing back from Peking at that time, complaining that life was appallingly lonely. Young Boursicot yearned for some friends outside the diplomatic circle and within the Chinese community for whom he quickly developed a liking. Eventually he met Shi Pei-pu at a reception given by the counsellor at the French Embassy. Shi Pei-pu was four years older than Boursicot and an established actress in the Peking Opera company with a reputation for being able to adapt to either male or female roles both in dancing and singing.

Shi Pei-pu came from a relatively wealthy Chinese family in the days before Mao Tse-tung's victory over all other opponents. She had been educated by Jesuit teachers and spoke French fluently. Immediately Boursicot struck up a friendship with Shi and soon became enthralled by the opera star's personality. So much so that he accepted that Shi was a woman. Yet, if he had not been so naïve he might have heeded the story that Shi told him: 'There was once a Chinese girl who disguised herself as a boy to help her brother in an examination, but could not recover her old identity and so she killed herself because of her horror of what had happened.' There are two versions as to how Shi commented on all this. One is that he said, 'Perhaps I am also a boy,' and the other is, 'Perhaps I am also really a girl.'

Obviously Boursicot became infatuated with Shi and within a few months he was having a passionate affair with the singer. Yet all the time Shi Pei-pu was really a man. Whether at some stage in his life there had been a sex change is still a mystery. Late in 1965 Boursicot was posted to Saudi Arabia, but he still exchanged letters with Shi. It was during this period that Shi wrote to him, saying that Boursicot had become the father of a boy. Boursicot was delighted and as a result of this information managed to get himself posted back to Peking as the Embassy archivist in 1969. By this time China had been transformed overnight by the so-called Cultural Revolution and Shi Pei-pu had been removed from the opera company. But, determined to be reunited with his lover, Boursicot bicycled through the streets of Peking until he found her.

This reunion was swiftly interrupted when Red Guards descended upon the pair and took them under escort to a political commissar. The commissar, being a realist as well as an activist, suggested that unless Boursicot started taking lessons from the teachings of Mao Tse-tung and co-operated with the Chinese government Shi would be sent to a labour camp. On the other hand, if the Frenchman agreed to help the Chinese by photocopying dispatches from the French Embassy, the couple would be free to meet whenever they wished.

Such was his infatuation for and devotion to Shi Pei-pu that Boursicot agreed and handed over copies of a large number of documents to the Chinese. Not that the documents were very important (at least, according to the French they were not), as they were supposed to include such trivial items as orders for such equipment as ice-buckets and mirrors for the French Embassy. Nonetheless one can only imagine that when in 1972 Boursicot was posted to Ulan Bator the Chinese would want something much more positive in the way of intelligence. For Ulan Bator was one place in China where he might be expected to get some reports on French probes into the secrets of Chinese nuclear developments at Lop Nor. Here Boursicot was in the ideal position not only for obtaining intelligence but also for passing it back, as he was the Ambassador's chief assistant in more ways than one: adviser, chauffeur, typist, accountant and responsible for taking the diplomatic bag to Peking for transmission to Paris. But when questioned on the subject of his stay in Ulan Bator, Boursicot said that this was 'not a serious post. We had a floor in a tourist hotel and when we went out we left the keys at the front desk.'[1]

Maybe not much of importance went to the Chinese intelligence officer who controlled Boursicot, though it is hard to believe that he was not pressed to deliver much more information than he admitted. As the prosecutor later alleged at the trial, 'For a secret service all information is important.'

Eventually Boursicot returned to France and in 1982 he

arranged a lecture tour for Shi Pei-pu to make in France, the subject being Chinese opera. Shi Pei-pu arrived in Paris with the 'son', Shi Du Du, and they lived happily in Boursicot's apartment in the Boulevard Raspail on the Left Bank. All went well until there was a question of Boursicot being promoted to an important post in the French Foreign Ministry. It was then the DST began taking an interest in the vetting of the Frenchman and as a result both he and Shi Pei-pu were charged with espionage. Yet it is extremely doubtful whether any charge would have been brought against either of them but for the mystery concerning the sex of Shi Pei-pu: it was this which initially caused DST officers to be suspicious, and not any hints of espionage. The singer claimed to be a female even though registered on her Chinese records as a male. Medical tests were ordered and these proved Shi Pei-pu was a man. It had only been through the usual checks on a person's suitability for promotion that Boursicot's private life had been examined and it was from this that all else developed. Suspicion grew when it transpired that the 'son' alleged to have been born out of the liaison between Boursicot and the opera singer was an orphan bought by Shi Pei-pu in a village market in Sinkiang.

Yet Boursicot insistently declared that he was not a homosexual and even produced as a witness a French married woman with whom he had had an affair to testify that he had 'normal tastes'. Long after his arrest, and despite what he was told by interrogating officers, he remained convinced that his lover was a woman, even declaring that he would 'cut his head off' if he was proved wrong.[2]

It would seem that Boursicot was totally mesmerized by Shi Pei-pu, so much so that possibly he had convinced himself that his lover was a woman. Yet in all other respects he was a normal person, picked out as a candidate for promotion and conscientious in his work. Yet when Shi Pei-pu arrived in court to face the charge, he was dressed in a formal man's striped grey suit. Eventually both he and Boursicot were sentenced to six years' imprisonment some two-and-a-half years after they had originally been arrested, an incredible delay in obtaining a sentence one way or another. Indeed, it is this very delay which suggests that behind the scenes there was much more important evidence than ever came out at the trial.

Not long afterwards President Mitterand announced that he had granted an amnesty to Shi Pei-pu. After all, the opera singer had not initiated the espionage.

In February 1983, an officer of the DGSE, Lieutenant-Colonel Bernard Nut, aged forty-seven, was found dead with a bullet in his head in the snow-covered foothills of the Alps some forty-eight miles north of Nice. The first impression was that this was a case of suicide as an autopsy revealed that he was suffering from serious heart and liver trouble. Every attempt was made to hush up the mystery of how he met his death, despite the fact that evidence pointed to murder rather than suicide. He was shot in the back of the head, his revolver was found more than seven feet from his body, there was no trace of gunpowder on his hands and there were three empty cartridges in the gun. One significant report from Paris was, 'It is thought that his Secret Service colleagues may have already taken away key evidence.'3

A month later new evidence from ballistic experts led police to believe that Colonel Nut did not commit suicide, but was murdered. Following this revelation a commentator on the French state-owned television service quoted sources in the DGSE as saying that Nut was killed 'while on a mission'. This was followed by a statement in *France-Soir* that he was killed 'while on duty'.

Nut's cover had been admirably maintained as far as his neighbours were concerned: to them he was an industrial engineer, happily married and the father of three children. His real work was to handle counter-espionage for the Alpine Affairs Bureau of the service, and this included helping to protect some of France's most sensitive intelligence targets such as the nuclear-submarine station at Toulon, the electronics complex where military weapons were manufactured, and the nuclear missile arsenal on the Albion plateau. It was known that he had helped to uncover a number of KGB spies, including Viktor Pronin, who had been working undercover as an Aeroflot official in Rome. Only days before Nut's death

Italian police announced that they had caught Pronin with microfilms of Western defence plans.[4]

No adequate explanation was ever given of why Colonel Nut might have been murdered, despite the vague hints already mentioned. Some prejudiced American Intelligence observers suggested this was a case of an internal feud in the DGSE ending with the settlement of the matter by a killing, but this was mere speculation without any evidence. Everything that is known about this affair suggests that Nut had a rendezvous with someone in the hill country behind Nice and he was actually seen at about 8 P.M. on the night of his death, sitting alone behind the wheel of his car close to the place where his body was later found. *Le Bon et Vrai* believes that Colonel Nut had helped the Italians to discover the 'Bulgarian Connection' in the attempted assassination of Pope John Paul II in May 1981, and adds, 'He may have known so much about this that someone inside the KGB felt it was essential to silence him for all time.'

Inexplicable incidents which concern, however slightly, the Intelligence Services of France, are of frequent occurrence. Somehow most of them are left totally unexplained. On 1 December 1983 Mr Niall Campbell, employed by the British company, ICI, was reported as having vanished from his hotel in Paris. The next day he was found drowned at Brest, 375 miles away, about one hundred yards from a secret French naval base for nuclear submarines. The rocks where his body was found were in an area normally prohibited for any unauthorized person. Captain Joseph Le Sech of the Brest naval police stated that they had 'not ruled out a possible link with espionage' and the British Foreign Office at the same time took the unusual step of denying that Mr Campbell had been involved with British Intelligence.[5]

Mr Campbell had been on a routine two-day visit to Paris to collect business statistics when he disappeared on 1 December. He was expected to catch a plane to return home at 9 P.M. that day. Police trying to draw a picture of what might have happened learned that he left his hotel with only about three hundred francs on him, enough to buy a ticket by rail to Brest. This would have cost him 254 francs and when his body was recovered a 50-franc note was in his pocket. He would certainly not have had enough money to hire a car. Police took the view that he must have been kidnapped in Paris, driven to Brest and then killed. His family were certainly sure that he had been murdered, all of them saying he was not the type to commit suicide and had no reason for doing so.

The previous month the Mayor of Brest had made a verbal protest about acts of espionage in the area on the part of the Soviet Union and other Eastern bloc states and this may have led to allegations of a link between Mr Campbell's death and espionage. The British press paid little heed to these rumours, but the French media revelled in them and one headline was 'The dead Englishman and a whiff of espionage'. Pierre Prier of the Parisian *Journal de Dimanche* commented: 'The French love mystery and intrigue, they love to romanticize and speculate. This story lets them do it.'

Speculation there certainly was: the French news agency, *Agence France-Presse*, circulated a story suggesting that Britons were being lured to France and offered jobs for British Intelligence. Without giving details of any possible plot of this nature, the agency gave accounts of eight unsolved killings which, it claimed, might have had spying as a common thread, all involving Britons. Wildly sensational though this story was, it was given some credibility when Mr John Graham, a 27-year-old British accountant, was also found drowned some few days later in the River Seine.

John Graham disappeared from his Paris hotel two days before Niall Campbell. There was, however, no link between the two men. Both left all their vital documents behind in their hotels and told hotel staff they would be returning shortly. A curious feature was that Niall Campbell's signet ring inscribed with a boar's head had been removed from his finger before he died. When it was learned that Mr Campbell had visited Amsterdam on a number of occasions in recent months there was further speculation that his death might be connected with the drug-smuggling racket, Amsterdam being a key centre in that trade. The theory was that he might have been acting as an agent for the French, either for the customs or for one of the Intelligence Services, giving them vital information on drug-trafficking. Three months earlier the French authorities seized a Panamanian cargo ship with 1,600 kilograms of cannabis on board. The ship was taken to Brest and one of the alleged drug-ring leaders leapt to temporary freedom as the ship approached the port, swimming ashore very close to the spot where Mr Campbell's body was found.

Almost equally mysterious was the obscure but tenuous link between the former SDECE and the attempted assassination of Pope John Paul II when he was shot and wounded in St Peter's Square in Rome in May 1981. In December 1982 the Comte de Marenches, then no longer in French Intelligence, claimed that he warned the Pope of a Communist assassination plot. He told this author: 'I sent a general and a colonel to the Vatican to tell the Pope personally of the danger', adding that he had made an earlier if more indirect warning to the Pope in June 1979.

Le Bon et Vrai not only confirmed this story, but added that it was made clear to the Pontiff that the threat to his life would come from Bulgaria. 'This information came from one of our own agents in Sofia and it was confirmed by reports from elsewhere, not at the time, but more recently and since the attempted assassination.'

Admittedly de Marenches' statement came at a time when the so-called Bulgarian Connection with the attempted killing of the Pope was being bruited around Europe, and when four Italian Government ministers were being questioned about this. At the same time two French Intelligence officers interviewed by the news magazine, *Le Nouvel Observateur*, asserted that Moscow was terrified of the Pope who, they said, gave the issue of Poland 'an international echo and repercussions . . . We believe the Kremlin tried to liquidate him without the crime being traced to Moscow . . . for all the clues would lead to Bulgaria.'[6]

This last statement one finds rather hard to accept. Certainly the Russians could never have been happy with the idea of there being a Polish Pope, who could become the figurehead for revolt for many Poles. On the other hand it is inconceivable that they would want clues pointing in the direction of a Bulgarian-manipulated assassination attempt, as this could only too easily be used to suggest the Soviet Union was employing Bulgarians for this purpose. The man who wounded Pope John Paul II was Mehmet Ali Agca, a Turk said to be working for the Grey Wolves, an organization of fanatical Turkish nationalists. It was surely only in this direction that Moscow hoped people would seek the men behind the killer.

Then the story leaked that behind the Turk was a Bulgarian Connection, the implication being that Bulgarian agents employed him as the marksman. All at once the intelligence services of the Western world started seeking the truth about the alleged implication of a plot by the Bulgarian Secret Service. It was the Turk who first alleged that not only the Bulgarians but the KGB were involved in planning the murder. But the evidence he supplied concerning three Bulgarians in Rome was purely circumstantial. Naturally, the Bulgarians officially and indignantly denied everything. Then Oleg Bitov, the former editor of *Literatournaja Gazeta* in Moscow, who had defected to Britain in 1983 claiming he was protesting against lack of freedom in Russia, returned to Moscow and at a press conference alleged he had been kidnapped and beaten by British agents. This move came some few weeks before an Italian judge was supposed to release a report implicating the Kremlin, if only indirectly, in the assassination attempt. Bitov's story was that the Bulgarian Connection had been invented by a former Bulgarian citizen, John Dimi Panitza, European director of *Reader's Digest*! (This account could of course be disinformation, and should be treated with caution.)

As to how the French and de Marenches found out about the plot against the Pope, the probability is that some at least of this intelligence came from a cosmopolitan Italian who worked for the SDECE as well as the Italian Secret Service, SISMI, and whose contacts extended from the P-2 secret masonic lodge on the right to informants in Bulgaria and Albania on the left. The Comte de Marenches' statement seems to have been borne out by the Vatican who admitted that three months before Agca struck they had been warned that an attack on the Pope's life was likely. What is even more interesting is that in July 1978 the Vatican had also been warned of a plot by Red Army terrorists in Frankfurt to kidnap Pope Paul VI and fly him to

Tripoli in Libya, where he would be held hostage until certain Palestinian terrorists were released from jail.

Later reports to French Intelligence suggested a possible link-up between Libyans and Bulgarians to assassinate Pope John Paul II. But the puzzle that has never been satisfactorily answered is whether in 1979 and afterwards the Libyans were acting primarily on their own initiative, or whether they were being used by Russians and Bulgarians.

An extraordinary incident occurred in June 1984 when President Mitterand was visiting London. The Frenchmen who were acting as his bodyguards had their guns taken from them by City of London police officers. One report described them as 'secret service men',[7] adding that this affair was expected to cause a row between British and French security chiefs as British police had always maintained that bodyguards for foreign dignitaries visiting Britain should not use or carry weapons of any kind. But this claim hardly stood up in view of the fact that it had already been disclosed that the Home Secretary had allowed at least two Americans accompanying President Reagan to carry guns when he had been in Britain for a summit meeting. The French were, of course, fully aware of this.

In fact the real cause of all this somewhat unnecessary bother was an incident of a few years earlier on the occasion of a visit to London by the previous French President, Giscard d'Estaing. At this time the British Government through representatives in the Ministry of Defence was trying to convince the sceptical French that dogs could sniff out explosives. The British were also trying to sell them the bomb-detecting gear which had been installed in the House of Commons. Following these talks, the French set out secretly to test the efficiency of the British bomb-sniffing dogs. The armed officers then protecting the President came from a special group called the *Service des Voyages Officielles*, which was answerable to the Ministry of the Interior and consisted of police officers. But a French explosives expert, almost certainly coming under the orders of Commandant Prouteau who then ran the GIGN special anti-terrorist group of the *Gendarmerie*, managed to hide a 150-gram charge from his technical bomb kit in the grounds of the

French Embassy in London. The dogs found the charge and the experiment ended satisfactorily on all counts. But someone made a fuss when this was discovered and later that same morning the French explosives expert was asked to go to a police station where he was interrogated and only spared further questioning when the French Ambassador intervened directly.[8]

The facts as given in the French press were not shown to be incorrect by the British authorities and the whole incident seems to have been worked up into quite an unnecessary skirmish between French and British security men and the police.

Later in 1984 a DC 8 belonging to the private French air transport, SFAIR, was seized at the airport in Athens and its crew were arrested for illegal arms traffic. It was alleged that the plane was carrying arms from Italy to Oman, which was indicated as the destination on the crates, but that Botswana was named as the destination on the flight papers. Many of the officers at Greek airports and customs are left-wingers who sometimes turn a blind eye to terrorists passing through Greece, but immediately clamp down on any suspicion of material which might be going to enemies of the left. In this instance Botswana's government formally denied that the arms were to enter its country, but it was generally believed that these supplies were intended to go to the anti-government ZANU rebels of Joshua Nkomo in Zimbabwe, and that he would have taken delivery of the weapons in Botswana.[9]

SFAIR has previously been involved in other clandestine operations in Africa, for example providing air transport to the Biafran rebels in 1967 and much later to French mercenaries operating in Chad under the suspected direction of the DGSE. It would seem that at times the Action Division was providing mercenaries for long-range desert groups fighting in Chad, supporting right-wing rebels in Angola, aiding anti-Vietnamese fighters in Cambodia and even supplying arms to anti-Soviet rebels in Afghanistan.

The Comte de Marenches had been equally concerned about Angola during his own headship of the SDECE, so much so that for a time there were somewhat strained relations between

him and President Giscard d'Estaing. The President was doubtful whether Savimbi, the Angolan leader, was reliable and if he
would stay in office: there were even suggestions that he was
lukewarm on support for Angola because he did not want to
offend the Russians who were supplying men and money to the
people fighting Savimbi. De Marenches' view had always been
that the Western Alliance should back those African nations
fighting against Marxist guerrillas and indeed that, instead of a
North Atlantic Treaty Organization, the word 'North' should
be dropped and the Alliance extended to include such nations
in the southern hemisphere as Angola. 'Savimbi is first and
foremost a true black African, whereas the Communist
bourgeoisie of Luanda is mostly made up of half-castes,' said
de Marenches when justifying his support for Angola. Then he
was asked by the President for proof that Savimbi was master
in his own country and was waging an effective campaign. 'The
man I despatched to take photos that would provide incontro-
vertible evidence did his job admirably. He trekked across a
large part of the Angolan bush on foot for three months . . .
The shots he brought back to me showed Savimbi's men along
the track of the Benguela railroad laying explosives so as to
blow up the track and destroy the bridges.'[10]

There were further cases of Soviet espionage directed at
France in 1984–5. In April 1984 a Tupolev 134 of the Soviet
airline Aeroflot strayed forty-five miles off course into prohibited air space, flying low over the naval base at Toulon where
France's first nuclear attack submarine was in dock. The plane
was supposed to be on a flight from Moscow to Marseille via
Budapest and the pilot ignored several warnings from civilian
air traffic controllers that it had gone into a restricted area. A
senior air traffic controller expressed the opinion that a naviga-
tion error was unlikely.

This incident appeared to typify a particularly strenuous
effort at this time both by the Soviet GRU and the KGB to
capture French military secrets. Then in March 1985 a French
businessman, Leonid Tavera, was jailed for five years for selling
trade and military secrets to the Soviet Union. At the trial he
admitted doing business with Vladimir Sapozhnikov, a member
of the Russian Military Intelligence. It was stated that no vital

secrets had been passed to Moscow, and as a result Tavara was given an extremely lenient sentence.

Much more serious was the case of Vladimir Zolotarenko, the 53-year-old son of White Russian emigrés, who was sentenced to ten years' imprisonment after being convicted of espionage in August 1985. He worked as a clerk in the photocopying department of the Advisory Group for Aerospace Research and Development, a NATO body based in Paris, and was said to have passed important technological and military secrets to the USSR over a period of sixteen years. He may have been a relatively low-grade spy, but the quantity of material he passed on was tremendously important. Once again the DST had scored a victory and they showed up the laxity of security measures employed by the organization AGARD, for which he worked. It was easy for him to keep copies of top secret papers for himself and to go through the wastepaper baskets at the end of each day for discarded papers that might be important. It was discovered that no check or search was made on employees as they entered or left the building. Zolotarenko actually admitted: 'It was enough to tempt the devil,' a curious manner of expressing what he meant. Worse still, it was learned that Zolotarenko had been recommended for his AGARD job by none less than Francis Roussilhe, the NATO employee who had already been sentenced to twenty years in jail for espionage. Not even after Roussilhe had been sentenced had anyone checked back on Zolotarenko.

Once again UNESCO had supplied the key man to link up with Zolotarenko, as his prime contact was Valentin Lvov, a KGB agent working under the cover of a junior member of the USSR UNESCO delegation. It emerged from DST inquiries that most of such intelligence leaked to the Russians was going to VPK, the Russian commission for military industry. This much was largely confirmed, if only indirectly, in an article in a monthly review published by the French Committee for National Defence Studies. This article was almost certainly the work of a senior French counter-espionage official. According to the author, the VPK, headed by Leonid Smirnov, one of the vice-presidents of the Soviet Council of Ministers, is composed of twelve ministers with direct involvement in the Russians' attempt to gain scientific and technological intelligence from ministries, institutes, factories and all other sources around the world. The main thrust of the article was that the Russians were very sophisticated in their current methods of obtaining such information. It stated that, 'Preceding estimates of the scientific and technological standards reached by the USSR, in both the military and civil sectors, must be revised significantly upwards, both in terms of quality and quantity.'[11] The article ended with the advice that the Western world should adopt new measures to protect itself against 'this constantly growing aggression'.

The Greenpeace Affair

Agents of the DGSE sank this boat. They acted on orders. This truth was hidden from state counsellor Tricot . . . a new head of the DGSE will be named at the next Cabinet meeting. His prime task will be to reorganize all of these services.

> French Government statement by M. Fabius

1985 was yet another of those many years when the French Intelligence Services were propelled into serious trouble. Not just by one incident, but by many. Yet of all these incidents that of the sinking of the Greenpeace campaign ship, *Rainbow Warrior*, was the most devastating of all.

It was on 10 July 1985 that agents of the DGSE planted a bomb whch sank the *Rainbow Warrior* in Auckland harbour in New Zealand and at the same time caused the death of the ship's photographer, Fernando Pereira, who after the first explosion went below decks to rescue his cameras and was killed by a second blast.

Greenpeace, the environmental pressure group, had a strong anti-nuclear stance. Its case was that the dumping of nuclear waste should be totally outlawed which, of course, would make life impossible for all developers of nuclear power. Further, Greenpeace and its ally, Friends of the Earth, claimed that British nuclear reactors could be less safe than the Russian reactor destroyed at Chernobyl, and it must be admitted that despite the organization's claims to be devoted to preserving the purity of the environment everywhere, some of its members were relatively quiet on Soviet breaches of environmental safeguards. French Intelligence had discovered that there were links between Greenpeace and a special parliamentary committee in Stockholm which worked with the Olof Palme Commission of which Georgi Arbatov, head of the Soviet, USA and

Canada Institute, was a member. In other words the French had some good reasons for suspecting that Greenpeace was quick to condemn the West for pollution and despoiling of the environment, but much less anxious to criticize the USSR.

On the other hand Greenpeace complained that the French had perpetually threatened its organization. In September 1987 Greenpeace set out a series of charges against the French for actions prior to the sinking of the *Rainbow Warrior*. In 1972 they alleged that a French minesweeper rammed *Greenpeace III* when it was sailing to protest against Pacific nuclear tests, adding that a year later French commandos boarded the boat and 'savagely beat our crew members: one was partially blinded by a rifle butt'.[1]

Some years earlier, they claimed, '*Rainbow Warrior* had been rammed as she attempted to block the entry of nuclear waste to Cherbourg.' Greenpeace also said that in 1983 the *Rainbow Warrior*, 'pursued by a warship escaped yet again when the USSR detained seven of our anti-whaling campaigners in Siberia'.[2] This last story is still lacking in many vital details; nor was much made of it at the time.

Greenpeace International planned to send the *Rainbow Warrior* into the French nuclear test zone in the South Pacific both to monitor and to protest, and it was also planning to enter French territorial waters. Obviously the French security and intelligence services were concerned about this, not least because it had been reported that the ship planned to lead a whole armada of vessels into the area of the tests. In recent years French secret agents had kept a constant watch on the activities of the Greenpeace movement. Some of these agents had reported that the *Rainbow Warrior* might have aboard sophisticated equipment for spying on the progress made by the French in the development of a neutron bomb and that Greenpeace might bring back disturbing and damaging reports about the high levels of radiation in test areas which they would present as a danger to the population of the islands of the Pacific.

Close watch was kept on the movements of the *Rainbow Warrior* by the French, and there can be no doubt that the fact that the ship had visited Vanuatu in the Pacific earlier on in

1985 must have alerted the DGSE and reinforced their desire to find out exactly what was being planned. This Pacific archipelago, formerly known as the New Hebrides, was now governed by Father Walter Lini, an Anglican priest who had become Prime Minister. Not only had he set up his own intelligence service, but had shown friendship towards the Soviet Union and regarded Cuba and Libya as allies. Indeed, two years after these events it was revealed that a Libyan delegation had visited Vanuatu in 1985 with the aim of extending its programme of terrorist and intelligence-gathering training for this area of the Pacific, including the Kanak liberation movement from New Caledonia and militants in Irian Jaya fighting against the Indonesian Government. French Intelligence, let it be said, had got information on such plans long before most other Western Intelligence Services.

The DGSE passed the problem of keeping the ship under close surveillance to the Action Division of the service which had its own marine commando base in Corsica where teams of undercover saboteurs were trained. The officer who ordered this operation of surveillance was an assistant to the head of the DGSE, one General Roger Emin, according to French sources.[3] The man who carried out the planning of the mission was Colonel Serge Codet who picked his team from among the Special Action members at the Cercottes camp near Orléans.

The first member of the team to arrive in New Zealand was Christine Cabon, an Army lieutenant attached to the Action Division. Her role was something of a mystery. She reached Auckland in mid-April 1985 under the name of Frédérique Bonlieu, introducing herself as a geologist and a supporter of ecological campaigns, so she soon made friends with members of Greenpeace. Armed with a letter of introduction from a leading French pacifist, she was soon able to join Greenpeace as a part-time assistant. However, anxious to obtain intelligence further afield in the Pacific, on 24 May she left New Zealand for the French Polynesian island of Tahiti.

Then on 22 June two further moves were made by the DGSE. First of all the yacht *Ouvea*, registered in the French Pacific territory of New Caledonia, arrived at the remote harbour of Parengarenga in the extreme north of New Zealand with five Frenchmen aboard. These included a DGSE crew comprising Roger Verge, a sergeant-major who used the name Raymond Velche, and two sergeants, all three attached to the Aspretto frogman school in Corsica. Their mission was to report on the Greenpeace ships and to see whether it would be possible to send a boat into the Greenpeace armada at some stage, presumably to upset their plans, or alternatively for Roger Verge to get himself chosen as the skipper of a Greenpeace ship.

Secondly, on 22 June, a French-speaking couple carrying Swiss passports in the names of Alain Jacques and Sophie-Claire Turenge, arrived in Auckland from London, claiming to be on honeymoon. They hired a camper van and spent two weeks in the north of the island. These two were not man and wife, but were both DGSE officers and their real names were Major Alain Mafart and Captain Dominique Prieur. The former was an instructor at the DGSE naval training school in Corsica, while Prieur was the wife of a French Defence Ministry worker. It was later officially stated by the French in the report on the incident by Bernard Tricot, a magistrate and civil servant, that orders from the DGSE to these two, given on 14 June, were that their mission was to report on the number, characteristics and plans of the boats accompanying *Rainbow Warrior* to Mururoa, to identify the crew and the political, scientific and journalistic abilities of those involved in the campaign and to report on its impact in New Zealand. There can be no doubt that French Intelligence was worried about the change in New Zealand's attitude to international defence problems since the new Prime Minister, David Lange, had adopted an anti-nuclear stance and had withdrawn his country from the weekly meetings in London of the Joint Allied Intelligence Committee.

On 28 June the *Ouvea* sailed to Whangarei, one hundred miles north of Auckland. Here, it was later noted, the skipper hired a car and in one week covered journeys of some nine hundred miles around the island, but for what purpose is unclear. Then on 6 July the *Rainbow Warrior* sailed into Auckland Harbour from Vanuatu. From then onwards French agents kept watch on the ship and decided to find out whether the New Zealand Government, in view of Lange's anti-nuclear policies, might be involved in some way. No one could deny that the French had a legitimate right to find out just what was happening. After all, Greenpeace International was not a small, amateurish concern: it had branches of its organization in no fewer than fifteen countries and its budget suggested that it could raise something like seven and a half million pounds. The *Rainbow Warrior* had been bought as its flagship by the British branch of the organization.

Three days after the *Rainbow Warrior* arrived in Auckland on 6 July the *Ouvea* left New Zealand for the Australian island of Norfolk, 750 miles to the north. It was on the following day that, just before midnight, an explosion tore a hole in the *Rainbow Warrior* below the waterline. Twelve members of Greenpeace escaped to the quayside and the Portuguese photographer Pereira was the only casualty.

There still remains something of a mystery about the presence of two French agents other than Mafart and Prieur, who were sent to Auckland. What their precise mission was is in doubt, whether to ensure the *Rainbow Warrior* was put out of action, or to help cover the tracks of Mafart and Prieur. Undercover evidence suggests that they were both experienced frogmen, officers of the DGSE, and that this separate mission was known as *Mission Oxygène*, the name being derived from the oxygen masks they used.

The *Rainbow Warrior* was sunk by two magnetic mines while alongside the dock at Auckland. Certainly as far as Mafart and Prieur were concerned the mission misfired badly as they were swiftly caught within hours by the harbour police. Instead of escaping in a yacht and leaving no clues, they abandoned a rubber dinghy, an oxygen cylinder and a life-jacket, all of the type used by the French Navy, which were, of course, duly discovered. They themselves were found in a camper van not far from the harbour. Coded phone numbers found on the couple after their arrest led New Zealand detectives to the view that they were employed by French Intelligence. Soon New Zealand's own Security Intelligence Service got on the trail. Studies of telephone records on their computer network showed the couple had dialled an official number of the DGSE from their hotel room and enabled them to confirm that Mafart and Prieur were French agents.

Mafart and Prieur were duly charged with carrying false passports on 15 July. Meanwhile New Zealand police went to Norfolk Island to interrogate members of the *Ouvea* crew. Not until 23 July were Mafart and Prieur charged with murder and arson and remanded in Auckland's Mount Eden Prison. Three days later the New Zealand police issued warrants for the arrest of the *Ouvea* crew on charges of arson and murder through use of explosives. By this time the New Zealanders had enough evidence to suggest the *Ouvea* crew were in some way involved in the attack on *Rainbow Warrior*.

The day after these warrants were issued Fredérique Bonlieu, who had switched over to working with an archaeological team in a kibbutz in Israel, suddenly flew off to New York. New Zealand police had been about to ask the Israeli police to hold her for questioning. Meanwhile the *Ouvea*, supposed to be on its way back to French Caledonia, disappeared in mid-ocean, presumably scuttled by its crew. It was thought that the crew had previously arranged to be rescued by another ship.

By this time the story of the sinking of the *Rainbow Warrior* had had a profound effect in Paris. The French Defence Ministry preserved silence despite all manner of reports in the press that the two people arrested were DGSE members. President Mitterand asked the Prime Minister, Fabius, to mount a rigorous inquiry into the whole affair. Fabius, in his turn, appointed a former Secretary-General at the Elysée Palace, Bernard Tricot, who had been an aide to General de Gaulle, to investigate the matter.

Meanwhile various rather improbable smoke-screens were thrown up in the French media, some of them doubtless originating from the DGSE. There were two attempts to incriminate or discredit the British. The first was to imply that the British were in some way responsible for the bombing of the ship, while the second suggested that the French had been betrayed by British Intelligence who got news of the mission and informed New Zealand. Some suggested that the bombing of *Rainbow Warrior* was an attempt by the British to retaliate against the supply of French Exocet missiles to Argentina during the Falklands War. There was even a suggestion that the deaths of Niall Campbell and Robert Graham might have been connected with all this.

Yet the only evidence which could be produced that in any way linked the British with this episode was that a Zodiac inflatable boat with an outboard engine found in Auckland harbour just after the sinking of the ship had apparently been bought in Brent, North London, by a French-speaking man whom the owner of the shop thought he could identify from photographs as Alain Mafart. The French alleged that the salesman at this shop who actually sold the inflatable craft was a former British secret agent. It would seem that the easily identifiable British-built boat was deliberately left for the New Zealanders to pick up.

Sir Geoffrey Howe, the British Foreign Secretary, described French press and television reports about British involvement in the affair as 'patently absurd' and based on 'disinformation'.

At the same time President Mitterand was assuring the New Zealand Prime Minister that France would cooperate fully with the inquiry. Next day the New Zealand Government demanded the extradition from France of those involved in the affair, to which Paris replied that the French did not extradite their own nationals. Then *Le Monde* quoted a number of DGSE agents as saying that a traitor within the service had betrayed the *Rainbow Warrior* operation to British Intelligence, who had passed on the information to New Zealand.[4]

Once speculation starts on a subject like this it soon mushrooms into an ever-increasing array of unsubstantiated allegations. One report even suggested that the whole affair had been organized by the Russians to discredit the French. This can almost certainly be ruled out in view of the fact that the French have long since admitted responsibility for the affair. Nevertheless the attempts to put the blame on the British do raise a variety of questions. Why, for example, should the DGSE send a man to London, of all places, to buy the rubber dinghy? Surely the obvious and safest place to get one was the frogman school in Corsica. Had the French always used British-built dinghies of this kind? Again, this seems improbable. Yet the facts are that a Frenchman named Andries, an underwater sabotage expert, using the name of Eric Andreine, flew to London from Paris to buy this craft on 29 May 1985. He stayed at the Vanderbilt Hotel in Kensington and, when he went to the shop in Brent, claimed to be the representative of a Belgian diving company, paying £1,400 in new fifty-pound notes for a grey Zodiac dinghy and a second-hand outboard motor.[5]

Confirmation of the statements in the previous paragraph comes quite independently from a New Zealand security officer who told the author that, 'We established that Andries was the man who made the purchase, but what was more damning for him was the fact that he telephoned the DGSE in Paris from his hotel in London.' Eventually the Tricot report on the sinking of the *Rainbow Warrior* also confirmed that Gerald Andries was one of the crew of the *Ouvea* and that the name Andries was a pseudonym. On other occasions this agent called himself Eric Audrenc.

The London visit still seems a very strange business, almost as though the DGSE agent was being used to draw attention not only to himself and the fact that he was buying such a boat in Britain, but to his links with the DGSE. Why should he take the risk of telephoning the DGSE in Paris from his hotel when he was on such an assignment? Or was this just carelessness on his part?

Bernard Tricot's 1985 report generally exonerated the French Government and DGSE from any responsibility for the sinking of this ship. But it gave a somewhat devious explanation of the affair: 'Certitudes are, alas, slight . . . but as far as my information goes at present there was no official French responsibility.' Tricot agreed that the announcement that Greenpeace was resuming demonstrations 'certainly irritated a large number of military and civilian personnel' and stressed that France had a legal right to deny access to its territorial waters in the Pacific and to intensify research on the positions and movements of Greenpeace. His report claimed that Captain Prieur and Major Mafart were 'innocent', though it acknowledged that five DGSE agents were in New Zealand to spy on Greenpeace's activities.

The report was condemned by an Opposition deputy, Alain

Madelin, as one which 'takes the French for imbeciles'. However, the French as a whole accepted the verdict for what it was, taking the view that such matters were much best left to the professionals to handle. Indeed, reporting on an opinion poll carried out by *Figaro*, the *International Herald Tribune* revealed that 'a national consensus apparently supports the Government's readiness to use violence in overt and covert operations to protect the nuclear testing ground in the Pacific'.[6]

Tricot's report also mentioned a series of meetings between Charles Hernu, the Defence Minister, and the DGSE's director-general, Admiral Lacoste. The Defence Minister was said to have given verbal orders to increase intelligence on Greenpeace, but Admiral Lacoste was alleged to have gone further by telling his agents to 'reflect on the ways and means of countering them'. The report did, however, confirm the true identities of the man and woman arrested by the New Zealand police as Alain and Sophie Turenge, the names given on their bogus Swiss passports.

Laurent Fabius, the French Prime Minister, then made a statement in which he asked the New Zealand Government to give him all the evidence in its possession on the sinking of the Greenpeace vessel. 'The French Government is determined that nothing should remain in the dark,' he added. This was a pious hope, no less, no more. But at least Fabius took some action. He made a statement that:

Agents of the DGSE sank this boat. They acted on orders. This truth was hidden from state counsellor Tricot. I have told the President about these serious facts and we have decided that immediate measures must be taken. Firstly, a new head of the DGSE will be named at the next Cabinet meeting. His prime task will be to reorganize all of these services. Secondly, the Government favours the creation of a parliamentary commission of inquiry. The people who merely carried out the act must, of course, be exempted from blame, as it would be unacceptable to expose members of the military who only obeyed orders and who, in the past, have sometimes carried out very dangerous missions on behalf of our country.

This statement eased the whole situation. Mr Lange, the New Zealand Prime Minister, concurred that Fabius's statement was 'conciliatory', though 'not an apology'. The new

Zealand detective-superintendent in charge of inquiries into the affair, Allan Galbraith, said that the Tricot report revealed information which the New Zealand police had not had beforehand. Another viewpoint was put by the former Gaullist Prime Minister, Chaban Delmas, who declared that, 'What Greenpeace is doing at Mururoa has nothing to do with ecology. The aim is to get us out of the Pacific.' But response to the Tricot report in the media was critical, ranging from *Libération*'s 'Tricot washes whiter' to *Figaro* asserting that it was 'a bit glib'. After such comments in the media the New Zealand Premier seemed to change his mind again, giving a television interview in which he alleged that, 'France has killed our friendship. We have always considered France an honourable country, but this is no longer the case today.'

There could be no doubt that the Rainbow affair was an extraordinarily untypical French blunder which only made Greenpeace more militant, alienated the New Zealanders and helped the French cause not one iota. Even if the agents had not been caught it would not have helped their cause very much. Two excuses have been put forward for this blunder by *Le Bon et Vrai*:

I imagine that for once the DGSE underestimated New Zealand Intelligence. Maybe they thought they would only be up against an incompetent police force, whereas New Zealand, though it does not have an external Intelligence Service, has a very competent Security Intelligence Service internally, comprising both police and army personnel. They have a computer network for studying telephone calls. On the other hand I have the feeling that some form of disinformation was given to DGSE which caused them to risk this clumsy bombing of the *Rainbow Warrior*. The question is, who gave the disinformation?

Le Bon et Vrai was not at that time in any of the French Intelligence Services, so he was speculating.

When Tricot failed lamentably to get Mitterand out of trouble, the President was forced to make the changes in appointments hinted at by Fabius. Firstly, Charles Hernu, very much an Army man, was replaced as Minister of Defence by Paul Quelès, of the Air Force Reserve, the son of an artillery officer and a graduate of the Polytechnic engineering school.

Secondly, Admiral Lacoste was sacked from his post as the head of the DGSE and in his place General René Imbot was appointed. Two years earlier General Imbot had been made Army Chief of Staff. Sixty years of age, General Imbot had seen action with the Maquis in World War II and had later served in Algeria and Indo-China. His appointment was designed to pacify military opinion, for President Mitterand was most anxious to counteract any malaise in the French Army. Malaise is almost a code word in that Army and does not really denote a lack of morale, or deterioration within the service, but is rather the Army hierarchy's way of disassociating itself from the government of the day. This is done by nothing more positive than exuding discontent and lending tacit support to anyone who might help to bring that government down. It is the kind of malaise which affected some senior officers in the British Army concerning Ulster in the years just before World War I until the detachment of Ulster from the rest of Ireland. The new Defence Minister had the right background to win the approval of the Army. Curiously, for a modern democracy, French generals still hold far more power, however subtly used, than do modern British generals. Imbot had a reputation for toughness, was popular in the Army and was very much a no-nonsense administrator.

As usual when a new man is appointed to take over the DGSE, his brief was 'to restore order', a phrase which is now becoming a cliché. Naturally, this phrase also included instructions to clear up the Greenpeace affair and to cope with the various revelations which were coming out in the world's media. Questions were being asked in some quarters about whether there was some attempt to sabotage and destroy the DGSE, and, if so, who was involved – members of that service, or a foreign nation? Did they wish to destroy the service for political reasons, or to destabilize France? Such questions were asked partly because to many people the incident seemed an inexplicable blunder for the French to have made, and partly because many within the French nation sought to find some excuse or alibi. General Imbot lost little time in hitting back. Though he had no instant answers on the day he took over and did not pretend that he had, within a matter of two days he gave the impression that he had uncovered a plot. Within five days of his appointment he made a totally unexpected appearance on French television and declared:

> To my great stupefaction, I have discovered – and I am weighing my words – a veritable malignant operation of destabilization in our Secret Services. I would even say of destruction of our Secret Services.
>
> Naturally, I have also found those who need to be punished. I have cut off the rotten branches. I now have a united, close-knit team around me . . . From now on any information that is said to have come from, or to have been given by, this Service is a lie, because I have put bolts on all the Service's doors.[7]

By any standards this was a remarkable statement for any Secret Service chief in the world to make, and even more remarkable coming from a modern Frenchman. What did it mean? Naturally, media correspondents asked direct questions such as whether any foreign powers were involved in this alleged sabotage attempt. To these he simply replied: 'I will say no more. I am the head of the Secret Services.'[8]

Yet to complicate matters, only a few hours before General Imbot's statements on French television, the Elysée Palace had issued a brief communiqué which indicated that the Greenpeace catastrophe was a closed subject, and that there was nothing further to say about it.

The search for the informants inside the service who had allegedly leaked material to the media was intensified at this time. General Imbot himself said that more agents were involved than the three who had already been arrested and charged. Those already arrested and questioned included Colonel Fournier, deputy head of the counter-espionage section; Captain Borras of the DGSE; and a warrant officer, Richard Guollet, a former leader of the frogmen's unit at the training centre in Corsica.

No doubt both the Elysée Palace, the Government and some members of the Intelligence Services thought this was a good moment to make all-round changes to satisfy everyone. Unfortunately this meant the end of the road for Yves Bonnet, who had been head of the DST since 1982. It was Bonnet who had orchestrated the expulsion of the forty-seven Russian diplomats in April 1983: his formidable dossier on Soviet espionage alone forced Mitterand to act in such a forthright manner. But poor Bonnet, who was moved to the post of Prefect in a department in Brittany, had clashed with both the *Gendarmerie* and the DGSE. This was as much due to his success in uncovering so many spies as anything else – it caused intense jealousy – and some in the DGSE obviously felt that Bonnet knew rather more than they did, and this irked them.

Bonnet was replaced in August 1985 by Rémy Patraud, a graduate of France's top seminary for civil servants, the *École Nationale d'Administration* (ENA). He had previously been *chef de cabinet* to Claude Cheysson, then Foreign Secretary. France is never short of highly skilled and intelligent candidates for all manner of jobs, discreetly waiting for the right opportunity. But that is the secret of French education. When General Imbot referred to 'cutting off the rotten branches', he was mainly referring to the lower ranks of the DGSE in which a number of changes were made over the next few months though they were, generally speaking, discreetly unannounced.

The French Foreign Minister, Roland Dumas, had meanwhile used his negotiating skills to get the charges against Mafart and Prieur reduced from murder to manslaughter. These negotiations were undoubtedly helped by a story leaked to *Le Monde* which claimed that it was another pair of DGSE operators who had actually carried out the bombing attack and who had made a safe getaway to France immediately afterwards. New Zealand's Premier, David Lange, reacted fiercely to criticism within his own country when the charges were changed and denied categorically that there had been any deal between the two countries. The mystery of the other pair of DGSE operators has never been satisfactorily cleared up and it would be foolish to speculate further on this matter. But there can be no doubt that manslaughter rather than murder was the obvious charge by any standards of justice: the aim was to put *Rainbow Warrior* out of action, not to murder the crew. Some in New Zealand thought the murder charges had been dropped so that New Zealand could go on selling lamb to Common Market countries. But the real fear in Auckland was that a murder charge could easily fail because there was insufficient evidence. Possibly the story in *Le Monde* helped the French in this instance.

On 22 November 1985 the two French Secret Service agents who took part in the bomb attack which sank the *Rainbow Warrior* were sentenced to ten years' imprisonment in New Zealand. But there was always an uneasy feeling in New Zealand that somehow, somewhere, the French would cunningly produce two other people in another part of the world who would say, 'We did it, the others were just used as a cover.' Even Sir Roland Davison, New Zealand's Chief Justice, after the trial made the somewhat strange comment that, 'The courts must make it plain that persons coming into this country cannot expect a short holiday at the expense of the Government and return home as heroes.'

Later the French Prime Minister gave the impression that orders for an attack had actually been given and he implied that he had been deceived by the former Defence Minister, Hernu. Curiously enough, very little was made by the French media of the possibility that Soviet Russia might be the key to all this. Russia had long been stirring up racial and anti-Western feeling all over the Pacific, not only in New Caledonia and the islands, but in New Zealand, too, hoping to play on the anti-nuclear sympathies of Prime Minister Lange. The latter had already withdrawn New Zealand's support for the ANZUS Treaty and quarrelled with the USA, Britain and even Australia on defence issues. Had Soviet agents infiltrated Greenpeace? If the French could do this, there is no reason to doubt that the Soviet Union could, too. The Soviets are more interested in French nuclear technology than Greenpeace could possibly be. It may well be that the French had learned that the Soviet Union had infiltrated Greenpeace and that this was the reason for swift, sudden and unorthodox methods. *Le Bon et Vrai* thinks: '[This is] more than likely from my knowledge of how the minds of the aggros in the service would react to such information. "Sink it," they would say, and then decide how to do just that. But in doing just that in a hurry they could easily come unstuck. It has happened before and it will happen again. You see, French agents tend to say to themselves, "Fortune favours the brave."'

Nevertheless, France fought hard in defence of its two agents caught in New Zealand. Even during the trial the story continued to be subtly leaked that the two caught were not the two who had actually sunk the *Rainbow Warrior*, and that the latter had escaped without being discovered. This story is being propagated even to this day. Once sentences had been passed, negotiations to assist the agents were pursued with great diligence.

After lengthy talks, exchanges of views and a certain amount of subtle pressure, in 1987 the French succeeded, with a letter of apology and a payment of £4,500,000, in freeing their two agents from New Zealand jails and transferring them to the French-owned South Pacific atoll of Hoa, a supply base for French nuclear tests on Mururoa. Here friends were allowed to meet them. It was a major success for highly skilled French negotiating tactics with implied threats that New Zealand butter and mutton markets might suffer if a deal did not get through. The warning on this instance was a sudden cancellation by the French of an order for New Zealand to supply meat and potatoes to New Caledonia. To make things seem all right to the outside world this bargain was carried out through the offices of the United Nations with its Secretary-General, Señor Javier Pérez de Cuellar, guaranteeing the plan by actually announcing it.

Then in September 1987 came a report that Major Mafart and Captain Prieur were secretly training military divers for sabotage operations on their paradise prison island, and that Mafart was the director of this school.[9] On a visit to Tahiti, Jacques Chirac, the new Prime Minister, said that the French Army had every reason to be proud of the two officers involved in the sinking of the *Rainbow Warrior*. Finally, in December 1987, it was announced that Major Mafart had been flown back to Paris from Hoa on 'humanitarian and medical grounds' because he needed medical treatment. New Zealand immediately complained that this was a breach of the UN-negotiated agreement that the major and Captain Prieur should be held for three years on Hoa. At the same time there was speculation that Dominique Prieur might follow her fellow-agent back to France. One of the stipulations of the agreement was that

Prieur could automatically be returned home in the event of illness or pregnancy. The French think of every possibility: since the 1986 agreement did not forbid conjugal visits, Captain Prieur was soon joined by her husband. Then in May 1988, during the pre-election campaign in France, Prime Minister Jacques Chirac arranged for Captain Prieur to be flown home on the grounds that she was pregnant.

A month earlier it was announced that Major Alain Mafart had won entry to France's elite School of War, which trains most of the nation's top military officers, the suggestion being that he was destined for senior service in the not too distant future.

28
The Ariane Space Programme At Risk

The Secret Services are following up the connection between those who gave the orders and those who got the documents. There have definitely been some leaks and transfers of information.

Fréderic d'Alles, President of Aerospace[1]

Despite some setbacks and frustrations between 1986 and 1987 both the DST and the DGSE achieved some considerable successes. In February 1986 a retired non-commissioned officer of the French Air Force was arrested for spying for the Soviet Union as a result of DST inquiries. A few days later France expelled four Soviet Embassy staff in Paris in connection with this same affair which involved the passing of information on the Brest submarine base to the USSR. The following day Mikhail Gorbachev, the Soviet leader, replied by expelling four French envoys from Moscow as a retaliation. Following this Jacques Berthelot, the Mayor of Brest, cancelled a friendship agreement between Brest and the Estonian port of Tallin because he believed that his city was an important target for observation for the Soviet Union.

Then in March 1987 the DST, aided considerably by the DGSE, revealed that a major Soviet spy ring had been gathering information on French defence priorities and the Ariane European space programme. Five people, including two women of Russian and Romanian origin, were charged in Rouen with spying. None of the arrested people worked at the Ariane rocket plant at Vernon, some fifty miles northwest of Paris, but three of the accused were employees of the National Institute for Statistics and Economic Analysis, and would have been able to examine the accounts of defence contractors and thus collect financial secrets on defence-related industries which could have revealed French military development plans.

The Ariane programme was controlled by the Ariane space consortium for the thirteen-member European Space Agency. The third stage of its rocket project used a motor fuelled by liquid oxygen and it was in this aspect in which the Soviet Union, also experimenting in this sphere, was most interested.

The two women arrested were Ludmilla Varyguine, the Russian wife of Pierre Verdier, director of the French National Statistical Institute in Rouen, who was also arrested, and Antonetta Manole, a Romanian who also worked at the Institute. The other two were Michel Fleury, who worked at the Institute's headquarters in Paris, and Jean-Michel Haury. The key to the whole case lay with Antonetta Manole, a secretary at the Institute who also ran a Romania–Normandy friendship society in Rouen.

A diplomatic row between Paris and Moscow continued for some days. Moscow had suddenly announced it was expelling six French diplomats, this being an attempt to force the French into admitting that they had expelled six Soviet nationals and not three as previously announced. Thereupon the French Ministry of Foreign Affairs confirmed that France was expelling six, only three of whom were diplomats. *Pravda* accused France of deliberately manufacturing 'spy mania', saying that this was the means by which 'the man in the street can be frightened again and made to believe that the arms race is wise', meaning presumably that it was necessary.

Two months later the French Government announced that it had decided to drop all charges against Ludmilla Varyguine after Moscow had consistently maintained that the charges against her were totally unfounded.

Behind all these charges against Madame Varyguine lay the story of a rejected lover. It had begun with the marriage at Jaroslav on the Volga of Ludmilla Varyguine, who worked for the local Water Board, and a young French engineer, Pierre Verdier. The couple had met for the first time six months previously at a New Year's party in Moscow. Since then, though, Verdier had had to return to his post in the Rouen branch of the INSEF, the French statistics agency. However, having decided he wanted to marry the Russian woman he had seen so little of, his first task had to be to end an existing and long-standing love affair with a fellow worker, Antonetta Manole, a Romanian poetess who was married to an unemployed factory worker.

There was, however, a serious snag about breaking off this affair. Manole (or Nina, as she was more often known) had already recruited Verdier to a Soviet spy network in the north of France. But Verdier took the view that Nina would not dare expose him because she could not do this without incriminating herself. So he went ahead with marriage plans despite threats from Nina.

Here he erred totally, for, apart from the menace of what Nina might do, once he was married to Ludmilla he put himself even further under Soviet control. For what Nina cunningly did was to tell Colonel Valery Konorev, the assistant air attaché at the Soviet embassy in Paris, that Verdier was secretly working for France as well as the Soviet Union. The colonel, perhaps a little unfortunately from a Soviet viewpoint, paid little heed to this, probably thinking it was merely a woman's jealousy causing her to invent stories. He should have realized that if he did not at least pretend to go along with her, Nina might well take other action. She did: she wrote to the French Premier, Jacques Chirac, telling him that Verdier was passing information to the Russians.

The matter was handed over to the DST who once again smelt a Romanian Connection linked to Soviet espionage. But it was not the INSEF in which the Soviets were most interested but another organization outside Rouen at Vernon – the Société Européenne de Propulsion, a firm which designed the engine for the European space rocket Ariane. It was following this discovery that the DST moved in and made arrests, including Nina herself.

Each year satellite espionage had become increasingly vital to all national security systems, and as probes into outer space continued, so satellite competition between the great powers increased. The Soviet Union had given priority to their own drive for satellite-manufacture intelligence in recent years, concentrating especially on Ariane.

In 1986-7, following another squabble inside the Intelligence Services, some further changes were made. General Imbot stayed on as head of the DGSE, but some heads fell in both the DGSE and the DST. General René Emin, head of Intelligence (not quite so important a post as it sounds) stepped down and was replaced by General Jean Pons. Special Operations, always a tricky organization to tackle, was taken over by Colonel Jean Heinrich. A former fighter pilot, General François Mermet, was appointed to a key post on the foreign administration side of the DGSE.

Meanwhile General Imbot had found out that the DGSE's secret ship at Aspretto in Corsica had fed false information and misleading navigational charts to the Prefect whose job it was to keep track from his Toulon headquarters of the movements of every vessel in the area. The DGSE did this to keep their own movements secret. A further cause of anger in the ranks of the French Navy was that DGSE agents had fitted limpet mines on the French Mediterranean Fleet's own target ships as part of training operations. The Admiral in charge was furious, but can the up-and-coming agents be blamed for showing such enterprise, or gaining such experience?

It was about this time that there was a suggestion in some influential quarters that the Comte de Marenches should be brought back into the Intelligence Services in some capacity. On balance, it seems unlikely that he would have agreed, and it may be only coincidence or markedly significant that in 1986, while in retirement at Grasse, he should have made a sensational statement in an interview with Christine Ockrent, one of France's most important media personalities. For years he had declined to make any comments at all, but in this statement he told of having discovered some ten tons of files in a chamber vault in the SDECE headquarters relating to French people who had collaborated with the Germans. He described 'distressing discoveries' of treachery and cowardice by people who still held respected positions in French life.[2]

This statement was given the widest publicity in France. How was it, people asked, that such files had been neglected for so long? Why were they not discovered before and had someone deliberately kept them out of sight? What was equally puzzling was that, as this book has shown, the French Secret Service usually destroys what it wishes to keep quiet: it does not hoard such material. Then again it was not clear why de Marenches was making this information public.

To complete a puzzling story there was no indication of what had been, or would be, done with the files. Had they since been destroyed? The Comte de Marenches mentioned no names, but he added: 'I found some people who are very well set up now, who seemed to have been and who claim to have been patriots and Resistance fighters and who were in fact being paid by the Germans.'[3]

There was an indignant response from Colonel Paillole, who had been head of counter-espionage in France at the end of the war. 'Absolutely all German files seized during the Liberation have been examined,' he claimed. He was certain that they were tracked down in vehicles which the Germans abandoned in their retreat, saying that at the end of the war there was enough evidence to charge 4,598 French men and women for espionage and treason and to condemn 756 to death.[4]

The French Defence Minister, André Giraud, said that if the files still existed, they should be transferred to his ministry for examination. Jacques Chaban-Delmas, a former Prime Minister and Resistance worker, criticized de Marenches for 'casting suspicion on all surviving members of the Resistance'. In giving his own version of events both before and after he had been head of the service, de Marenches broke what had been a tradition of silence. Nonetheless, his comments and suggestions were statesmanlike, leaving only the puzzle of why he had chosen to bring up the subject of the discovery of the files on collaborators with the enemy in World War II. Certainly this was not a mischievous revelation, though undoubtedly it was a warning to some in high places, for he made it clear that he refused in any way to exploit these archives, or to produce names.

Because of his criticism of the Intelligence Service when he was interviewed in 1986, de Marenches was asked by a correspondent of *Le Monde* whether he felt that his predecessor and his successor were incompetent or inefficient. His reply was that

It was notoriously well known that until 1970 [the date when he took over the SDECE], the service had suffered much after the war. It

suffered from what I call the *millefeuilles*, with far too many people
squabbling among themselves . . . In the special services we have not
got to be of the right or the left or the centre in politics . . . I do not
compare myself with my predecessors. I was given full powers by the
President of the Republic to remould the service.[5]

The Increasing Threat of Terrorism

It is essential that we defend our country from the frightening dangers of terrorism . . . a last word to our leaders: they must not hide the facts which essentially concern public opinion . . . After all, the French are adults.

The Comte de Marenches[1]

The Comte de Marenches put his finger effectively on one of the major problems of the day when he gave this warning in the late 1980s. By the beginning of 1986 French Intelligence, in both the DGSE and the DST, was trying to develop new techniques in combating terrorism. One theory was – to twist around an old saying – 'if you want to beat them, join them'. Thus in April 1986 the DGSE authorized one of their agents, a Libyan, to bomb the offices of Air France in Lisbon in order to establish his credibility as a patriotic Libyan terrorist. Meanwhile he continued to report back to Paris on the activities of various Libyan and other Arab terrorists in Europe.

This agent was Syrian-born Farid Hassan, leader of a Libyan-backed terrorist group called the Call of Jesus Christ. The previous October Hassan had travelled to France from Spain to mastermind the bombing of a synagogue in the Rue Copernic in Paris, but his plan had collapsed when he was arrested with two others by French Intelligence agents soon after his arrival. It was after interrogation that Hassan agreed to become a French undercover agent in exchange for his freedom. This was once again one of those inspired gambles which the French seem able to pull off rather better than most other nations, and where their senior intelligence officers show themselves to be highly perceptive.

On 11 April 1986 Hassan placed bombs in the offices of Air

France in Lisbon and at the same time a DGSE agent monitored the bombing to make sure that nobody inside was hurt.
This ruse was apparently successful, as it is now known from
statements by the Spanish police that Hassan's group was later
promised the equivalent of £45,000 from the Libyan Intelligence Bureau in Madrid to finance a terrorist campaign in
Spain and Portugal. Whether the group did co-operate with the
French, or whether Hassan duped them into believing the
bombing was genuine, is not fully clear. Later that same year,
two members of the Call of Jesus Christ were arrested while on
an assignment to place bombs in the Madrid branch of the
Bank of America. It was this incident which led to Hassan's
arrest by the Spanish police and in the interrogation which
followed he claimed he was a French agent. It is impossible to
say how useful Hassan was to the French in their drive against
terrorism, nor would it be helpful to speculate. What can be
said is that by infiltrating terrorist groups the French have very
often gained more than those security services who rely solely
on orthodox methods.

Terrorism had once again proved a major problem for the
Intelligence Services in 1986. The previous year the DST had
arrested a member of a West German group responsible for
several anti-NATO bombings: he was said to be the leader of
various right-wing organizations which in some curious way had
become linked with left-wing groups in Western Europe and
the *Factions Armées Revolutionnaire Libanaises* (FARL). He
had been hiding in the United Kingdom to avoid arrest before
he was caught by the French.[2]

There had also been problems with the Basque terrorists
following the refusal of the Spanish police and Intelligence
Service to cooperate with their French counterparts in repress-
ing all forms of terrorism based in their respective countries.
Then in October 1986 the head of anti-terrorist operations
inside the Elysée Palace, Lieutenant-Colonel Christian Prouteau, was charged with 'suborning a witness'. This referred to a
case in which three Irish citizens had been arrested in the
Vincennes area of Paris in 1982 and charged with suspected
terrorism after the alleged discovery of weapons and explosives
in an apartment.

Nine months later the three, Mary Reid, Stephen King and Michael Plunkett, had been released as a result of what was called 'bungling' by the *Gendarmerie*. Later in 1986 Colonel Prouteau, who had founded the GIGN, a special commando division of the anti-terrorist *Gendarmerie*, was specifically blamed by another *Gendarmerie* officer for having bungled the case. It was all very mysterious and, as there had been a delay of over three years before these accusations were made, the affair smelt of a deliberate intrigue probably connected with the Presidential elections which were shortly to be held. Colonel Prouteau categorically denied all connection with the case, saying he had never been given any orders concerning it.[3]

In March 1987 the Lebanese terrorist chief, Georges Ibrahim Abdallah, was sentenced to life imprisonment in Paris. A few days later it was announced that the French Government had successfully censored some twenty-five pages of a book alleging that the DGSE had planted an agent to act as lawyer for Abdallah. Charles Pasqua, Minister of the Interior, and André Giraud, the Defence Minister, won a court injunction concerning the book, *The Black Agent, A Mole in the Abdallah Affair*, by Laurent Gally. During the court hearing Patrick Devedjian, the lawyer for the two ministers, alleged that the pages in question had been compiled from internal notes of both the DGSE and the DST. 'These notes give the names of a number of agents whose lives could be put in danger,' he commented.

Abdallah was a professional terrorist and a hit-man for the fanatical Marxist organization FARL; he had been found guilty of complicity in the murders of two diplomats and the attempted murder of another.

Two days later came an admission from the lawyer who had represented Abdallah, Jean-Paul Mazurier, that he had been a full-time agent of the DGSE since 1984. He revealed a further scandal behind the trial of Abdallah in that there had been a feud between the DGSE and the DST on this question, as the DST had refused to co-operate in tracking down Abdallah's extremist associates. Mazurier also asserted that he had acted as a go-between for Abdallah and his organization, travelling to Belgrade, Geneva, Rome and Damascus to smuggle messages from the Lyon prison where Abdallah was serving a four-year sentence for a previous offence. While doing this he secretly passed on all such information to his spymaster in Paris.

Discussing the affair on French television, he said he had supported the claims of Middle Eastern revolutionary movements, but had volunteered to become a double-agent because he could not accept anti-European terrorism as a weapon of achieving this. In a message to Abdallah in the book the lawyer said: 'The humiliation of your brothers will not be relieved by the mutilation of mine.'[4]

The Black Agent had contained Mazurier's confession and undoubtedly what angered the Minister of the Interior was that this directly contradicted evidence given at the trial on behalf of the DST suggesting that Abdallah was 'small fry', and also stating that, 'While the DST was seeking the bombers in Paris who killed or injured more than two hundred people, the DGSE was in direct contact with Abdallah's leading lieutenants, including Jacqueline Esber, who was said to have murdered an Israeli diplomat in Prais. The DGSE refused to hand over any information.'[5]

The book by Laurent Gally told how a French lawyer violated his professional oath and became an agent of the DGSE. It should perhaps once again be stressed that in a world in which common sense and a duty to one's own country are of paramount importance an oath such as this could be legitimately broken on moral grounds. This should apply equally to lawyer or priest. Jean-Paul Mazurier came from a middle-class family. First he went to a medical school, then switched to the law. It was after setting up a small legal practice that he was visited one day by Abdallah and recruited into FARL. Not wishing to be a party to terrorist acts, Mazurier contacted the DGSE and then his double life began. To maintain his cover, he successfully defended terrorists in Italy and handled FARL's business in Damascus, Trieste and Paris, all the while acting for the DGSE.

Clearly his problems began once the DST and the DGSE again antagonized one another, each tending to blame the other for mistakes. Mazurier, whose future at the bar was put at risk because of this, was full of remorse for his part in it and said he actually risked being killed for what he had disclosed. He added that twice previously the Syrians had tried to kill him.

It was perhaps tragic that so vital and contemporary a problem as terrorism should not be tackled by united espionage and counter-espionage services. Yet it must be realized that the French impatience for quick decisions, even snap decisions which may result in catastrophe, characterizes these anti-terrorist policies. Whereas the Anglo-Saxons (both British and American) allow themselves to become immobilized by the moral dilemmas of coping with terrorism, the French method of taking action regardless of possible consequences probably pays larger dividends more quickly. At any rate, it is certainly true that despite the Abdallah upset both the DGSE and the DST made considerable advances in tackling terrorism in 1987 and 1988. Just as they had used their highly effective computer systems to sniff out suspect capital in Swiss accounts a year or two before, so in 1987 they began to concentrate on using these systems to combat the problem of terrorism.

It would be tantamount to aiding terrorism to go into too many details of how French Intelligence computer systems are now being used in Paris to combat terrorism. Suffice to say that the computer system consists of two identical programs which enable the services to have instant access to information on terrorists such as biographical details, the code-names under which they operate and their methods and movements. While these systems are identical, they allow for double-checks to be made on each: the one program can help to check or supplement the other, and the combined database provides cross-referencing.

The DGSE casts its net wide in looking for clues on terrorism around the world. One of its successes related to the case of the Swedish Prime Minister, Olof Palme, who was shot dead in 1986 and whose assassin was never caught. It was a curious case in that usually Olof Palme kept the Swedish security police informed of his movements. The day he was killed he had not done so. Nobody outside his family and household staff knew his plans for that evening. Yet as the Palmes reached the corner of a street, shots were fired. A passing taxi-driver remembered three people standing on the corner. He heard a shot and then saw a man run off towards a pedestrian tunnel.

The DGSE's interest in Palme was largely because of his close relationships with a number of suspected Middle Eastern and European terrorists. A well-known womanizer, he was consorting with at least two women suspected of being agents of a Middle Eastern power. In addition the French well knew he had a number of dubious contacts behind the Iron Curtain.

The French discovered that there was a link between Palme's murder and the arms trade with the Middle East in which they themselves were concerned. There was evidence that Palme had contacts in two terrorist groups concerned with Europe just as much as the Middle East, one called Little Girls from the Suburbs and the other Children of the Economic Miracle (examples of the kind of satire in which the more sophisticated terrorist societies of today indulge). Everything about his murder pointed to a political killing, the most likely perpetrators being an Iranian group. Palme had been trying to stop the proliferation of nuclear arms amongst non-aligned nations and he had also become involved in trying to open up international banking laws so that there could be no hidden accounts. Moreover, Iran could only pay for arms with oil and Palme refused to permit the importation of Iranian oil by Sweden. Three weeks before Palme's death an Iranian military mission had gone to Sweden and had protested strongly against Palme's action in blocking the delivery of arms to Iran. French inquiries suggested that in planning Palme's death an Iranian group had made a deal either with some European terrorist organization or an anti-Communist group inside Scandinavia who would have supplied the hit-man. The computer system had helped enormously in pointing the way to such an answer to Palme's murder, but, more importantly, it provided various clues to future terrorist activities.

In February 1987 the DST had by patient and diligent planning tracked down some nineteen men and women belonging to the *Action Directe* terrorist group which was linked to a number of other terrorist organizations, including the West German Red Army Faction. Prior to this the *Action Directe* had made several successful attacks, including the assassination of General René Audran, deputy director of the French Defence Ministry's arms sales department, in 1985. Shortly after this incident François le Mouel, one of France's most respected police commissioners, was appointed the head of a special anti-terrorist co-ordinating unit, and he immediately attributed the fact that only one *Action Directe* suspect had been arrested since December 1984 to a crippling lack of skilled infiltrators able to penetrate the network.

By 1987 many earlier mistakes had been rectified and in February of that year the DST had located the *Action Directe* group in a remote farmhouse near the village of Vitry-aux-Loges some twenty-five miles east of Orléans. They caught four of the group's leaders, Jean-Marc Rouillan, Nathalie Menigon, Georges Cipriani and Joelle Aubron. This was a devastating blow to the organization which for a long time previously had been divided into two wings, one national, concerned with France, and the other dubbed international, which had links with all manner of terrorist groups in various parts of Europe, such as Belgium's CCC (Communist Combatant Cells), the Middle East and even the Far East. The farmhouse at Vitry had been rented in November 1984 by Georges Cipriani, using Belgian papers in the name of Eric Oerdeil. The police who raided the place found weapons, ammunition and explosives as well as stacks of papers which revealed lists of potential victims, addresses of safe houses, accounts and financial records including an IOU from the Red Army Faction for a sum in Deutschmarks equivalent to about £65,000.

The DST had to guard against a possible bombing campaign during the trial of these people. This risk was finally disposed of when in November 1987 the DST arrested in Lyon Max Frérot, the explosives expert of the *Action Directe*. It was a splendid coup, but it by no means ended the threat of terrorism. 'The principal three terrorist groups have clearly been dealt with, but that does not mean extreme left-wing terrorism is dead. On the contrary, I think it will return,' stated Ian

Geldard of the London-based Institute for the Study of Terrorism.[6]

The trial of the five leading members of the *Action Directe* dragged on until it became a grisly charade with the accused going on a hunger strike that lasted eighty-six days. By this time they were reduced to little more than total emaciation and had to be brought to court on stretchers. During proceedings they dozed off so frequently that the judge more than once summoned a doctor to make sure they were still alive. The five were not being forcibly fed, but they were being fed intravenously at their own request, this being with large doses of glucose. Then in February 1988 a special court in Paris imposed sentences on them ranging from life imprisonment to thirteen years in jail.

During 1987 the new director of the DST, Bernard Gerard, visited Damascus to discuss terrorist bombings in Paris with the Syrian authorities. This was widely regarded as a somewhat futile mission, with France continuing to express goodwill towards Syria while being fully aware that Syria was involved in some terrorist attacks. Certainly this was not an auspicious moment to hold such talks, just when France was accusing the brothers of Georges Abdallah, serving his prison sentence, of having organized some of the earlier bombings in Paris. Nor was the logic of this mission clear to the outside world in the light of Prime Minister Chirac's statement that there was no evidence of Syrian responsibility for such bombings, coupled with a warning that France would not deal with states using terrorists against it. But what may appear illogical to the outside world often appears logical to France. The French view, always optimistic even in defeat, is that even when one ostensibly takes a categoric stand such as Chirac's, there is always room for talk and manoeuvre. Quite often this works when Anglo-Saxon moral pigheadedness fails. To some extent Chirac's work paid off in the early summer of 1988 when Syria brought about a ceasefire in Lebanon.

In November 1987 a report by the French Army controller, General Jean-François Barba, revealed that President Mitterand and his former Defence Minister, Charles Hernu, had known about illegal arms sales to Iran, but had done nothing.

The Barba report had been ordered by the new government after it had been disclosed a year earlier that the Luchaire arms company had sold some 500,000 artillery shells to Iran, using false end-user certificates and in contravention of a French arms embargo on Tehran. These sales had brought in some 700 million francs to France between 1983 and 1986.

This sum did not include commission payments made to French and Iranian intermediaries through an Italian bank in Switzerland. It was even alleged that some of this money had found its way back to France to provide funds for the Socialist Party to fight the next Parliamentary elections. Hernu denied that he had known anything about arms sales to Iran, but this statement was somewhat weakened when the former Socialist Foreign Minister, Roland Dumas, confessed that he had known of the deals and that in 1985 he had managed to dissuade *Le Canard Enchaîné* from publishing the story because he feared it would jeopardize negotiations for the release of French hostages held by Iranian sympathizers in the Lebanon. If Dumas knew about this, it seems unlikely that either the President or the Defence Minister did not also know.

But no country in the world can play a double game more effectively than France. It was true that in the autumn of 1987 it was believed in many quarters that France had been secretly trying to strike a deal with Iran to free its own hostages in Lebanon and that this had made the British fear that their own policy of no negotiation with terrorists was weakened. The truth was that the British had absolutely no influence whatsoever in trying to get their own hostages released. Compared to the French, they were hopelessly outclassed in this highly skilled operation.

In September 1987, following diplomatic moves by the DGSE, Hojatoleslam Ali Akbar, the Speaker of the Iranian Parliament, stated publicly that, 'For the first time French officials, using Pakistan as an intermediary, sought to make a deal with Iran during several days of clandestine negotiations in Geneva.'[7]

According to the Speaker, a French official had offered to allow home a senior Iranian diplomat, Wahid Gordji, wanted for questioning about a wave of terrorist bombings in Paris a

year before, in return for the release of five French hostages
held by pro-Iranian terrorists in Lebanon. This statement by
the Iranian Speaker was published in the French magazine,
Jeune Afrique, and seemed a clear and public indication of
France's intention to deal with Iran. Gordji was at the time
taking refuge inside the Iranian Embassy in Paris.

Then in December 1987 France acted with surprising swift-
ness in ridding itself of no less than twenty-six known opponents
of the Ayatollah Khomeini then residing in Paris by arresting
them and putting seventeen of them on a plane for Gabon, a
former French colony in Equatorial Africa. Included among
these Iranians was one with refugee status in Britain. The
French Government's official statement was that these people
were expelled because they constituted a threat to public order.
Not surprisingly this was interpreted as being part of a secret
deal between Paris and Tehran for the release of the French
hostages held in Lebanon. The people arrested by the French
were all said to be members of the People's Mujahedeen, the
resistance group fighting the Ayatollah's regime in Iran. There
was a sequel to this in January 1988, when the French Prime
Minister signed an order releasing fifteen Iranians and three
Turks from house arrest in Gabon.

A few months before this the DST had been given a totally
different problem. Maryse Villard, a 44-year-old administrative
secretary in the office of the Prime Minister, Jacques Chirac,
had been charged with passing secret documents to her Iranian
lover. As long ago as June 1986 French customs officers at the
Franco-German border had searched her bags and found a
classified document relating to France's role in the Iran–Iraq
hostilites. The DST was immediately consulted and Villard was
taken back to Paris under close arrest. It was alleged that her
lover was a member of the Ayatollah's Security Service.

How, people asked, had it been possible for this secret to be
kept for more than a year? After her arrest she had been
released for a brief spell while inquiries were made and then
rearrested on 29 July 1986. Ever since then she had been in
prison, yet nobody had asked questions about her whereabouts
or seemed interested in her fate. Undoubtedly at this period it
was a subject of considerable embarrassment for the French

government, especially on the home front, and for that reason great pains had been taken to hush things up. Only slowly, bit by bit, did the story emerge in late October 1987. The man behind this was said to be a handsome Iranian working for the Iranian Nico petrol company who had seduced no fewer than three confidential secretaries working inside the Paris headquarters of UNESCO, as well as Villard.

In November 1987 French Intelligence was able to do the British a good turn by seizing a leading member of the IRA on a ship carrying more than 150 tons of weapons and explosives, including twenty Soviet-manufactured SAM-7 anti-aircraft missiles. He was Gabriel Cleary who was using a stolen Irish passport. He was a crew member of the coaster *Eksund*, which was seized off Brittany. Along with four other men, he was arrested and charged with illegally transporting arms to be used for 'disturbing public order by intimidation and terror'.[8]

These missiles were undoubtedly ordered by the IRA to attack British helicopters along the Northern Ireland border with the Irish Republic. Cleary, a known IRA gun-running expert, had already served a lengthy sentence in the Irish Republic after being connected with an explosives find in the mid-1970s. The *Eksund* was a Panamanian-registered vessel which had spent ten years carrying grain across the Baltic and had been bought by an Irishman from its Swedish owner shortly before the capture of the ship.

Terrorism undoubtedly takes up a great deal of time for many of the Western world's secret services today, for it is far too big a problem to be left to the police. Equally it is too complicated a problem solely for the counter-espionage services to cope with. When terrorist organizations operate in several countries at the same time the external intelligence services are forced to take cognizance of this. In France public responsibility for the DGSE is generally shared equally by the President and the Prime Minister, though this principle has on occasions been challenged. Sometimes, but not always, such responsibility is extended to include the Minister of Defence. On the whole this is a much tidier way of doing things than the British practice which, in effect, tends to divide responsibility between the

Foreign Secretary and the Prime Minister, with the Defence Minister often being ignored. The French Intelligence and Security Services have learned to mistrust their Foreign Office and not to rely upon it, whereas the British have sometimes failed in the world of intelligence as a result of paying too much heed to their Foreign Office. The further away from Foreign Office interference any Secret Service can keep, the better it is. In any case diplomatic protocol establishes the principle that they should be apart, even if this is often broken. Foreign Offices and Intelligence Services may have the wish to help their countries in common, but their methods of carrying this out must frequently clash and sometimes even make them, marginally at least, in opposition.

The Comte de Marenches consistently took the view in his retirement from the service that the drive against terrorism was of supreme importance and that France was more vulnerable than most nations in facing this problem.[9]

Perhaps one can usefully point to the fact that those engaged in intelligence work in France have positively concentrated on future needs in the past few years. In no sphere has this been more usefully demonstrated than in the fight against terrorism, which, worldwide, threatens to become a greater menace to peace than any threat of war from the big powers in the years to come. It was the French, backed by their Intelligence Services, who brought about the many improvements in the Trevi group, the EC organization for co-operation against terrorism. Until 1985 Trevi had shown few signs of coping with these problems effectively. Then Jacques Chirac, the French Premier, gave a positive lead to Trevi and suggested various initiatives. It was then agreed during the period when France held the chairmanship of Trevi in 1987 that the co-operation of the USA and non-EC countries should be sought. This was France's reply to American criticism of what it had seen as Europe's inability to tackle terrorism inside its borders.

Though this may not easily be grasped by the outside world, it is the talent of French Intelligence Services for looking to the future when internally the outlook is bleak, under siege or confused, that is one of their greatest assets. While the mass of

French people are occasionally overcome by pessimism – as in 1870, 1940 and in the past decade concerning terrorism in their midst – the optimism of their Intelligence Services is something to which they owe a great deal.

Chapter Notes

INTRODUCTION

1 *Daily Telegraph*, 26 October 1987.

CHAPTER 1

1 *Life of Richelieu*, Gabriel Hanataux, London, 1893.

CHAPTER 2

1 *De la manière de négocier avec les souverains*, François de Callières, Paris, 1716.
2 *Ibid*.
3 'Mr Secretary Thurloe', article in *Macmillan's Magazine*, LXX, 1894.
4 *Histoire de France principalement pendant le XVI et le XVII siècle*, Ranke, translated by J J Procat, Paris, 1888.
5 Cited in *Secret Diplomacy: Record of Espionage and Double-Dealing: 1500–1815*, J E Thomson and S K Padover, Jarrolds, London, 1937.
6 *Abrégé de la correspondance diplomatique de Dubois*, 2 vols, edited by Sévelinges, Paris, 1815.
7 *Ibid*.
8 An unabridged edition of *La correspondance de Dubois*, Paris, 1897.

CHAPTER 3

1 'Le Cabinet secret de Louis XV en Hollande', by P Coquelle, *Revue d'histoire diplomatique*, XV, 1901. See also *Secret Diplomacy*, Thomson and Padover.
2 *Ibid*.

CHAPTER 4

1 *The Memoirs of the Chevalier d'Eon*, Frédéric Gaillardet, translated 1970.
2 *The Strange Career of the Chevalier d'Eon de Beaumont*, Captain J Buchan Telfer, RN, Longman, Green & Co., London, 1885.
3 *Ibid.*
4 *Ibid.*
5 *The Enigma of the Age: the Strange Story of the Chevalier d'Eon*, Cynthia Cox, 1966.

CHAPTER 5

1 *Histoire philosophique de la révolution française*, F Desodoards.
2 *Babeuf et le socialisme en 1796*, Edouard Fleury.
3 *Ibid.*
4 *A Social History of Madness*, Roy Porter, Weidenfeld & Nicolson, London, 1987.

CHAPTER 6

1 *Lettres Inédites de Napoléon Ier*, 2 vols, L Lecestre, Paris, 1897.
2 *Talleyrand's Memoirs, Nineteenth Century*, XXIX, Lord Acton, 1891.
3 *Ibid.*
4 *Ibid.*
5 *La Police secrète du Premier Empire: bulletins quotidiens adressés par Fouché à l'Empéreur*, Librairie Académique, Paris, 1908.
6 *A Hirszerzés és Kémkedés Törtenete* (The History of Intelligence and Espionage), 2 vols, Franklin Society, Budapest, 1936.
7 *Ibid.*

CHAPTER 7

1 *Mémoires*, François Vidocq, Paris, 1838.
2 *Rapports militaires écrits de Berlin*, Colonel Baron Stoffel, *Bibliothèque Nationale*, Paris.
3 *Les Services de Renseignements: 1871–1944*, Henri Navarre, Plon, Paris, 1978.
4 *Ibid.*
5 Annexes of the *Service de Renseignements*.
6 *Mysteries of Police & Crime*, vol 1, Arthur Griffiths.

CHAPTER 8

1 *La Libre Parole*, 31 October 1894, Paris.
2 *Dreyfus*, Walther Steinthal. Also *Cinq Années de Ma Vie*, Alfred Dreyfus.
3 *Les Dessous de l'Affaire Dreyfus*, Ferdinand Esterhazy, Fayard Frères, Paris, 1898.
4 *Secret and Urgent, the Story of Codes and Ciphers*, Fletcher Pratt, Robert Hale, London, 1939.
5 Cavaignac after his resignation wrote *La Formation de la Prusse Contemporaine, 1891–8.*
6 *Les Services de Renseignements*, Navarre.

CHAPTER 9

1 Cited by R W Rowan and Robert S Deindorfer in *Secret Service: 33 Centuries of Espionage*, Hawthorn Books Inc., New York, 1967.
2 *Les Services de Renseignments*, Navarre.
3 See *Secret and Urgent, the Story of Codes and Ciphers*, Pratt.
4 *Ibid.*
5 *La Guerre Secrète*, Michel Garder. See also Annexes of *Les Services de Renseignements*.

CHAPTER 10

1 Annexes of the *Services de Renseignements*.
2 *Guerre des cerveaux: en missions spéciales*, C Lucieto, 1926.
3 *Ibid.* Also cited in German documents of the period.

4 *Encyclopaedia of Espionage*, Ronald Seth, New English Library, London, 1972.
5 Extracts from the *Bulletin de Renseignements du Poste SR de Belfort*, 10 February 1916.
6 *Treason and Tragedy*, George Adam, Jonathan Cape, London, 1929.

CHAPTER 11

1 Churchill wrote these words in his foreword to Marthe McKenna's book, *I was a Spy*, Jarrolds, London, 1933.
2 *Take Nine Spies*, Sir Fitzroy Maclean, Weidenfeld & Nicolson, London, 1978.
3 *The Underworld of Paris*, Alfred Morain.
4 *Ibid.*
5 *Ma vie d'espionnage au service de la France*, Marthe Richer, Paris, 1936.
6 *Agents secrètes: L'affaire Fauquenot-Birckel*, Paul Durand, Paris, 1937.
7 *Secret Services of Europe*, Robert Boucard, London, 1940.

CHAPTER 12

1 *Treason and Tragedy*, Adam.
2 Cited from French press reports in *A History of the Russian Secret Service*, Richard Deacon, Frederick Muller, London, 1972.
3 *Le Réarmament Clandestin du Reich: 1930–35*, Georges Castellan, Plon, Paris, 1954.
4 *Le Deuxième Bureau au Travail*, General Gauché, Amiot-Dumard, Paris, 1953.
5 *Services Spéciaux 1935–45*, Paul Paillole, Éditions Robert Laffont, Paris, 1975.
6 *Le Deuxième Bureau au Travail*, Gauché.
7 *Code-Name Marianne*, Edita Katona with Patrick Macnaghten, Collins & Harvill Press, London, 1976.
8 *Ibid.*
9 *Treason and Tragedy*, Adam.

10 *Services Spéciaux 1935–45*, Paillole.
11 *Treason and Tragedy*, Adam.

CHAPTER 13

1 Public Records Office, London: FO 800/317, H/XV/312.
2 *Ibid*.
3 Letter to the author from Miss Elka Schrijver, 27 March 1981.
4 *Ibid*.
5 *Second Bureau*, P J Stead, Evans, London, 1959.
6 Cited in official French archives, 27 June 1940, which state: '*Le Cinquième Bureau cesse d'exister à la date du 27 juin – Un SR camouflé est constitué immédiatement avec un personnel de qualité prélevé sur les éléments d'active de l'ancien Cinquième Bureau. I: prend, sauf impossibilités momentanées pour certaines d'entre elles, les tâches dont le Cinquième Bureau était chargé à la veille de sa dissolution.*'
7 *Le Sacrifice du Matin*, Guillain de Bénouville, Robert Laffont, Paris, 1975.
8 See *Bulletin de l'Amicale des Anciens Membres des Services de Sécurité Militaire et des Réseaux*, TF No. 1.

CHAPTER 14

1 *Chemins Secrets*, Colonel Georges Groussard, Bader-Dufour, Paris, 1948.
2 *MI6: British Secret Service Operations 1909–45*, Nigel West, Weidenfeld & Nicolson, London, 1983.
3 *The Second World War*, Sir Winston Churchill, vol 3, Educational Books, London, 1950.
4 Both Dewavrin and Renault-Roulier were on friendly terms with Dansey. See *Trente Ans Après*, Rémy, Librairie Académique Perrin, Paris, 1974.
5 See *Ten Thousand Eyes*, Richard Collier, Collins, London, 1958.

6 *Second Bureau*, Stead.
7 *Chemins Secrets*, Groussard.
8 *Second Bureau*, Stead.
9 *Ibid*.
10 *Le Monde*, Paris, 17 February 1966. See also *2e Bureau, Londres*, Colonel Passy, Solar, Monte Carlo, 1947.
11 *Envers et Contre Tout*, vol 2, *Souvenirs et Documents sur la France Libre, 1942–4*, Jacques Soustelle, Robert Laffont, Paris, 1950.

CHAPTER 15

1 *Le Sacrifice du Matin*, de Bénouville.
2 *Moondrop to Gascony*, Anne-Marie Walters, London, 1946.
3 Article entitled 'Resistance Author Hits at Critics', *Sunday Telegraph*, 1 May 1966, by M R D Foot.
4 Cited by Sam White in his Paris Column, *Evening Standard*, 6 May 1966.
5 *SOE in France*, M R D Foot, HMSO, London, 1966.
6 *L'Enigme Jean Moulin*, Henri Frenay, Robert Laffont, Paris.
7 Letter to the author from Jacques Bergier, 9 November 1977. Bergier was a member of the *Comité des Intellectuels Antifascistes de France*, founded during the Spanish Civil War.
8 Personal communication to the author by 'Roger', an ex-member of the INSA anti-fascist secret group which existed in Switzerland in the early 1930s.
9 Letter to Jacques Bergier from General de Gaulle, 21 June 1955.
10 *Secret Weapons – Secret Agents*, Jacques Bergier, Hurst & Blackett, London, 1956.
11 *Ibid*.

CHAPTER 16

1 *Le Monde*, 17 February 1966.
2 Jacques Soustelle in an interview with V S Naipaul in the *Daily Telegraph*, 26 January 1968.

3 *Ibid*.

4 Article entitled 'Genesis of the French Service SDECE' by Laughlin Campbell, *Foreign Intelligence Literary Scene*, vol 5, no. 3, 1986.

5 Report by staff reporter, Paris, in *Daily Express*, 6 May 1946.

6 *Daily Telegraph*, 12 September 1946.

7 Article entitled 'Torture in Duke Street', by John Ellison, *Daily Express*, 4 April 1967. Dewavrin showed the author of this article a photocopy of official records of these claims.

8 *Trente Ans Après*, Rémy.

9 *Daily Express*, 4 April 1967.

10 *Ibid*.

11 This information was obtained by the author personally and printed in a feature called 'Inside Information' in the London *Daily Sketch* some time between late November 1948 and the end of January 1949. As both Glubb Pasha and King Abdullah were still alive at that time and no denial was made by either to the best of my knowledge, one must assume the information was accurate.

12 Professor Douglas Porch in a review of *La Piscine: Les Services Secrets Français 1944–84*, Roger Faligot and Pascal Krop, Seuil, Paris, 1985, published in the *International Journal of Intelligence and Counterintelligence*, vol 1, no. 2, 1986, Intel Publishing Group, Pennsylvania.

CHAPTER 17

1 *The Espionage Establishment*, David Wise and Thomas B Ross, Random House, New York, 1967.

2 'Draining the Swimming Pool', book review by Douglas Porch in the *International Journal of Intelligence and Counterintelligence*, vol 1, no. 2, 1986.

3 *Mr France: The Life and Times of France's Dynamic Post-War Premier*, Donald McCormick, Jarrolds, London, 1955.

4 *Ibid*.

CHAPTER 18

1 *Sunday Times*, London, 12 July 1959.
2 Article by Eric Scott in the *Daily Worker*, London, 4 August 1959.
3 Quoted in *The Times*, London, 25 August 1959.
4 Quoted in *The Times*, London, 17 September 1960.
5 *Evening Standard*, London, 5 April 1960.
6 Article entitled 'The Secret War of the Red Hand', by Peter Stephens, *Daily Mirror*, London, 27 October 1959.
7 *Ibid*.
8 *Daily Mail*, London, 20 October 1959.
9 *Ibid*.
10 *Welt am Sonntag*, Bonn, 2 November 1959.
11 *The Times*, London, 29 January 1960.

CHAPTER 19

1 Soustelle in an interview with V S Naipaul, *Daily Telegraph*, London, 26 January 1968.
2 *The Times*, London, 26 May 1958 and 10 June 1958.
3 *L'Express*, Paris, 14 January 1960.
4 *Daily Telegraph*, London, 26 January 1968.
5 Report from Alan Tillier, *Sunday Telegraph* correspondent in Geneva, including an interview with Soustelle.
6 Professor Douglas Porch in a review of *La Piscine: Les Services Secrets Français 1944–84*, Faligot and Krop, published in the *International Journal of Intelligence and Counterintelligence*, vol 1, no. 2.
7 *Daily Telegraph*, London, 20 January 1966.

CHAPTER 20

1 *Le Canard Enchaîné*, Paris, April 1968.
2 *Topaz*, Leon Uris, McGraw Hill, New York, 1962.
3 Details of this affair were given by Yuri Krotkov to a US Senate Investigating Committee, and released for publication in January 1971. See also article by Krotkov entitled

'Secrets of Russia's Security Police' in the *Sunday Telegraph*, London, 13 September 1970.

4 *Daily Telegraph*, London, 10 May 1965; *Daily Mirror*, London, 10 May 1965.

5 *Daily Telegraph*, London, March 1968, and especially 15 April 1968.

6 *News of the World*, London, 10 April 1966.

7 *Ibid*.

8 *Ibid*.

9 Article entitled 'The Soviet Agent Close to de Gaulle', by Thyraud de Vosjoli, *Sunday Times Review*, London, 21 April 1968.

10 *Le Canard Enchaîné*, Paris, April 1968.

11 *De Gaulle*, Brian Crozier, Charles Scribner, New York, 1973.

12 *Lamia*, Philippe Thyraud de Vosjoli, Little, Brown, Boston, 1970.

CHAPTER 21

1 *The Times*, London, 26 October 1968.

2 *Ibid*.

3 *The Times*, London, 30 November 1967.

4 *The Times*, London, 15 June 1955.

5 *The Times*, London, 15 January 1972.

6 *Cinq Ans à la Tête de la DST: La Mission Impossible*, Jean Rochet, Plon, Paris, 1985.

7 French television: *Dossiers de l'Écran* programme, 27 January 1971.

8 *Guardian*, London, 30 January 1971, article by Nesta Roberts entitled 'Spycatcher Spills the Beans'.

9 *The People*, London, report from Jack Gee in Paris, 31 January 1971.

CHAPTER 22

1 *The Times*, London, 27 November 1971.

2 *Ibid*.

3 *Ibid*.

4 *Daily Telegraph*, London, 27 November 1971.
5 *Le Secret des Princes*, Alexandre Comte de Marenches, Éditions Stock, Paris, 1986.
6 Article entitled 'French Led Secret Campaign to Back Smith' by James Macmanus, *Sunday Telegraph*, London, 6 September 1987.
7 *Le Secret des Princes*, de Marenches.
8 *Serving Secretly*, Ken Flower, John Murray, London, 1987.
9 *Ibid*.
10 Cited from Leroy-Finville's memoirs in *The Observer*, London, 1 May 1981.
11 *The Evil Empire: The Third World War Now*, Comte de Marenches and Christine Ockrent, Sidgwick & Jackson, London, 1988.
12 *Guardian*, London, 4 December 1971.
13 *News of the World*, London, 27 May 1973. As a point of interest, the *News of the World* has been extremely well served by its Paris correspondents since 1945.
14 *L'Express*, Paris, 4 October 1971.
15 *Ibid*.

CHAPTER 23

1 *Observer*, London, 16 January 1977, and *Guardian*, London, 11 January 1977.
2 *Guardian*, 11 January 1977.
3 *Le Nouvele Observateur*, Paris, 18 January 1976, and *The Times*, London, 19 January 1976.
4 *Ibid*.
5 *Daily Express*, London, 14 January 1976.
6 *Daily Express*, London, 16 July 1975.
7 *Le Secret des Princes*, de Marenches.
8 *Le Monde*, Paris, 23 February 1978.
9 *The Times*, London, 10 September 1980.
10 *The Times*, London, 6 March 1980, and *Observer*, London, 15 February 1980.

CHAPTER 24

1 *Sunday Times*, London, 31 May 1981.
2 *Alpha*, no. 5, London 1979.

3 *Omni*, vol 8, no. 4, 1986: article by Sherry Baker, entitled 'UFO Update'.
4 *Flying Saucer Review*, vol 30, no. 3, 1984, article by Gordon Creighton entitled 'Another French Report on GEPAN'.
5 *Sunday Express*, London, 24 July 1983, article entitled 'Flying Saucer Has the Boffins Baffled', by David Paskov, Paris.
6 *Ibid*.
7 *France-Soir*, Paris, 11 November 1982.

CHAPTER 25

1 *Le Canard Enchaîné*, Paris, 28 November 1984.
2 Interview on Swiss television, 14 April 1983.
3 *Le KGB en France*, Thierry Wolton, Bernard Grasset, Paris, 1986.
4 *The Evil Empire*, de Marenches and Ockrent.
5 *Sunday Times*, London, 20 June 1982.
6 *The Times*, London, 1 September 1982.
7 *Guardian*, London, 1 September 1982.
8 *The Times*, London, 3 September 1982. Also *Quotidien de Paris* and *France-Soir*, Paris, 2 September 1982.

CHAPTER 26

1 *Sunday Times*, London, 11 May 1986.
2 *Ibid*.
3 *The Times*, London, 24 February 1983.
4 *Daily Telegraph*, London, 20 February 1983.
5 *Daily Mail*, London, 12 December 1983.
6 *Le Nouvel Observateur*, Paris, December 1982.
7 *Sunday Telegraph*, London, 10 June 1984.
8 *Le Monde*, Paris, 26 October 1984.
9 *Le Matin de Paris*, Paris, 19 October 1984.
10 *The Evil Empire*, de Marenches and Ockrent.
11 Article by Henri Regnard in *Défense Nationale*, Paris, December 1984.

CHAPTER 27

1 Greenpeace campaign sheet, September 1987.
2 *Ibid*.
3 *Le Point*, Paris, 12 August 1985.
4 *Le Monde*, Paris, 17 August 1985.
5 *Observer*, London, 1 September 1985.
6 *International Herald Tribune*, Paris, 21 August 1985.
7 *The Times*, London, 30 September 1985.
8 *Ibid*.
9 *Daily Express*, London, 1 September 1987, report from a New Zealand correspondent.

CHAPTER 28

1 *Daily Telegraph*, London, 21 March 1987.
2 *Le Secret des Princes*, de Marenches.
3 *Ibid*.
4 *Sunday Times*, London, 12 October 1986.
5 Interview with the Comte de Marenches by Jacques Isnard in *Le Monde*, Paris, 14 October 1986.

CHAPTER 29

1 Interview with the Comte de Marenches by Jacques Isnard in *Le Monde*, Paris, 14 October 1986.
2 *De Knipselkrant*, Holland, 24 April 1985 and 8 May 1985.
3 *Daily Telegraph*, London, 30 October 1986.
4 *Guardian*, London, 6 March 1987.
5 *Ibid*.
6 Article entitled 'Terror 88: the Fight Moves On', by Niall Ferguson, *Daily Telegraph*, London, 22 January 1988.
7 *Sunday Telegraph*, London, 27 September 1987.
8 *Daily Telegraph*, London, 4 November 1987.
9 *Le Secret des Princes*, de Marenches.

Bibliography

ADAM, George, *Treason and Tragedy*, Jonathan Cape, London, 1929.

ALLARD, P, *Quand Hitler espionne la France*, Éditions de France, Paris, 1939.

AUER, M, *L'Oeil invisible: les appareils photographiques d'espionnages*, EPR, Paris, 1978.

BERGIER, Jacques, *Secret Weapons – Secret Agents*, Hurst & Blackett, London, 1956.

—*Je ne suis pas une légende*, Retz, Paris, 1977.

BERJAUD, L, *Boutin, agent de Napoleon I*, Paris, 1950.

BERNET, Philippe, *SDECE – Service 7*, Presses de la Cité, Paris.

BERTRAND, Gustave, *Enigma ou La Plus Grande Enigme de la Guerre, 1939–45*, Plon, Paris, 1973.

CHURCHILL, Sir Winston, *The Second World War*, vols 1–6, Cassell, London, 1958.

COLLIER, Richard, *Ten Thousand Eyes*, Collins, London, 1958.

DAUDET, Léon, *L'avant Guerre: études et documents sur l'espionnage Juif–Allemand–Français depuis Dreyfus*, Nouvelle Librairie Nationale, Paris, 1913.

DE BÉNOUVILLE, Guillain, *Le Sacrifice du Matin*, Robert Laffont, Paris, 1947.

DE MARENCHES, Comte Alexandre, *Le Secret des Princes* (with Christine Ockrent), Éditions Stock, Paris, 1986. Also *The Evil Empire: The Third World War Now*, Sidgwick & Jackson, London, 1988.

DE VIDEMAREST, Pierre, *L'Espionnage Soviétique en France 1944–69*, Éditions Latines, Paris, 1969.

DE VOSJOLI, Philippe Thyraud, *Lamia*, Little, Brown, Boston, 1970.

FALIGOT, Roger, and KROP, Pascal, *La Piscine: Les Services Secrets Français 1944–84*, Éditions du Seuil, Paris, 1985.

FOOT, M R D, *SOE in France*, HMSO, London, 1966.

FOUCHÉ, J, *La Police secrète du Premier Empire: (1804–7): bulletins quotidiens addressés à l' Empéreur*, Perrin, Paris, 1908–22, 3 vols.

GARDER, Michel, *Le Guerre Secrète des Services Spéciaux Français 1939–45*, Paris, 1967.

GAUCHÉ, General, *Le Deuxième Bureau au Travail*, Amiot-Dumard, Paris, 1953.

GROUSSARD, Colonel Georges, *Chemins Secrets*, Bader-Dufour, Paris, 1948.

HANATAUX, Gabriel, *Life of Richelieu*, London, 1893.

HAUTERIVE, E d', *Police secrète du Premier Empire*, Grassion, Paris, 1963.

KATONA, Edita, with MACNAGHTEN, Patrick, *Code-Name Marianne*, Collins & Harvill Press, London, 1976.

LADOUX, Commandant, *Mes Souvenirs*, Éditions de France, Paris, 1939.

LAURENT, Gally, *The Black Agent: Traitor to an Unjust Cause*, André Deutsch, London, 1988.

LÉCESTRE, I, *Lettres Inédites de Napoleon Ier*, 2 vols, Paris, 1987.

McCORMICK, Donald, *Mr France: the Life and Times of France's Dynamic Post-War Premier*, Jarrolds, London, 1976.

MELNIK, Constantin, *La Troisième Rome*, Grasset, Paris, 1986.

MOSSARD, Comte Émile, *Les Espionnes à Paris: Verité sur Mata Hari*, A Michel, Paris, 1922.

MULLER, P, *L'Espionnage sous Napoleon I: Schulmeister*, Paris, 1896.

NAVARRE, Henri, *Le Service de Renseignements 1871–1944*, Plon, Paris, 1978.

NORD, P, *Mes Camarades sont morts 1943–4*, Librairie des Champs Elysées, Paris, 1949.

PAILLOLE, Paul, *Services Spéciaux 1939–45*, Éditions Robert Laffont, Paris, 1975.

PASSY, Colonel, *Missions Secrètes en France: Souvenir du BCRA*, Plon, Paris, 1951.

—*2e Bureau Londres*, Solar, Monte Carlo, 1947

PERI, Gabriel, *Des Bandits Hitlerians*, published clandestinely, 1943.

PILCH, J, *A Hirszerzés és Kemkedés Története* (The History of Intelligence and Espionage), Franklin Society, Budapest, 2 vols, 1936.

PINGAUD, I, *Un Agent secrète: d'Antraigues*, Paris, 1894.

PRATT, Fletcher, *Secret and Urgent: the Story of Codes and Ciphers*, Robert Hale, London, 1939.

RÉMY, Colonel, *Trente Ans Après*, Librairie Académique Perrin, Paris, 1974.

RICHER, Marthe, *Ma Vie d'éspionne au service de la France*, Paris, 1936.

ROCHET, Jean, *Cinq ans à la tête de la DST, 1967–72: la mission impossible*, Plon, Paris, 1985.

SAXE, Maurice, *Les Rêveries ou Mémoires sur l'Art de la Guerre*, published posthumously at The Hague, 1756.

SOUSTELLE, Jacques, *Envers et Contre Tout*, vol 2, *Souvenirs et Documents sur la France Libre 1942–44*, Robert Laffont, Paris, 1950.

STEAD, Philip John, *Second Bureau*, Evans, London, 1959.

TELFER, Captain J Buchan, RN, *The Strange Career of the Chevalier d'Eon de Beaumont*, Longman, Green & Co., London, 1895.

THOMSON, J W, and PADOVER, S K, *Secret Diplomacy: A Record of Espionage and Double-Dealing, 1500–1815*, Jarrolds, London, 1937.

Also consulted: various other books as cited in the Chapter Notes; La Bibliothéque Nationale, Paris; the Archives of the International Institute for Strategic Studies; the National Intelligence Study Center, Washington; the Public Records Office, London.

Index

Index